# SHORTHAND

## ALEXANDER L. SHEFF

### CENTURY EDITION

Speedwriting Publishing Co., Inc.
55 West 42nd Street, New York 36, N. Y.

# NOTICE

You are now studying a course in "SPEEDWRIT-ING" which identifies the best known and, in our opinion, the most efficient system of ABC shorthand. It is known throughout the United States and abroad under the distinguishing trade mark and service mark "SPEEDWRITING".

"SPEEDWRITING" is the registered trade mark of the School of Speedwriting, Inc. and identifies the books and publications of that organization and the term "SPEEDWRITING" means that system of instruction and teaching.

*Shorthand Plates Written by* 7

Agnes J. de Vito

Printed in the United States of America.

ii

# CONTENTS

# A

a . . . . . . . . . . . .

aback . . . . . . . .

abaft . . . . . . . . . .

abandon . . . . . . . .

abandonment . . .

abase . . . . . . . . . .

abasement . . . . . .

abash . . . . . . . . . .

abate . . . . . . . . . .

abatement . . . . . .

abattoir . . . . . . . .

abbess . . . . . . . . .

abbey . . . . . . . . . .

abbot . . . . . . . . . .

abbreviate . . . . . .

abbreviation . . . .

abdicate . . . . . . . .

abdication . . . .

abdomen . . . . . . .

abduct . . . . . . . . .

abduction . . . . . .

abed . . . . . . . . . .

aberration . . . . . .

abet . . . . . . . . . . .

abeyance . . . . . . .

abhor . . . . . . . . .

abide . . . . . . . . .

ability . . . . . . . . . .

abject . . . . . . . . . .

abjection . . . . . . .

abjuration . . . . . .

abjure . . . . . . . . .

ablation . . . . . . . .

ablative . . . . . . . .

ablaze . . . . . . . . .

able . . . . . . . . . . .

ablution . . . . . . . .

abnegate . . . . . . .

abnegation . . . . .

abnormal . . . . . . .

aboard . . . . . . . . .

abode . . . . . . . . .

abolish . . . . . . . .

abolition . . . . . . .

abolitionist . . . . .

abominable . . . . .

abominate . . .

abomination . .

aboriginal . . . .

aborigines . . . . .

abortion . . . . .

abortive . . . . .

abound . . . . . .

about . . . . . . .

above . . . . . . .

abrade . . . . . .

abrasion . . . . .

abrasive . . . . .

abreast . . . . .

abridge . . . . .

abridgment . .

abroad . . . . . .

abrogate . . . . .

abrogation . . .

abrupt . . . . . .

abruptly . . . . .

abruptness . . .

abscess . . . . .

abscond . . . . .

absence . . . . .

absent . . . . . .

absolute . . . . .

absolution . . .

absolve . . . . .

absorb . . . . . .

absorbent . . . .

absorption . . .

abstain . . . . . .

abstemious . . .

abstinence . . .

abstract . . . . .

abstraction . . .

absurd . . . . . .

absurdity . . . .

abundance . . .

abundant . . . .

abuse . . . . . . .

abusive . . . . . .

abut . . . . . . . .

abutment . . . . .

abyss . . . . . . . .

academic . . . . .

ACADEMIC

**ACADEMY**

| | |
|---|---|
| academy........ *akd* | accredit ..... *acr* |
| accede......... *xd* | accretion........ *akj* |
| accelerate....... *xla* | accrue.......... *aku* |
| acceleration..... *xly* | accumbent...... *akb-* |
| accent.......... *x-* | accumulate...... *akla* |
| accentuate...... *x-a* | accumulating.... *akla* |
| accentuation.... *x-1* | accumulation .... *akly* |
| accept.......... *xp* | accumulative..... *aklv* |
| acceptable...... *xpb* | accumulator...... *Akla* |
| acceptance...... *xp* | accuracy........ *akus,* |
| acceptation...... *xply* | accurate........ *akua* |
| access.......... *x'* | accursed........ *akr,* |
| accessible...... *xsb* | accusation...... *akzj* |
| accession....... *xy* | accusative....... *akzv* |
| accessory....... *xd* *xsy* | accuse......... *akz* |
| accidence....... *xd* | accuser......... *Akz* |
| accident....... *xd-* | accustom....... *aks,* |
| accidental...... *xd-l* | ace............ *as* |
| acclaim........ *akla* | acerbity........ *asb)* |
| acclamation..... *akly* | acetic.......... *asj* |
| acclimatize...... *aklz* | acetylene........ *astln* |
| acclivity........ *aklv)* | ache........... *ak* |
| accommodate.... *akda* | achieve......... *ace* |
| accommodating.. *akda* | achievement..... *ace-* |
| accommodation.. *akdj* | acid............ *asd* |
| accommodative.. *akdv* | acidity.......... *asd)* |
| accommodator... *Akda* | acknowledge..... *ak* |
| accompaniment.. *aco-* | acknowledgment.. *ak-* |
| accompany...... *aco* | acme........... *akse* |
| accomplice...... *akps* | acorn........... *akn* |
| accomplish...... *akpj* | acoustic......... *aks5* |
| accomplisher.... *Akpj* | acquaint........ *aq-* |
| accomplishment. *akpj-* | acquaintance..... *aq-/* |
| accord.......... *akj* | acquiescence..... *aqs* |
| accordance...... *akj/* | acquiescent...... *aqs-* |
| accordant....... *akj-* *Akj* | acquire......... *aqe* |
| accorder........ | acquisition...... *aqzj* |
| according....... *akj* | acquisitive...... *aqzv* |
| accordingly.... . *-akjl* | acquit.......... *aql* |
| accordion...... .*akjn* | acquittal........ *aqtl* |
| accost........ . *ak,* | acre............ *ak* |
| account........ *akl* | acrimonious..... *akmx* |
| accountable..... *aklb* | acrimony........ *akm,* |
| accountant...... *akl-* | acrobat......... *akbl* |
| accoutre........ *Aku* | acropolis........ *akpls* |
| accoutrements... *Aku--* | across.......... *ak'* |

**ACROSS**

ACROSTIC

| | |
|---|---|
| acrostic........ | *aks* |
| act............ | *ak* |
| acting........ | *ak* |
| action........ | *aks* |
| actionable..... | *akb* |
| active........ | *akv* |
| activity....... | *akv)* |
| actor.......... | *ak* |
| actress........ | *ak'* |
| actual......... | *akl* |
| actuary........ | *aky* |
| actuate........ | *ako* |
| acumen........ | *akm* |
| acute.......... | *aku* |
| adage......... | *ady* |
| adamant....... | *ads-* |
| adamantine.... | *ad-m* |
| adapt.......... | *adp* |
| adaptable...... | *adpb* |
| adaptability... | *adpb)* |
| adaptation..... | *adpy* |
| add.......... | *ad* |
| addendum.... | *ad—* |
| adder........ | *ad* |
| addition...... | *ady* |
| additional..... | *adyl* |
| addict........ | *adk* |
| addle......... | *adl* |
| address....... | *ad'* |
| adduce....... | *ads* |
| adept........ | *adp* |
| adequacy..... | *adqs* |
| adequate...... | *adqa* |
| adequateness.. | *adqa'* |
| adhere....... | *adhe* |
| adherence.... | *adhe/* |
| adherent...... | *adhe-* |
| adhesion...... | *adhy* |
| adieu......... | *adu* |
| adipose....... | *adpz* |
| adjacent...... | *ajs-* |
| adjective (adj). | *ajkv* |
| adjoin........ | *ajyn* |
| adjourn....... | *ajrn* |
| adjudge...... | *ajj* |
| adjudicate.... | *adjka* |

| | |
|---|---|
| adjudication.... | *ajdk* |
| adjudicator..... | *ajdka* |
| adjunct........ | *ajq* |
| adjure........ | *aju* |
| adjust.......... | *aj,* |
| adjustment..... | *ajs-* |
| adjutant........ | *ajt-* |
| administer...... | *amS* |
| administrate.... | *amSa* |
| administrator... | *amSar* |
| admirable....... | *arb* |
| admiral........ | *arl* |
| admiration...... | *arj!* |
| admire........ | *ar* |
| admirer........ | *ar* |
| admissible...... | *arsb* |
| admissibility.... | *arsb)* |
| admission...... | *ary* |
| admit.......... | *arl* |
| admittance...... | *arl* |
| admixture....... | *aru* |
| admonish....... | *amz* |
| admonition...... | *amy* |
| admonitory...... | *amly* |
| ado............ | *adu* |
| adobe.......... | *adt* |
| adolescence..... | *adls* |
| adopt.......... | *adp* |
| adoption........ | *adpy* |
| adorable........ | *adot* |
| adoration....... | *adoy* |
| adore.......... | *ado* |
| adorn.......... | *adrn* |
| adornment...... | *adrn-* |
| adroit.......... | *adyt* |
| adulation....... | *adly* |
| adulatory....... | *adlly* |
| adult.......... | *adll* |
| adulterate....... | *adla* |
| adulteration..... | *adly* |
| adulterator...... | *adlar* |
| adultery........ | *adlly* |
| advance........ | *av* |
| advancement.... | *av-* |
| advantage....... | *avy* |
| advantageous.... | *avyx* |

ADVANTAGEOUS

ADVENT

| | |
|---|---|
| advent........ | affluence....... |
| adventitious... | affluent........ |
| adventure..... | afford.... .... |
| adventurer.... | afforestation.... |
| adventuresome | affray......... |
| adventurous .. | affright........ |
| adverb (adv).. | affront......... |
| adversary..... | afield...x...... |
| adverse....... | afire.......... |
| adversity..... | aflame......... |
| advertise..... | afloat.......... |
| advertisement | afoot.......... |
| advertiser..... | afore.......... |
| advice........ | aforesaid....... |
| advisable..... | aforetime...... |
| advise........ | afraid......... |
| adviser....... | afresh......... |
| advocacy...... | aft........... |
| advocate...... | *after*.......... |
| adze......... | afterclap....... |
| aerate........ | after-damp..... |
| aeration...... | aftermath...... |
| aerial........ | aftermost....... |
| aerie......... | *afternoon*....... |
| aeriform...... | afterthought.... |
| aerodrome.... | afterward....... |
| aerolite....... | *again*.......... |
| aeronaut...... | *against*........ |
| aeronautics... | agape.......... |
| aeroplane..... | agate.......... |
| aesthetic...... | *age*........... |
| afar.......... | aged.......... |
| affable........ | agency......... |
| affair......... | agent (agt)..... |
| affect......... | age-old........ |
| affectation... | agglomerate..... |
| affection...... | agglutinate...... |
| affectionate... | aggrandize..... |
| affiant........ | *aggrandizement*.. |
| affidavit...... | aggravate...... |
| affiliate....... | aggravation.... |
| affinity....... | aggregate...... |
| affirm........ | aggregation..... |
| affix.......... | aggression...... |
| afflict......... | aggressive...... |
| affliction...... | aggressiveness.. |

**AGGRESSIVENESS**

## AGGRESSOR

| | | | |
|---|---|---|---|
| aggressor.... | *agsr* | ale............ | *al* |
| aggrieve..... | *agv* | alert......... | *al,* |
| aghast....... | *ag,* | alfalfa........ | *alflf* |
| agile........ | *agl* | algebra (alg)... | *algb* |
| agitate....... | *agta* | alias.......... | *alis* |
| aglow........ | *aglo* | alibi.......... | *albi* |
| ago......... | *ag* | alien.......... | *aln* |
| agony....... | *agn,* | alienable...... | *alnb* |
| agree........ | *ag* | alienate........ | *alna* |
| agreeable..... | *agb* | alienist........ | *aln,* |
| agreement.... | *ag-* | alight......... | *ali* |
| agricultural... | *agkllul* | align......... | *ali* |
| agriculture... | *agkllu* | alignment..... | *ali-* |
| aground...... | *agr—* | alike......... | *alk* |
| ague........ | *agu* | aliment........ | *al-* |
| ah.......... | *ah* | alimentary.... | *al-y* |
| aha......... | *aha* | alimony....... | *alm,* |
| ahead....... | *ahd* | aliquot....... | *algt* |
| aid......... | *ad* | alive......... | *ale* |
| aigrette...... | *agl* | alkali......... | *alkle* |
| ail.......... | *al* | alkaline....... | *alkle* |
| aim......... | *a* | all............ | *al* |
| air......... | *a* | allay......... | *ala* |
| airplane...... | *apn* | allegation...... | *algs* |
| airy......... | *a,* | allege........ | *alg* |
| aisle........ | *il* | allegiance..... | *alg* |
| ajar........ | *aja* | allegory....... | *algy* |
| akimbo...... | *ak bo* | alleviate...... | *alva* |
| akin........ | *akn* | alley......... | *al,* |
| alabaster..... | *albs* | alliance........ | *ale* |
| alacrity...... | *alk)* | allied........ | *ali* |
| alarm....... | *alr* | alligator...... | *alga* |
| alarmist...... | *alr,* | alliteration.... | *alt* |
| alas........ | *als* | allocate....... | *alka* |
| alb.......... | *alb* | allot......... | *all* |
| albatross..... | *albi,* | allotment..... | *all-* |
| albeit........ | *albl* | allow......... | *l* |
| albino....... | *albno* | allowable..... | *lb* |
| album....... | *albs* | allowance..... | *l* |
| albumen..... | *alb m* | alloy......... | *aly* |
| alchemy...... | *alk* | allude........ | *ald* |
| alcohol....... | *alkl* | allure........ | *alu* |
| alcoholic..... | *alklk* | allusion....... | *alj* |
| alcove....... | *alko* | allusive....... | *alsv* |
| alder........ | *al* | alluvial....... | *alvl* |
| alderman..... | *al-* | alluvium...... | *alv* |

**ALLUVIUM**

**ALLY**

| | |
|---|---|
| ally | *(shorthand)* |
| almanac | *(shorthand)* |
| almighty | *(shorthand)* |
| almond | *(shorthand)* |
| *almost* | *(shorthand)* |
| alms | *(shorthand)* |
| aloes | *(shorthand)* |
| aloft | *(shorthand)* |
| *alone* | *(shorthand)* |
| *along* | *(shorthand)* |
| alongside | *(shorthand)* |
| aloof | *(shorthand)* |
| aloud | *(shorthand)* |
| alp | *(shorthand)* |
| alpaca | *(shorthand)* |
| alphabet | *(shorthand)* |
| alpine | *(shorthand)* |
| *already* | *(shorthand)* |
| also | *(shorthand)* |
| altar | *(shorthand)* |
| alter | *(shorthand)* |
| alteration | *(shorthand)* |
| alterative | *(shorthand)* |
| altercate | *(shorthand)* |
| altercation | *(shorthand)* |
| alternate | *(shorthand)* |
| alternation | *(shorthand)* |
| alternative | *(shorthand)* |
| *although* | *(shorthand)* |
| altitude | *(shorthand)* |
| alto | *(shorthand)* |
| altogether | *(shorthand)* |
| alum | *(shorthand)* |
| aluminum | *(shorthand)* |
| alumni | *(shorthand)* |
| alumnus | *(shorthand)* |
| *always* | *(shorthand)* |
| *am* | *(shorthand)* |
| amain | *(shorthand)* |
| amalgam | *(shorthand)* |
| amalgamate | *(shorthand)* |
| amalgamation | *(shorthand)* |
| amanuensis | *(shorthand)* |
| amass | *(shorthand)* |
| amateur | *(shorthand)* |
| amatory | *(shorthand)* |

| | |
|---|---|
| amaze | *(shorthand)* |
| amazement | *(shorthand)* |
| ambassador | *(shorthand)* |
| amber | *(shorthand)* |
| ambiguity | *(shorthand)* |
| ambiguous | *(shorthand)* |
| ambition | *(shorthand)* |
| *ambitious* | *(shorthand)* |
| amble | *(shorthand)* |
| ambuscade | *(shorthand)* |
| ambush | *(shorthand)* |
| ameliorate | *(shorthand)* |
| amelioration | *(shorthand)* |
| ameliorative | *(shorthand)* |
| amen | *(shorthand)* |
| amenable | *(shorthand)* |
| amend | *(shorthand)* |
| amendment | *(shorthand)* |
| amenity | *(shorthand)* |
| *America* | *(shorthand)* |
| *American* | *(shorthand)* |
| Americanization | *(shorthand)* |
| amiability | *(shorthand)* |
| amiable | *(shorthand)* |
| amicable | *(shorthand)* |
| amid | *(shorthand)* |
| amidst | *(shorthand)* |
| amiss | *(shorthand)* |
| amity | *(shorthand)* |
| ammonia | *(shorthand)* |
| ammunition | *(shorthand)* |
| amnesia | *(shorthand)* |
| amnesty | *(shorthand)* |
| amnesties | *(shorthand)* |
| *among* | *(shorthand)* |
| amongst | *(shorthand)* |
| amorous | *(shorthand)* |
| amorphous | *(shorthand)* |
| amortize | *(shorthand)* |
| *amount* | *(shorthand)* |
| ampere | *(shorthand)* |
| amphibious | *(shorthand)* |
| amphitheater | *(shorthand)* |
| ample | *(shorthand)* |
| amplification | *(shorthand)* |
| amplify | *(shorthand)* |

**AMPLIFY**

AMPLITUDE

| | | | |
|---|---|---|---|
| amplitude....... | | animosity...... | |
| amputate....... | | animus....... | |
| amulet......... | | anise......... | |
| amuse......... | | aniseed...... | |
| amusement..... | | anker......... | |
| *an*............. | | ankle......... | |
| anachronism.... | | annal......... | |
| anaemia........ | | annalist........ | |
| anaesthetic...... | | anneal (anele).. | |
| anagram........ | | annex........ | |
| analogous....... | | annihilate...... | |
| analogy......... | | annihilation.... | |
| analyse......... | | anniversary.... | |
| analysis........ | | annotate....... | |
| analyst......... | | annotation..... | |
| analytic........ | | announce...... | |
| analytical...... | | announcement.. | |
| anarchist...... | | annoy......... | |
| anarchy........ | | annoyance.... | |
| anathema...... | | annual........ | |
| anatomical..... | | annuitant...... | |
| anatomy....... | | annuity........ | |
| ancestor........ | | annul......... | |
| anchor......... | | annunciate..... | |
| anchorage...... | | annunciation... | |
| anchovy........ | | anode........ | |
| ancient........ | | anodyne....... | |
| *and*............ | | anoint........ | |
| andante........ | | anomalous..... | |
| andirons........ | | anomaly..... .. | |
| anecdote....... | | anon.......... | |
| anele (anneal)... | | anonymity..... | |
| anemone........ | | anonymous..... | |
| anew.......... | | anonymously... | |
| angel.......... | | *another*........ | |
| angelic......... | | *answer*........ | |
| anger.......... | | ant........... | |
| angle.......... | | antagonism.... | |
| angrily......... | | antagonist..... | |
| angry.......... | | *antagonistic*.... | |
| anguish........ | | antagonize..... | |
| animadversion... | | antarctic....... | |
| animadvert...... | | antecedent..... | |
| *animal*.......... | | antechamber... | |
| animate........ | | antedate....... | |
| animation....... | | antediluvian.... | |

**ANTEDILUVIAN**

**ANTELOPE**

|  | |
|---|---|
| antelope | *a-lp* |
| antemeridian | *a-rrdn* |
| antenna | *a-na* |
| antennae | *a-ne* |
| antepenult | *a-pnll* |
| antepenultimate | *a-pnllra* |
| anterior | *u-* |
| anteroom | *a-rn* |
| anthem | *al* |
| anthology | *alol* |
| anthracite | *alsi* |
| anthrax | *alx* |
| anthropology | *alpol* |
| anti | *a-* |
| antic | *a-k* |
| Antichrist | *a-k,* |
| antichristian | *a-kscn* |
| anticipant | *a-sp-* |
| anticipate | *a-spa* |
| anticipation | *a-spy* |
| anticipative | *a-spv* |
| anticipator | *a-spa* |
| anticlimax | *a-klx* |
| antidote | *a-do* |
| antimony | *a-m,* |
| antipathetic | *a-pt* |
| antipathic | *a-plk* |
| antipathy | *a-pl,* |
| antiquary | *a-qy* |
| antiquate | *a-qa* |
| antiquated | *a-qa* |
| antique | *a-k* |
| antiquity | *a-q)* |
| antiseptic | *a-spk* |
| antithesis | *a-lss* |
| antithetical | *a-ttk* |
| antitoxin | *a-lxn* |
| antler | *a-l* |
| anvil | *avl* |
| anxiety | *ax)* |
| anxious | *ax* |
| any | *n,* |
| anybody | *n, bd,* |
| anyhow | *n, h* |
| anyone | *n, l* |
| anything | *n,* |

|  | |
|---|---|
| anyway | *n, a* |
| anywhere | *n, r* |
| aorta | *a/a* |
| apace | *aps* |
| apart | *ap/* |
| apartment (apt) | *ap/-* |
| apathetic | *apt* |
| apathy | *apt,* |
| ape | *ap* |
| aperient | *ap-* |
| aperture | *aplu* |
| apex | *apx* |
| aphorism | *afz* |
| apiary | *apy* |
| apiece | *aps* |
| apocalypse | *apklps* |
| apologetic | *apot* |
| apologist | *apol,* |
| apologize | *apolz* |
| apology | *apol* |
| apoplexy | *appx,* |
| apostasy | *apss,* |
| apostate | *apsa* |
| apostle | *apsl* |
| apostleship | *apsl)* |
| apostolic | *apslk* |
| apostrophe | *apsfe* |
| apostrophize | *apsfz* |
| apothecary | *aplky* |
| apotheosis | *apless* |
| appall | *apl* |
| appalling | *apl* |
| apparatus | *a/lx* |
| apparel | *a/l* |
| apparent | *a/-* |
| apparition | *a/1* |
| appeal | *apl* |
| appear | *ap/* |
| appearance | *ap* |
| appease | *apz* |
| appellant | *apl-* |
| appellation | *apl* |
| append | *ap—* |
| appendicitis | *ap—si)* |
| appendix | *ap—x* |
| appertain | *apln* |

**APPERTAIN**

| | | | |
|---|---|---|---|
| appetite...... .. | *apli* | aquarium........ | *aqy* *aqT* |
| applaud........ | *apsd* | aquatic........... | |
| applause....... | *apz* | aqueduct......... | *aqdk* |
| *apple*.......... | *ap* | aquiline........... | *aqli* *ab* |
| appliance...... | *api* | arable............ | |
| applicability.... | *apkb)* | arbiter............ | *Ab* |
| applicable...... | *apkb* | arbitrary.......... | *Aby* *Aba* |
| applicant....... | *apk-* | arbitrate.......... | |
| application..... | *apkj* | arbitration........ | *Aby* *Ab* |
| applied........ | *api* | arbor............. | |
| apply.......... | *api* | arboretum. ....... | *Abl* |
| appoint........ | *apy-* | arboriculture...... | *Abkllu* |
| appointment.... | *apy--* | arbutus........... | *ablx* |
| apportion...... | *apj* | arc............... | *ak* |
| apposition...... | *apzj* | arch.............. | *ac* |
| appraise....... | *apz* | archaeology....... | *akol* |
| appreciable..... | *apzb* | archaic........... | *akk* |
| appreciate...... | *apza* | archbishop....... | *aclzp* |
| appreciation.... | *apzj* | archer............ | *Ac* |
| appreciative.... | *apzv* | arching........... | *ac* |
| apprehend...... | *aph-* | archipelago....... | *akplq* |
| apprehension... | *aphy* | architect.......... | *aklk* |
| apprehensive... | *aphv* | architecture....... | *akllu* |
| apprentice..... | *ap-s* | archway.......... | *ac a* |
| apprize........ | *apz* | arctic............. | *akT* |
| approach....... | *apc* | ardent............ | *ad-* |
| approachable... | *apcb* | ardor............. | *A* |
| approbation.... | *apby* | *are*............... | *r* |
| appropriate..... | *appa* | area.............. | *are* |
| appropriation... | *appj* | arena............. | *arna* |
| approval....... | *apvl* | aren't............. | *r-* |
| approve........ | *apv* | arguable.......... | *aqub* |
| approximate.... | *apx* | argue............. | *aqu* |
| approximately... | *apx* | arguer............ | *Aqu aqu* |
| approximation.. | *apxy* | arguing........... | |
| appurtenance... | *apnl* | argument......... | *aq-* |
| apricot......... | *apkl* | argumentative..... | *aq-v* |
| April.......... | *ap* | arid.............. | *ad* |
| apron.......... | *apn* | aright............ | *ari* |
| apropos........ | *appo* | arise.............. | *arz* |
| apse........... | *aps* | aristocracy........ | *asks,* |
| apt............ | *ap* | aristocrat......... | *askl* |
| aptitude....... | *apld* | aristocratic........ | *askT* |
| aqua.......... | *aq* | arithmetic (arith).. | *arlT* |
| aquamarine.... | *aq vn* | ark.............. | *ak* |
| aquarelle....... | *aqrl* | *arm*.............. | *a* |

## ARMAMENT

| | | | |
|---|---|---|---|
| armament | *as-* | asbestos | *asbss* |
| armature | *arlu* | ascend | *as—* |
| armful | *arf* | ascension | *asy* |
| armhole | *arhl* | ascent | *as-* |
| armistice | *arss* | ascertain | *asln* |
| armor | *ar* | ascribe | *askb* |
| armorial | *a rgl* | ascription | *askpy* |
| army | *ar,* | ash | *az* |
| aroma | *arra* | ashamed | *aza* |
| aromatic | *art* | ashes | *azs* |
| arose | *arz* | ashore | *azo* |
| around | *r* | aside | *asd* |
| arouse | *arz* | ask | *sk* |
| arraign | *arn* | askance | *sk* |
| arraigner | *arn* | askew | *sku* |
| arrange | *ary* | aslant | *asl-* |
| arrangement | *ary-* | asleep | *aslp* |
| arranger | *ary* | asp | *as* |
| arrant | *a -* | asparagus | *asgx* |
| array | *ara* | aspect | *ask* |
| arrear | *are* | aspen | *asn* |
| arrest | *ar,* | asperity | *as)* |
| arrestment | *ars-* | aspersion | *asy* |
| arrival | *rvl* | asphalt | *asfll* |
| arrive | *rv* | aspirate | *asa* |
| arrogance | *aq/* | aspiration | *asy* |
| arrogant | *aq-* | aspire | *asu* |
| arrow | *ao* | ass | *a'* |
| arsenal | *asnl* | assail | *asl* |
| arsenic | *asnk* | assailant | *asl-* |
| arson | *asn* | assassinate | *assna* |
| art | *a/* | assault | *asll* |
| artery | *a/y* | assay | *asa* |
| artful | *a/f* | assemblage | *asrby* |
| artichoke | *a/ck* | assemble | *asrb* |
| article (art) | *a/K* | assembly | *asrb* |
| articulate | *a/kla* | assent | *as-* |
| articulation | *a/kly* | assert | *as/* |
| artifice | *a/fs* | assertion | *asy* |
| artificial | *a/fx* | assess | *as'* |
| artillery | *a/ly* | assessment | *ass-* |
| artisan | *a/sn* | assets | *asls* |
| artist | *a/,* | asseverate | *asva* |
| artistic | *a/S* | assiduous | *asdu* |
| artless | *a/l'* | assign | *asn* |
| as (s) | *as* | assignation | *asgny* |

## ASSIGNATION

ASSIGNMENT

| | |
|---|---|
| assignment.... *asn-* | atonement..... *aln-* |
| assimilate..... *asrla* | atrocious....... *ax* |
| assist......... *as,* | atrocity......... *as)* |
| assistance..... *ass/* | attach......... *alc* |
| assistant...... *ass-* | attachment..... *alc-* |
| assize........ *asz* | attack........ *alk* |
| associate...... *asza* | attain........ *aln* |
| association.... *aszl* | attainable...... *alnb* |
| assort........ *as/* | attainment..... *aln-* |
| assortment.... *as/-* | attempt........ *als* |
| assuage....... *asy* | attend......... *al—/* |
| assume....... *asu* | attendance..... *al—/* |
| assumption.... *asy* | attendant...... *al—-* |
| assurance..... *azu* | attention....... *aly* |
| assure........ *azu* | attentive....... *at-b* |
| assuredly..... *azul* | attenuate...... *alna* |
| aster......... *aS* | attest......... *al,* |
| asterisk....... *aSsk* | attestation..... *alsy* |
| astern........ *aSn* | attic.......... *aT* |
| asteroid...... *aSyd* | attire......... *ale* |
| asthma....... *asra* | attitude........ *attd* |
| asthmatic..... *as T* | attorney (atty).. *an,* |
| astonish...... *asn* | attract........ *ak* |
| astonishment.. *asn-* | attraction...... *aky* |
| astound....... *as—* | attractive...... *akv* |
| astral........ *aSl* | attribute....... *abu* |
| astray........ *aSa* | attribution..... *aby* |
| astride....... *aSd* | attributive..... *abv* |
| astringent..... *asy-* | auburn........ *abrn* |
| astrology...... *aSol* | auction........ *aky* |
| astronomy..... *aSn,* | auctioneer..... *akje* |
| astute........ *asu* | audacious...... *adx* |
| astuteness.... *asu* | audacity........ *ads)* |
| asunder...... *asll* | audible........ *adb* |
| asylum....... *asl* | audience...... *ad* |
| *at*........... *l* | audit.......... *adl* |
| ate.......... *al* | auditor........ *ad* |
| atheism....... *alz* | auditorium..... *adly* |
| atheist........ *al,* | auditory....... *adly* |
| athirst........ *alr,* | aught......... *al* |
| athlete....... *alle* | augment....... *aq-* |
| athletic....... *allT* | augmentation... *aq-y* |
| Atlantic....... *all-k* | augury........ *agy* |
| atmosphere... *alrsf* | *August*........ *aq* |
| atom......... *als* | aunt.......... *a-* |
| atone......... *aln* | auricle........ *ark* |

**AURICLE**

## AURICULAR

| Word | Shorthand | Word | Shorthand |
|---|---|---|---|
| auricular | *Ork* | avenger | *avg* |
| aurist | *as,* | avenue | *av* |
| aurora | *arra* | aver | *av* |
| auspice | *ass* | average | *av* |
| auspices | *asss* | averse | *avrs* |
| auspicious | *asx* | aversion | *avry* |
| austere | *ase* | avert | *avf* |
| austereness | *ase'* | aviary | *avy* |
| austerity | *asf)* | aviation | *avy* |
| austral | *asl* | aviator | *ava* |
| authentic | *al-k* | avidity | *avd)* |
| authenticate | *al-ka* | avocation | *avkf* |
| authenticity | *al-s)* | avoid | *avy* |
| author | *a,* | avoidable | *avyb* |
| authoress | *a'* | avoidance | *avy* |
| authoritative | *alv* | avoirdupois | *avdpy* |
| authority | *a)* | avow | *av* |
| authorization | *azf* | avowal | *avl* |
| authorize | *az* | avowedly | *avl* |
| authorship | *az* | await | *a-a* |
| auto | *alo* | awake | *a-k* |
| autobiography | *albgf,* | awaken | *a-kn* |
| autocracy | *alks,* | award | *a/* |
| autocrat | *alkl* | aware | *a-a* |
| autograph | *algf* | away | *a-a* |
| automatic | *alvt* | awe | *a* |
| automaton | *alvtn* | awful | *af* |
| automobile | *alvb* | awhile | *a-l* |
| autonomous | *alnvx* | awkward | *ak/* |
| autonomy | *alnv,* | awl | *al* |
| autopsy | *alps,* | awning | *an* |
| autumn | *alv* | awoke | *a-k* |
| autumnal | *alvml* | awry | *arv* |
| auxiliary | *axly* | axe | *ax* |
| avail | *avl* | axiom | *x-f* |
| available | *avlb* | axiomatic | *x-v* |
| avalanche | *avlc* | axis | *xs* |
| avarice | *avrs* | axle | *xl* |
| avaricious | *avrx* | ay | *i* |
| avaunt | *av-* | aye | *a* |
| avenge | *avy* | azure | *azf* |

## B

| Word | Shorthand | Word | Shorthand |
|---|---|---|---|
| babble | *bb* | babe | *bab* |
| babbler | *Bb* | baboon | *bbn* |

**BABOON**

## BABY

|  | |  |
|------|---|------|
| baby | | bandit |
| bachelor | | bandy |
| back | | bane |
| backbite | | bang |
| backbone | | bangle |
| backer | | banish |
| backslide | | banishment |
| backward | | banister |
| bacon | | banjo |
| bad | | bank |
| bade | | banker |
| badge | | bankrupt |
| badger | | bankruptcy |
| badness | | banner |
| baffle | | bannock |
| bag | | banquet |
| baggage | | banter |
| bail | | bantling |
| bait | | baptism |
| baize | | baptismal |
| bake | | Baptist |
| baker | | baptize |
| balance | | bar |
| balcony | | barb |
| bald | | barbarian |
| baldness | | barbarism |
| bale | | barbarous |
| balk | | barber |
| ball | | barbican |
| ballad | | bard |
| ballast | | bare |
| ballet | | barefaced |
| balloon | | barefoot |
| balloonist | | bareness |
| ballot | | bargain |
| balm | | barge |
| balmy | | baritone |
| balsam | | bark |
| baluster | | barley |
| balustrade | | barm |
| bamboo | | barn |
| ban | | barnacle |
| banal | | barnyard |
| banana | | barometer |
| band | | baron |
| bandage | | baronet (bart) |

**BARONET**

## BARONETCY

baronetcy (barts)
barony
barouche
barque
barrack
barrage
barrel (bbl)
barren
barrette
barricade
barrier
barrister
barrow
barter
basalt
base
baseball
*basement*
baseness
bashful
bashfulness
basic
basin
basis
bask
*basket*
bass
bastard
baste
basting
bastion
bat
batch
bate
bath
bathe
bathrobe
bathroom
batiste
baton
battalion
batten
batter
battery
*battle*
battlement

battleship
bauble
bawl
bay
bayonet
bazaar
*bo*
beach
beacon
bead
beading
beadle
beagle
beak
beam
bean
beanstalk
*bear*
beard
*bearer*
bearing
*beast*
*beastliness*
*beastly*
beat
beaten
beater
beating
beau
beauteous
*beautiful*
beautifully
*beautify*
*beauty*
beaver
became
*because*
beck
beckon
*become*
bed
bedaub
bedchamber
bedding
bedew
bedlam

**BEDLAM**

BEDRIDDEN

| | | | |
|---|---|---|---|
| bedridden.... | *bdrdn* | beleaguer..... | *Blg blf,* |
| bedroom..... | *bdr* | belfry........ | |
| bedspread.... | *bdspd* | belie........ | *ble* |
| bedstead..... | *bdsd* | belief........ | *blf* |
| bedtime...... | *bdle* | believe....... | *ble* |
| bee......... | *b* | believer....... | *Ble* |
| beech........ | *bec* | bell.......... | *bl* |
| beef......... | *bef* | belle......... | *bl* |
| been........ | *b be* | belligerent..... | *blg-* |
| beer......... | *be* | bellow........ | *blo* |
| beet......... | *be* | belly......... | *bl, blg* |
| beetle....... | *bll bes* | belong........ | |
| beeves....... | | beloved....... | *blō blo* |
| befall........ | *bfl* | below........ | |
| befell........ | *bfl bf* | belt.......... | *bll* |
| before....... | | belted........ | *blt bm* |
| beforehand... | *bfh—* | bemoan....... | |
| befriend..... | *bf—* | bench........ | *bc* |
| beg......... | *bg bf* | bend......... | *b—* |
| began....... | *bg* | beneath...... | *bnt* |
| beget........ | *bgt* | benediction.... | *bndkf* |
| beggar....... | *Bg* | benefactor..... | *bn 7k* |
| beggarly..... | *Bgl* | benefactress... | *bn 7k'* |
| begin........ | *bg* | benefice....... | *bnfs* |
| beginner..... | *Bg bgl* | beneficent..... | *bnfs-* |
| begird....... | | beneficial..... | *bfc* |
| begone...... | *bgn bgl* | beneficiary.... | *bnf zy* |
| begot........ | | benefit........ | *bnf* |
| begrudge.... | *bgl bgl* | benevolence... | *bnvl* |
| beguile...... | *bgl bgl* | benevolent.... | *bnvl-* |
| begun...... | *bgn* | benighted..... | *bnī* |
| behalf....... | *bhf* | benign........ | *bnn* |
| behave..... | *bha* | benignant..... | *bngn-* |
| behavior..... | *Bha* | benison....... | *bnsn* |
| bchead...... | *bhd* | bent......... | *b-* |
| beheld....... | *bhl* | benumb....... | *bns* |
| behest....... | *bh,* | benzine....... | *bnzn* |
| behind....... | *bh—* | bequeath..... | *bgl* |
| behold....... | *bhl* | bereave...... | *bre bre-* |
| behoof...... | *bhf* | bereavement.. | |
| behove...... | *bhv* | bereft........ | *brf* |
| being....... | *b* | berry......... | *by* |
| belabor...... | *bdal* | berth........ | *brt* |
| belated...... | *blā blc* | beseech...... | *bsc* |
| belch........ | | beseem....... | *bse bst* |
| beldam...... | *bld* | beset......... | |

BESET

## BESHREW

| | |
|---|---|
| beshrew | *bʒu* *bsd* |
| beside | |
| besides | *bsds* |
| besiege | *by* |
| besmear | *bsse* |
| besot | *bsl* |
| besought | *bsl* |
| bespatter | *b Sa* |
| bespeak | *bsk* |
| *best* | *b,* |
| bestial | *bsl* |
| bestir | *bs* |
| bestow | *bso* |
| bestride | *bsd* *bl* |
| bet | |
| betake | *btk* *blg* |
| bethink | |
| bethought | *btt* |
| betide | *bld* |
| betimes | *blis* |
| betoken | *blken* |
| betook | *btk* |
| betray | *Ba* |
| betrayal | *Bal* |
| betroth | *Bl* |
| betrothal | *Bll* |
| betrothed | *Bt* |
| betrothment | *Bl-* *Be* |
| *better* | *bl* |
| *between* | |
| betwixt | *blux* |
| bevel | *bvl* |
| beverage | *Bvy* *bv,* |
| bevy | |
| bewail | *bwl* |
| beware | *bwa* |
| bewildered | *b Wl* |
| bewilderment | *b Wl-* |
| bewitch | *bwc* |
| bewitchment | *bwc-* |
| bewray | *bra* |
| bey | *ba* |
| beyond | *by—* |
| bias | *bis* |
| bib | *bb* |
| bible | *bb* |

| | |
|---|---|
| bibliography | *bbgf,* *bble* |
| bibulous | |
| biceps | *bsps* |
| bicker | *Bk* |
| bicycle | *bsk* |
| bid | *bd* |
| bide | *bd* |
| bidden | *bdn* |
| biennial | *bnl* *be* |
| bier | |
| *big* | *bg* |
| bigamous | *bg x* |
| bigamy | *bg,* |
| *bigger* | *Bg* *bg,* *bu* |
| biggest | |
| bight | |
| *bigness* | *bg'* *bgl* |
| bigot | |
| bigotry | *Bgl* |
| bile | *bl* *ble* |
| bilious | |
| *bill* | *bl* *bll* |
| billet | |
| billiards | *bly//* *bln* |
| billion (B) | |
| billow | *blo* |
| bin | *bn* |
| bind | *bi—* |
| binder | *B—* |
| binds | *bi——* |
| binnacle | *bnk* |
| binomial | *bnl* |
| biography | *bgf,* *bol* |
| biology | |
| birch | *brc* *b/* |
| *bird* | |
| birdie | *b/,* *brl* |
| birth | |
| birthday | *brld* |
| birthplace | *brlpl* |
| birthright | *brbru* |
| biscuit | *bskl* *bsk* |
| bisect | |
| bisector | *Bsk* |
| bishop | *bZp* |
| bishopric | *bZpk* |

## BISHOPRIC

## BISMUTH

| | | | |
|---|---|---|---|
| bismuth....... | | blend......... | |
| bison......... | | *bless*........ | |
| *bit*.......... | | blessedness... | |
| bitch......... | | blessing...... | |
| bite.......... | | blest......... | |
| *bitter*........ | | blew......... | |
| bitterness..... | | blight........ | |
| bitumen....... | | *blind*........ | |
| bituminous.... | | blindly....... | |
| bivalve........ | | blindness..... | |
| bivouac........ | | blink........ | |
| *black*........ | | bliss........ | |
| blackberry.... | | blissful...... | |
| blackbird..... | | blister....... | |
| blackboard.... | | blithe....... | |
| blacken...... | | blizzard..... | |
| *blackness*..... | | bloat........ | |
| blacksmith... | | block........ | |
| blackthorn.... | | blockade..... | |
| blackguard.... | | blockhead.... | |
| bladder....... | | blond........ | |
| blade......... | | *blood*........ | |
| blamable..... | | bloodshed.... | |
| blame........ | | bloody....... | |
| blameless..... | | bloom....... | |
| blanch....... | | bloomer..... | |
| bland........ | | bloomers.... | |
| blandishment... | | blossom..... | |
| blank........ | | blot........ | |
| blanket...... | | blouse....... | |
| blare........ | | *blow*........ | |
| blaspheme.... | | *blower*....... | |
| blasphemy.... | | blubber...... | |
| blast........ | | bludgeon.... | |
| blasting...... | | *blue*........ | |
| blatant...... | | bluebell..... | |
| blaze........ | | bluebird.... | |
| blazon....... | | bluefish..... | |
| bleach....... | | *bluer*........ | |
| bleak........ | | bluff........ | |
| bleaker...... | | bluish....... | |
| blear........ | | blunder..... | |
| bleat........ | | blunderbuss... | |
| bled......... | | blunt........ | |
| bleed........ | | blur......... | |
| blemish...... | | blurred...... | |

**BLURRED**

**BLUSH**

| | |
|---|---|
| blush......... | |
| bluster....... | |
| boa.......... | |
| boar......... | |
| board....... | |
| hoarder...... | |
| boardwalk... | |
| boast........ | |
| boastful...... | |
| boat......... | |
| boatman..... | |
| boatswain.... | |
| bob......... | |
| bobbin....... | |
| bobolink...... | |
| bode......... | |
| bodice....... | |
| bodily....... | |
| bodkin....... | |
| body........ | |
| bodyguard.... | |
| bog......... | |
| boil......... | |
| boiler....... | |
| boisterous.... | |
| bold........ | |
| boldness..... | |
| boll........ | |
| bolster...... | |
| bolt........ | |
| bomb........ | |
| bombard..... | |
| bombardment.. | |
| bombast..... | |
| bona fide..... | |
| bonbon...... | |
| bond........ | |
| bondage..... | |
| bondman..... | |
| bone........ | |
| bonfire...... | |
| bonnet...... | |
| bonny....... | |
| bonus....... | |
| boo......... | |
| book........ | |

| | |
|---|---|
| bookcase...... | |
| booklet........ | |
| boom......... | |
| boon......... | |
| boor......... | |
| boorish....... | |
| boost........ | |
| boot......... | |
| booth........ | |
| booty........ | |
| bo-peep....... | |
| borax. ....... | |
| border....... | |
| bore........ | |
| boric........ | |
| born........ | |
| borne........ | |
| borough...... | |
| borrow....... | |
| borrower...... | |
| bosom........ | |
| boss......... | |
| botanical...... | |
| botanist....... | |
| botanize...... | |
| botany....... | |
| botch........ | |
| both........ | |
| bother....... | |
| bottle........ | |
| bottom....... | |
| bottomless..... | |
| bough........ | |
| bought....... | |
| boulder...... | |
| boulevard..... | |
| bounce....... | |
| bound....... | |
| boundary..... | |
| boundless..... | |
| boundlessness.. | |
| bounteous..... | |
| bountiful...... | |
| bounty....... | |
| bouquet...... | |
| bout........ | |

**BOUT**

## BOW

| | |
|---|---|
| bow | |
| bowels | |
| bower | |
| bowl | |
| box | |
| boxer | |
| boxroom | |
| boy | |
| boycott | |
| boyhood | |
| boyish | |
| brace | |
| bracelet | |
| bracket | |
| brackish | |
| brag | |
| braggart | |
| braid | |
| brail | |
| brain | |
| brake | |
| bramble | |
| bran | |
| branch | |
| brand | |
| brandish | |
| brandy | |
| brass | |
| brassiere | |
| bravado | |
| brave | |
| bravery | |
| bravo | |
| brawl | |
| brawn | |
| brawny | |
| bray | |
| brazen | |
| breach | |
| bread | |
| breadth | |
| break | |
| breakable | |
| breaker | |
| breakfast | |
| breakwater | |

| | |
|---|---|
| breast | |
| breastplate | |
| breath | |
| breathe | |
| breathless | |
| bred | |
| breech | |
| breeches | |
| breed | |
| breeding | |
| breeze | |
| breezy | |
| brethren | |
| breve | |
| brevet | |
| breviary | |
| brevity | |
| brew | |
| brewer | |
| brewery | |
| brewster | |
| briar | |
| bribe | |
| brick | |
| bridal | |
| bride | |
| bridegroom | |
| bridge | |
| bridle | |
| brief | |
| brig | |
| brigade | |
| brigadier | |
| brigand | |
| brigantine | |
| bright | |
| brighten | |
| brighter | |
| brightly | |
| brightness | |
| brilliancy | |
| brilliant | |
| brim | |
| brimstone | |
| brindle | |
| brine | |

**BRINE**

## BRING

|  | |  | |
|------|---|------|---|
| *bring* | | brutality | |
| bringer | | brutalize | |
| brink | | brute | |
| brisk | | brutish | |
| bristle | | bubble | |
| brittle | | buccaneer | |
| broach | | buck | |
| *broad* | | bucket | |
| broaden | | buckle | |
| *broader* | | buckler | |
| *broadly* | | buckram | |
| *broadness* | | buckwheat | |
| broadsword | | bud | |
| brocade | | budge | |
| broider | | budget | |
| broil | | buff | |
| broke | | buffalo | |
| broken | | buffer | |
| *brokenly* | | buffet | |
| broker | | buffoon | |
| brokerage | | buffoonery | |
| bronchitis | | bug | |
| bronze | | buggy | |
| brooch | | bugle | |
| brood | | build | |
| *brook* | | builder | |
| brooklet | | building | |
| broom | | built | |
| broth | | bulb | |
| *brother* | | bulbous | |
| brotherhood | | bulk | |
| brotherly | | bulky | |
| brougham | | bull | |
| *brought* | | bullet | |
| brow | | bulletin | |
| *brown* | | bullion | |
| browner | | bullock | |
| brownie | | bully | |
| browse | | bulwark | |
| bruin | | bumble | |
| bruise | | bump | |
| brunette | | bumper | |
| brunt | | bun | |
| brush | | bunch | |
| brushwood | | bundle | |
| brutal | | bung | |

## BUNG

BUNGALOW

| | |
|---|---|
| bungalow..... | |
| bungle........ | |
| bunion........ | |
| bunny........ | |
| bunting...... | |
| buoy......... | |
| buoyancy..... | |
| buoyant...... | |
| burden....... | |
| burdensome... | |
| bureau....... | |
| burgess....... | |
| burgher....... | |
| burglar....... | |
| burial........ | |
| buried........ | |
| burlesque..... | |
| burly......... | |
| *burn*......... | |
| *burner*........ | |
| burnish....... | |
| burr......... | |
| burrow....... | |
| bursar........ | |
| bursary....... | |
| burst......... | |
| bury......... | |
| bus.......... | |

| | |
|---|---|
| bush........ | |
| bushel (bu).. | |
| bushes...... | |
| bushing..... | |
| bushy....... | |
| busier....... | |
| busily....... | |
| business..... | |
| busk........ | |
| buskin....... | |
| bust........ | |
| bustle....... | |
| busy........ | |
| *but*......... | |
| butcher...... | |
| butler....... | |
| *butter*....... | |
| buttercup.... | |
| butterfly..... | |
| button....... | |
| buttress..... | |
| buxom....... | |
| *buy*........ | |
| *buyer*....... | |
| buzz........ | |
| buzzard...... | |
| *by*.........| |
| bye........ | |

## C

| | |
|---|---|
| cab.......... | |
| cabalistic..... | |
| cabbage....... | |
| cabin........ | |
| cabinet....... | |
| cable........ | |
| cackle....... | |
| cadaverous.... | |
| caddie........ | |
| cadence...... | |
| cadet......... | |
| cafe.......... | |
| cafeteria...... | |
| cage......... | |
| cajole........ | |

| | |
|---|---|
| cake........ | |
| calabash..... | |
| calamitous... | |
| calamity..... | |
| calcine...... | |
| calculate..... | |
| calculation... | |
| calculus..... | |
| caldron...... | |
| calendar..... | |
| calf......... | |
| calibre....... | |
| calico........ | |
| caliph....... | |
| call......... | |

CALL

## CALLER

| | | | |
|---|---|---|---|
| *caller* | *Kl* | canned | *k—* |
| callous | *klx* | canner | *Kn* |
| callow | *klo* | cannery | *kny* |
| calm | *ks* | cannibal | *knb* |
| calmness | *ks'* | cannibalism | *knbz* |
| calomel | *klbl* | cannibalistic | *knbS* |
| caloric | *Klyk* | cannon | *kn* |
| calumniate | *klma* | cannonade | *knd* |
| calumnious | *klmx* | cannot | *kn* |
| calumny | *klm,* | canny | *kn,* |
| calves | *Kvs* | canoe | *knu* |
| calyx | *klx* | canon | *kn* |
| cambric | *kbk* | canonical | *knl* |
| *came* | *k* | canopy | *knp,* |
| camel | *ksl* | canst | *k,* |
| camelopard | *kslp/* | can't | *k—* |
| cameo | *kro* | cantaloupe | *k—lp* |
| camera | *Kra* | canteen | *k—n* |
| cammomile | *knu* | canter | *K—* |
| camouflage | *krfly* | cantilever | *k—le* |
| camp | *krp* | canton | *k—n* |
| campaign | *krpn* | cantonments | *k—n——* |
| camper | *Krp* | canvas | *kvs* |
| camphor | *krf* | canyon | *kyn* |
| campus | *krpx* | cap | *kp* |
| *can* | *k* | capability | *kpb)* |
| canal | *knl* | capable | *kpb* |
| canard | *kn/* | capacious | *kpx* |
| canary | *kny* | capaciousness | *kpx'* |
| cancel | *ksl* | capacity | *kps)* |
| cancellation | *ksly* | cape | *kap* |
| cancer | *K/* | caper | *Kp* |
| cancerous | *K/x* | capillary | *kply* |
| candid | *k—d* | capital (cap) | *kpll* |
| candidacy | *k—ds,* | capitalism | *kpllz* |
| candidate | *k—da* | capitalist | *kpll,* |
| candidness | *k—d'* | capitation | *kply* |
| candle | *k—l* | capitol (cap) | *kpll* |
| candlestick | *k—lsk* | capitulate | *kplla* |
| candor | *K—* | capitulation | *kplly* |
| candy | *k—,* | capon | *kpn* |
| cane | *kn* | caprice | *kps* |
| canine | *knun* | capricious | *kpx* |
| canister | *kS* | capriciousness | *kpx'* |
| canker | *Kg* | capsize | *kpsz* |
| cankerous | *Kgx* | capsule | *kpsl* |

## CAPTAIN

| | | | |
|---|---|---|---|
| captain | | carpenter | |
| caption | | carpentry | |
| captious | | carpet | |
| captivate | | carriage | |
| captive | | carrier | |
| captivity | | carrion | |
| capture | | carrot | |
| car | | carry | |
| caramel | | cart | |
| carat | | cartage | |
| caravan | | carter | |
| caravansary | | cartilage | |
| carbine | | cartoon | |
| carbohydrate | | cartoonist | |
| carbolic | | cartridge | |
| carbon | | carve | |
| carbonic | | cascade | |
| carboniforous | | cascara | |
| carbonize | | case | |
| carbuncle | | case-hardened | |
| carburetor | | case-knife | |
| carcanet | | casement | |
| carcass | | cash | |
| card | | cash-book | |
| carder | | cash-boy | |
| cardboard | | cashier | |
| cardiac | | cashmere | |
| cardinal | | cask | |
| care | | casket | |
| career | | casque | |
| careful | | casserole | |
| carefully | | cassock | |
| carefulness | | cast | |
| careless | | castigate | |
| carelessness | | castigation | |
| caress | | castile | |
| caret | | castle | |
| cargo | | castor | |
| caricature | | casual | |
| carnage | | casualties | |
| carnal | | casualty | |
| carnation | | casuist | |
| carnival | | cat | |
| carnivorous | | catacomb | |
| carol | | catalogue | |
| carouse | | catapult | |

**CATAPULT**

### CATARACT

| | | | |
|---|---|---|---|
| cataract | *Kak* / *Ka* | cell | *sl* |
| catarrh | *Ka* | cellar | *Sl* |
| catastrophe | *klSfe* | celluloid | *sllyd* |
| catch | *kc* | cellulose | *slls* |
| catcher | *Kc* | cement | *s-* |
| catches | *kcs* | cemetery | *s-My* |
| catechism | *kikz* | cenotaph | *snif* |
| catechize | *kikz* | censer | |
| categorical | *klgrk* | censorious | *slyx s/y* |
| category | *klgy* | censorship | *s/y* |
| cater | *Ka* | censure | *su* |
| cathedral | *kldl* | census | *sx* |
| catkin | *klkn* | cent | *c* |
| catnip | *klnp* | centenary | *s-my* |
| cattle | *kll* | centennial | *s-nl* |
| caucus | *kkx* | center | *8-* |
| caught | *kal* | central | *8-l* |
| cauldron | *kldn* | centralization | *8-lzy* |
| cauliflower | *kl* | centralize | *8-lz* |
| causation | *kzy* | centrifugal | *8-fgl* |
| cause | *kz* | century | *s-y* |
| causeless | *kzl'* | cereal | *syl* |
| caustic | *kS* | cerebellum | *sbl* |
| cauterize | *Kaz* | cerebral | *sbl* |
| caution | *ky* | ceremonial | *s-ml* |
| cautious | *kx* | ceremonious | *s-mx* |
| cavalcade | *kvlkd* | ceremony | *s-m,* |
| cavalier | *kvle* | certain | *s/n* |
| cavalry | *kvlr,* | certainty | *s/-,* |
| cave | *ka* | certificate (cert) | *s/fka* |
| cavern | *kvrn* | certify | *s/f* |
| cavity | *kv)* | certitude | *s/ld* |
| caw | *ka* | cess | *s'* |
| cease | *ses* | cessation | *ssy* |
| ceaseless | *ssl'* | cesspool | *sspl* |
| cedar | *Sd* | chafe | *caf* |
| cede | *sd* | chaff | *cf* |
| ceiling | *sel* | chaffer | *cf* |
| celebrant | *slb-* | chaffinch | *cfc* |
| celebrate | *slba* | chagrin | *zgn* |
| celebration | *slby* | chain | *cn* |
| celebrity | *slb)* | chair | *ca* |
| celerity | *slr)* | chairman | *ca-* |
| celery | *sly* | chalice | *cls* |
| celestial | *slsx* | chalk | *cak* |
| celibacy | *slls,* | challenge | *cly* |

### CHALLENGE

## CHALLIS

| | | | |
|---|---|---|---|
| challis | | charitableness | |
| chamber | | charity | |
| chamberlain | | charlatan | |
| chambermaid | | charm | |
| chameleon | | chart | |
| chamois | | charter | |
| champ | | chartographer | |
| champaign | | chartography | |
| champion | | chartometer | |
| championship | | chary | |
| *chance* | | chase | |
| chancel | | chasm | |
| chancellor | | chaste | |
| chancery | | chasten | |
| chances | | chastise | |
| chandelier | | chastisement | |
| chandler | | chastity | |
| *change* | | chat | |
| changeable | | chateau | |
| *changeful* | | chattels | |
| channel | | chatter | |
| chant | | chauffeur | |
| chanticleer | | cheap | |
| chaos | | cheapen | |
| chaotic | | cheat | |
| chap | | *check* | |
| chapbook | | checkers | |
| chapel | | checkmate | |
| chaperon | | cheek | |
| chaplain | | cheer | |
| chaplet | | cheerful | |
| chaps | | cheerfulness | |
| chapter | | cheerily | |
| chapterhouse | | cheerless | |
| char | | cheery | |
| character | | cheese | |
| characteristic | | chemical | |
| characterize | | chemise | |
| charade | | chemist | |
| charcoal | | chemistry | |
| *charge* | | cheque | |
| *chargeable* | | chequer | |
| *charger* | | cherish | |
| chariot | | cherry | |
| charioteer | | cherub | |
| charitable | | cherubim | |

**CHERUBIM**

CHESS

| | | | |
|---|---|---|---|
| chess | *c'* | choleric | *Klk* |
| chest | *c,* | choose | *c3* |
| chestnut | *csnt* | chop | *cp* |
| chevalier | *Zvle* | chopper | *cp* |
| cheviot | *cvt* | choral | *krl* |
| chew | *cu* | chord | *k/ krs* |
| chicanery | *Zky* | chorister | |
| chick | *ck* | chorus | *kre* |
| chicken | *ckn* | chose | *c3* |
| chickory | *cky* | christen | *ksn* |
| chide | *cd* | Christian | *kscn* |
| chidden | *cdn* | christianity | *kscn)* |
| chief | *cef* | Christmas (Xmas) | *X ns* |
| chiefly | *cfl* | chromatic | *kt* |
| chieftain | *Zfn cftn* | chronic | *knk* |
| chiffon | *Zfn* | chronicle | *knt* |
| chiffonier | *Zfne* | chronologist | *knol,* |
| child | *cu* | chronology | *knol* |
| childhood | *cuhd* | chronometer | *knse* |
| childish | *cus* | chrysalis | *ksls* |
| childless | *cul'* | chrysanthemum | *kznl* |
| childlike | *culk* | chubby | *cb,* |
| children | *cl cul* | chuck | *ck* |
| chill | *cl* | chuckle | *ck* |
| chilliness | *cl'* | chum | *cn* |
| chilly | *cl,* | church | *crc* |
| chime | *cu* | churchman | *crc-* |
| chimer | *Cu* | churchyard | *crcy/ crl* |
| chimera | *kvra* | churl | |
| chimerical | *kvrk* | churlish | *crlz* |
| chimney | *cm,* | churn | *crn* |
| chin | *cn* | chute | *Zu* |
| china | *cuna* | cider | *Se* |
| chink | *cq* | cigar | *Sg* |
| chintz | *c-s* | cigarette | *Sgl* |
| chip | *cp* | cinch | *sc* |
| chiropodist | *krpd,* | cincture | *sglu* |
| chirp | *crp* | cinder | *s—* |
| chisel | *czl* | cinema | *snra* |
| chivalrous | *Zvlx* | cinnamon | *snm* |
| chivalry | *Zvlr,* | cipher | *sf* |
| chocolate | *ckla* | circle | *cl* |
| choice | *cys* | circlet | *Clt* |
| choir | *qr* | circuit | *Cl* |
| choke | *cok* | circuitous | *Clx* |
| cholera | *Kla* | circular | *Clr* |

## CIRCULATE

| | | | |
|---|---|---|---|
| circulate | | clammy | |
| circulation | | clamor | |
| circumcise | | clamorous | |
| circumcision | | clamp | |
| circumference | | clan | |
| circumflex | | clandestine | |
| circumflexion | | clang | |
| circumlocution | | clank | |
| circumlocutory | | clannish | |
| circumnavigable | | clansman | |
| circumnavigate | | clap | |
| circumnavigation | | clapper | |
| circumnavigator | | claret | |
| circumscribe | | clarification | |
| circumscription | | clarify | |
| circumscriptive | | clarion | |
| circumspect | | clarity | |
| circumspection | | clash | |
| circumspective | | clasp | |
| circumspectly | | class | |
| circumspectness | | classic | |
| circumstance | | classical | |
| circumstances | | classification | |
| circumstantial | | classify | |
| circumvent | | classmate | |
| circus | | clatter | |
| cirrus | | clause | |
| cist | | claw | |
| cistern | | clay | |
| citadel | | clean | |
| citation | | cleaner | |
| cite | | cleanliness | |
| citizen | | cleanness | |
| city (C) | | cleanse | |
| civic | | clear | |
| civil | | clearance | |
| civilian | | clearness | |
| civility | | cleave | |
| civilization | | cleaver | |
| civilize | | clef | |
| clack | | cleft | |
| clad | | clemency | |
| claim | | clement | |
| claimant | | clench | |
| clam | | clergy | |
| clamber | | clergyman | |

**CLERGYMAN**

## CLERK

|  | |  | |
|---|---|---|---|
| clerk | krk | clubman | klb |
| clever | kv | cluck | kk |
| clew | ku | clump | krp |
| click | ku | clumsy | krz |
| client | ku-l | clung | kq k8 |
| clientele | ku-l | cluster | |
| cliff | kf kra | clutch | kc |
| climate | | coach | koc |
| climax | krx | coachman | kc |
| climb | ku | coadjutor | kdy |
| clime | ku | coagulate | kgla |
| clinch | kec | coagulation | kgly |
| cling | kq knk | coal | kol |
| clinic | | coalesce | kls |
| clinical | knk kq | coalescence | kls |
| clink | | coalition | kly krs |
| clinker | kz kp | coarse | krs |
| clip | | coarseness | krs' ko, |
| cloak | kok | coast | ko, |
| clock | kk | coat | ko kox |
| clockmaker | kk kk | coax | kox |
| clod | kd | cob | kb |
| clog | kg | cobble | kb |
| cloister | kyS kos | cobbler | kb |
| close | kz | cobweb | kb b |
| close | kz kz | cocaine | kkn |
| closed | ks' | cock | kk |
| closeness | ks' Ks | cockade | kkd |
| closer | | cockatoo | kklu |
| closet | kzl kl | cockatrice | kkls |
| clot | kl | cockle | kK |
| cloth | kl kol | cocktail | kkll |
| clothe | | cocoa | kko |
| clothes | kz kl | coconut | kknl |
| clothing | kl | cocoon | kkn |
| cloud | k-d | cod | kd |
| cloudless | k-dl' | coddle | kdl |
| cloudy | k-d, | code | kd |
| clout | k-l | codfish | kdfS |
| clove | ko | codling | kdlg keg |
| cloven | kon | coequal | |
| clover | ko | coerce | kors |
| clown | k-n | coercion | kory |
| clownish | k-nz | coexist | kx, kfe |
| cloy | ky kb | coffee | kfe |
| club | | coffer | kf |

**COFFER**

## COFFIN

| | | | |
|---|---|---|---|
| coffin | *kfn* | colonial | *klnl* |
| cog | *kg* | colonist | *kln,* |
| cogent | *kj-* *kgla* | colonize | *klnz* |
| cogitate | | colonnade | *klnd* |
| cogitation | *kgly* | colony | *kln,* *Kl* |
| cognate | *kgna* | color | |
| cognition | *kgny* *kgnz/* | coloration | *Klg* *Kll'* |
| cognizance | | colorless | |
| cognizant | *kgnz-* *kgnz* | colt | *kll* |
| cognize | | column | *kls* |
| cognomen | *kgn-n* | coma | *ksa* |
| cohere | *khe* | comb | *ko* |
| coherent | *khe-* | combat | *kbl* |
| cohesion | *khj* *khsv* | combatant | *kbl-* |
| cohesive | | combative | *kbv* |
| cohort | *kh/* *kyf* | combe | *ko* |
| coif | | combination | *klbny* |
| coiffure | *kyfu* *kyl* | combine | *kbin* |
| coil | | combustible | *kbsb* |
| coin | *kyn* *kyry* | combustion | *kbsy* |
| coinage | | come | *k* |
| coincidence | *knsd* | comedian | *kdn* |
| coincident | *knsd-* | comedy | *kd,* *kel'* |
| coke | *kok* | comeliness | |
| colander | *Kl—* | comely | *kl* |
| cold | *kol* | comer | *K* |
| colder | *Kol,* | comet | *kl* |
| coldness | *kol'* | comfort | *kf/* *kf/b* |
| colic | *klk* | comfortable | *kf/b* |
| collapse | *klps* | comfortably | *kf/b* |
| collar | *Kl* | comforter | *Kf/* |
| collate | *kla* | comfortless | *kf/l'* *kel'* |
| collateral | *kLll* | comical | |
| collation | *kly* | coming | *k* |
| colleague | *klg* | comma | *ksa* |
| collect | *kk* | command | *k—* |
| collection | *kky* | commandant | *k—-.* |
| collective | *kkv* | commander | *K—* |
| college | *kly* | commemorate | *ksa* |
| collegiate | *klja* | commemoration | *ksy* |
| collide | *kld* | commemorative | *ksv* |
| collier | *klyr* *kly* | commence | *k* |
| collision | | commencement | *k-* |
| cologne | *kln* | commend | *k—* |
| colon | *kln* | commendable | *k—b* |
| colonel | *col* | commendation | *k—y* |

**COMMENDATION**

COMMENSURABLE

| | | | |
|---|---|---|---|
| commensurable.. | *k'ub* | compatible...... | *kplb* |
| commensurate... | *k'ua* | compatriot...... | *k'al* |
| comment....... | *k-* | compel......... | *kpl* |
| commentary..... | *k-y* *k-a* | compensate..... | *kpa* |
| commentator.... | | compensation.... | *kpl* *kpe* |
| commerce....... | *krs* | compete........ | |
| commercial..... | *kre* | competence..... | *kpl* *kpl* |
| commingle...... | *k-ngl* | competency.... | |
| commiserate.... | *ksa* | competent...... | *kpl-* |
| commiseration... | *ksy* | competition..... | *kply* |
| commissariat.... | *ksyl* | competitive..... | *kplv* |
| commissary..... | *ksy* *ky* *ky* | competitor...... | *Kpl* |
| commission..... | | compilation..... | *kpl* *kpl* |
| commissioner... | | compile......... | |
| commit......... | *kl* *k)* | complacence..... | *kps* |
| committee...... | | complacent...... | *kps-* |
| commodious..... | *kdx* | complain....... | *kpn* |
| commodity...... | *kd)* | complainant..... | *kpn-* |
| commodore..... | *kdo* | complaint....... | *kpa-* |
| common........ | *kn* | complement..... | *kp-* |
| commoner...... | *Kn* | complementary.. | *kp-y* |
| commonly...... | *knl* | complete........ | *kpe* |
| commonplace.... | *knpl* | completeness.... | *kpe'* |
| commonwealth.. | *kn-ll* | completion...... | *kpey* |
| commotion...... | *ky* *kn* | complex........ | *kpx* |
| commune....... | | complexion...... | *kpky* |
| communicate.... | *kuka* | complexity...... | *kpx)* |
| communication.. | *kuky* | compliance...... | *kpu* |
| communion..... | *knn* | compliant....... | *kpi-* |
| community...... | *kn)* | complicate...... | *kpka* |
| commutation.... | *kuy* | complication.... | *kpky* |
| commute....... | *ku* *ku* | complicity....... | *kps)* |
| commuter....... | *Ku* | compliment..... | *kp-* |
| compact........ | *kpk* | complimentary... | *kp-y* |
| compactness.... | *kpk'* | comply......... | *kpi* |
| companion...... | *kpnn* | component...... | *kpn-* |
| company........ | *co* | comport........ | *kpj* |
| comparable..... | *kPb* | comportment.... | *kpj-* |
| comparative..... | *k'v* | compose........ | *kpz* |
| comparatively... | *k'vl* | composite....... | *kpzl* |
| compare........ | *kpa* | composition..... | *kpzj* |
| comparison...... | *k'sn* | composure...... | *kpz* |
| compartment.... | *kp/-* | compound...... | *kp-* |
| compass........ | *kp'* | comprehend..... | *kphn* |
| compassion..... | *kpj* | comprehensible.. | *kphb* |
| compassionate... | *kpja* | comprehension... | *kphny* |

COMPREHENSION

31

COMPREHENSIVE

comprehensive.. *kph'o*
compress...... *kp'*
compressible.... *kpsb*
compression..... *kpj*
compressive..... *kpsv*
comprise........ *kpz*
compromisal.... *kprzl*
compromise..... *kprz* *kplj*
compulsion......
compunction.... *kpqj* *kpuj*
computation.....
compute........ *kpu*
comrade........ *krd*
comradeship.... *krdj*
con............ *k*
concave........ *kka*
conceal........ *ksl*
concealment..... *ksl-*
concede........ *ksd*
conceit........ *kse*
conceivable..... *kseb*
conceive........ *kse*
concentrate..... *ks-ra*
concentration.... *ks-ry*
concentric....... *ks-k*
concept......... *ksp*
conception...... *kspj*
concern......... *ksn*
concerning...... *ksn*
concert........ *ksj*
concession...... *ksj*
conciliate...... *ksla*
conciliation...... *kslj*
conciliatory..... *ksllj*
concise........ *kss*
conclave........ *kcv*
conclude........ *kcd*
conclusion...... *kcj*
conclusive...... *kcsv*
concord........ *kkj*
concordance..... *kkj*
concordant...... *kkj-*
concourse....... *kkrs*
concrete........ *kke*
concretion...... *kkj* *kqbn*
concubine.......

concupiscence... *kkps*
concur.......... *kk*
concurrence..... *kk*
concussion...... *kkj*
condemn....... *kd*
condemnation... *kdmy*
condensation.... *kd* *kd*
condense....... 
condescend..... *kds—*
condign........ *kdm*
condiment...... *kd-*
condition....... *kdj*
conditional...... *kdjl*
condole........ *kdl*
condolence...... *kdl*
condonation.... *kdmy*
condone....... *kdm*
conduce....... *kds*
conducive...... *kdsv*
conduct....... *kdk*
conduction.....*kdkj*
conductive.....*kdkv*
conductor...... *Kdk*
conduit........ *kdl*
cone.......... *kn*
confabulate..... *kfbla*
confection....... *kfkj*
confectioner..... *Kfkj*
confectionery.... *kfkjy*
confederacy.....*k Jds,*
confederate.....*kJda*
confederation... *kJdj*
confer.......... *kf*
conference......*kf* *kf'*
confess........ *kfj*
confession...... *kfj*
confessor....... *Kf'*
confide........ *kfd*
confidence...... *kfd*
confident...... *kfd-*
confidential..... *kfdx*
configuration.... *kfgj*
confine........ *kfi*
confinement..... *kfi-*
confiner........ *Kfi*
confirm........ *kfrs*

CONFIRM

## CONFIRMATION

confirmation..... *kfry*
confirmative..... *kfrw*
confiscate....... *kfska*
conflagration.... *kflg* *kflk*
conflict......... 
confluent........ *kflu-*
conform........ *kf*
contorm.... *kfy*
conformity...... *kf,)*
confound........ *kf-*
confounder...... *kf-*
confront........ *kf-*
confuse......... *kfz*
confusion...... *kfs* *kfuy*
confutation..... *kfuy*
confute...... *kfu*
congeal........ *kgl*
congenial....... *kgnl*
congenital...... *kgnll*
congest........ *kj,*
congestion...... *kjs* *kglra*
conglomerate.... 
congratulate..... *kglla*
congratulation... *kglly*
congratulatory... *kgilly*
congregate...... *kkga*
congregation.... *kkgy* *kg'*
congress........ 
congressional.... *kgjl*
congruent....... *kgu-*
congruity....... *kgu)*
conjecture...... *kjku*
conjoin......... *kjyn*
conjugal........ *kjgl*
conjugation..... *kjgj* *kjgj*
conjunction..... 
conjuncture..... *kjgu*
conjuration...... *kjuy*
conjure........ *kju*
connect........ *knk*
connection...... *knky*
connective...... *knkw*
connects........ *knks*
connivance...... *knv*
connive........ *knv*
connote........ *knl*

conquer.......... *Kg* *Kgr*
conqueror........ 
conquest......... *kg,* *ksgn)*
consanguinity..... 
conscience........ *kf* *kznx*
conscientious...... 
conscientiously.,,, *kznl* *kznx'*
conscientiousness.. 
conscious......... *kx* *kx'*
consciousness..... 
conscript......... *kskp*
conscription...... *kskpy*
consecrate........ *kska*
consecration...... *ksky*
consecutive....... *kskv*
consent........... *ks-*
consequence...... *ksg* *ksg-*
consequent........ 
consequential...... *ksgx* *ksvv*
conservative....... 
conservatory...... *ksvly*
conserve.......... *ksv* *ksv*
conserving........ 
consider.......... *Ks* *Ksb* *Ksb*
considerable...... 
considerably...... 
considerate....... *Ksa* *Ksy* *ksvn*
consideration...... 
consign........... 
consignment...... *ksvn-*
consist........... *ks,* *kss-*
consistent......... 
consistory........ *kssy*
consolation........ *ksly*
console........... *ksl* *kslda*
consolidate....... 
consolidation..... *ksldy*
consonant......... *ksn-*
consort........... *ks/*
conspicuous...... *kskx*
conspiracy........ *ksvs,*
conspirator....... *Ksv* *ksv*
conspire......... 
constable........ *ksb* *ks/*
constancy........ 
constant......... *ks-*

### CONSTANT

## CONSTELLATION

| | | | | |
|---|---|---|---|---|
| constellation | *ksl/ksny* | continent | *K-* |
| consternation | | continental | *K-l* |
| constipate | *kspa* | contingent | *Ky-* |
| constituency | *kslu* | continual | *Kul* |
| constitute | *kslu* | continuance | *Ku* |
| constitution | *ksly* | continuation | *Kuy* |
| constitutionality | *kslyl)* | continue | *Ku* |
| constrain | *ksn* | continuous | *Kux* |
| constraint | *ks-* | contort | *kl/* |
| constrict | *kSk* | contour | *klu* |
| constriction | *kSk/kSk* | contraband | *Kl—* |
| construct | | contract | *Kk* |
| construction | *kSk/kSkv* | contraction | *Kk/* |
| constructive | | contractor | *Kkr* |
| construe | *kSu* | contradict | *Kdk* |
| consul | *ksl* | contradiction | *Kdk/* |
| consular | *Ksl* | contrary | *Ky* |
| consulship | *ksl/ksll* | contrast | *K,* |
| consult | | contravene | *Kun* |
| consultation | *ksly* | contravention | *Kuy* |
| consume | *Ksu* | contribute | *Kbu* |
| consumer | *Ksu* | contributed | *Kbu* |
| consumption | *ks/klk* | contribution | *Kly* |
| contact | | contributive | *Kbv* |
| contagion | *klyn* | contrite | *Kl* |
| contagious | *klyr* | contrition | *Ky* |
| contain | *kln* | contrivance | *Ku* |
| container | *Kln* | contrive | *Ku* |
| contaminate | *klma* | control | *Kl* |
| contamination | *klmy* | controversy | *Kurs,* |
| contemplate | *klspa* | controvert | *Ku/klx* |
| contemplation | *klspy* | contumacious | |
| contemporaneous | *klspnx* | contumely | *klrl* |
| contemporary | *klspy* | contusion | *kly* |
| contempt | *kls* | conundrum | *k—rs* |
| contemptible | *klsb* | convalescent | *kvls-* |
| contemptuous | *klsx* | convene | *kvn* |
| contend | *kl—* | convenience | *kv* |
| content | *kl-l* | convenient | *kvn-* |
| contentedly | *kl—l* | convent | *kv-* |
| contention | *kly/kl--* | conventicle | *kv-K* |
| contentment | | convention | *kvy* |
| contest | *kl,* | conventionality | *kvyl)* |
| context | *klx* | converge | *kvy* |
| contiguity | *klgu)* | convergence | *kvy/kvrs-* |
| contiguous | *klgx* | conversant | |

34

| | | | |
|---|---|---|---|
| conversation ... | *kvrs* | coquette ........ | *kkl* |
| converse ...... | *kvrs* | coracle ........ | *kl* |
| convert ....... | *kv* | coral ......... | *krl* |
| convertible .... | *kv/t* | cord ......... | *k/* |
| convex ........ | *kvx* | cordage ........ | *k/j* |
| convey ........ | *kva* | cordial ......... | *k/l* |
| conveyance .... | *kva* | cordiality ....... | *k/l)* |
| convict ........ | *kvk* | cordon ......... | *k/n* |
| conviction ..... | *kvks* | corduroy ........ | *k/ry* |
| convince ....... | *kv* | core ........... | *ko* |
| convivial ...... | *kvvl* | cork ......... | *krk* |
| convocation.... | *kvks* | cormorant ....... | *k-r-* |
| convoke ....... | *kvk* | corn .......... | *kn* |
| convoy ........ | *kvy* | cornea ......... | *kne* |
| convulse ...... | *kvls* | cornel ......... | *knl* |
| convulsion ..... | *kvls* | corner ......... | *Kn* |
| convulsive ..... | *kvlsv* | cornet ......... | *knl* |
| cony ......... | *kn,* | cornicle ........ | *knk* |
| coo ......... | *ku* | cornucopia ..... | *knkpa* |
| cook ......... | *kk* | corollary ....... | *kly* |
| cooker ........ | *Kk* | corona ........ | *krna* |
| cooky ........ | *kk,* | coronation ...... | *kns* |
| cool ......... | *kul* | coroner ........ | *Kn* |
| cooler ........ | *Kl* | coronet ........ | *knl* |
| coolness ...... | *kl'* | corporal (corp).. | *kpl* |
| coom ......... | *ku* | corporate ....... | *kpa* |
| coop ......... | *kup* | corporation ..... | *kp/* |
| cooperate ..... | *kopa* | corps ......... | *ko* |
| cooperation ... | *kops* | corpse ......... | *kps* |
| cooperative .... | *kopv* | corpulence ...... | *kpl* |
| coordinate ..... | *kd/na* | corpulent ....... | *kpl-* |
| coordination ... | *kd/n* | corral ......... | *krl* |
| coordinative ... | *kd/nv* | correct ........ | *krk* |
| coot ......... | *ku* | correction ...... | *krks* |
| cope ......... | *kop* | corrective ...... | *krkv* |
| coping ........ | *kop* | correctly ....... | *krkl* |
| copious ........ | *kpx* | correctness ..... | *krk* |
| copper ........ | *Kp* | corrector ........ | *Krk* |
| copperas ...... | *kps* | correlation ..... | *krl* |
| copse ......... | *kps* | correlative ...... | *krlv* |
| copula ........ | *kpla* | correspond ...... | *ks-* |
| copulative ..... | *kplv* | correspondence.. | *ks-* |
| copy ......... | *kp,* | correspondent... | *ks--* |
| copyright ...... | *kpru* | corridor ........ | *Kr* |
| coquet ........ | *kkl* | corrigible ....... | *kjl* |
| coquetry ....... | *Kk,* | corroborate ..... | *kbra* |

## CORROBORATION

| | |
|---|---|
| corroboration... | *kbry* |
| corroborative.... | *kbrcv* |
| corroboratory... | *kbrly* |
| corrode......... | *krd* |
| corrosion....... | *kry* *krsv* |
| corrosive....... | |
| corrugate....... | *kga* |
| corrupt......... | *krp* |
| corruptible...... | *krpb* *krpy* |
| corruption...... | |
| corsair......... | *ksa* |
| corse.......... | *krs* |
| corset......... | *ksl* |
| corslet......... | *ksll* |
| cortege......... | *k/3* |
| cortex......... | *k/x* |
| coruscate....... | *kska* |
| corvette........ | *kvl* |
| cosmetic........ | *kz* |
| cosmopolitan.... | *ksrplln* |
| *cost*........... | *k,* *ksl* |
| costal......... | |
| costive........ | *ksv* *ksl* |
| *costly*........ | |
| costume........ | *ksu* |
| cosy........... | *kz,* |
| cot............ | *kl* |
| coterie........ | *kly* |
| cottage........ | *kly* *kln* |
| cotton......... | |
| cotyledon...... | *klldn* |
| couch......... | *krc* |
| cough......... | *kf* |
| *could*......... | *kd* |
| couldn't....... | *kd-* |
| couldst........ | *kd,* |
| coulter........ | *Kl* |
| council........ | *ksl* *ksl* |
| *counsel*....... | |
| counselor...... | *Ksl* |
| *count*......... | *kl* |
| countenance.... | *kl* |
| counter........ | *K* |
| counterbalance. | *Kbal* |
| counterfeit..... | *Kfl* |
| countermand... | *K—* |

| | |
|---|---|
| countersign.... | *Ksm* |
| counterstroke.. | *KSk* |
| countess....... | *ki'* *kll'* |
| countless...... | |
| *country*........ | *K* *kl,* |
| county......... | |
| coup........... | *ku* |
| couple......... | *kp* *kpl* |
| couplet........ | |
| coupling....... | *kpg* *kpn* |
| coupon........ | |
| courage....... | *kry* *kryx* |
| courageous..... | |
| *course*........ | *krs* *kl* |
| *court* (ct)...... | |
| courteous...... | *k/x* |
| courtesy....... | *k/s,* |
| courtier........ | *k/e* |
| courtmartial.... | *k/rx* |
| courtship...... | *k/?* *kzn* |
| cousin........ | |
| cove.......... | *ko* *kvn-* |
| covenant....... | |
| cover.......... | *Kv* *kv/* |
| covert......... | |
| covet......... | *kvl* *kvlx* |
| covetous....... | |
| covey......... | *kv,* |
| *cow*........... | *k/* |
| coward........ | *k/* *k/s* |
| cowardice...... | |
| cowboy........ | *k by* |
| cowl.......... | *k l* |
| cowslip........ | *k slp* |
| coxcomb....... | *kxk* |
| coy........... | *ky* *kzn* |
| cozen......... | |
| cozy.......... | *kz,* *kb* |
| crab.......... | *kk* *kk* |
| crack......... | |
| cracker........ | *kl* *kdl* |
| crackle........ | |
| cradle........ | |
| craft.......... | *kf* *kfss-* |
| craftsman...... | |
| crafty......... | *kf,* |

**CRAFTY**

## CRAG

| | | | |
|---|---|---|---|
| crag | | crescent | |
| cram | | cress | |
| cramp | | cresset | |
| cranberry | | crest | |
| crane | | crestfallen | |
| craniology | | cretaceous | |
| cranium | | cretonne | |
| crank | | crevasse | |
| cranny | | crevice | |
| crape | | crew | |
| crash | | crewel | |
| crass | | crib | |
| crate | | cribbage | |
| crater | | cricket | |
| cravat | | cried | |
| crave | | crier | |
| craven | | cries | |
| crawl | | crime | |
| crayon | | criminal | |
| craze | | criminate | |
| crazy | | criminology | |
| creak | | crimp | |
| cream | | crimson | |
| creamery | | cringe | |
| creamy | | crinkle | |
| crease | | crinoline | |
| create | | cripple | |
| creation | | crisis | |
| creative | | crisp | |
| creator | | criterion | |
| creature | | critic | |
| credence | | critical | |
| credential | | criticise | |
| credible | | criticism | |
| credit | | croak | |
| creditable | | crochet | |
| creditor | | crock | |
| credulity | | crockery | |
| credulous | | crocodile | |
| creed | | crocus | |
| creek | | croft | |
| creep | | crone | |
| cremation | | crook | |
| crepe | | crooked | |
| crept | | crop | |
| crescendo | | cross | |

## CROSS

| | | | |
|---|---|---|---|
| crosswise... | *ks z* | culinary........ | *klny* |
| crouch...... | *krc* | cull.......... | *kl* |
| croup....... | *kp* *reup* | culminate....... | *klma* |
| croupier.... | *Kp, ko* | culmination..... | *klmy* |
| crow....... | | culpable........ | *klpb* |
| crowbar.... | *koba* | culprit.......... | *klpl* |
| crowd...... | *krd* | cultivate........ | *kllva* |
| crown...... | *krn* | cultivation...... | *kllvy* |
| crucial...... | *kuk* | culture......... | *kllu* |
| crucible..... | *ksb* | cumber.......... | *Kb* |
| crucifixion.. | *ksfkj* | cumberless...... | *Kbl'* |
| crucify...... | *ksf* *kd* | cumbersome.... | *Kbs* |
| crude....... | *kd )* | cumbrous....... | *Kbx* |
| crudity..... | | cumulate....... | *kla* |
| cruel....... | *kul* | cumulation...... | *kly kn* |
| cruelty..... | *kll, kul* | cunning........ | |
| cruet....... | | cup.......... | *kp kpb/* |
| cruise...... | *kz kl* | cupboard....... | |
| cruller...... | | cupidity........ | *kpd ) kpla* |
| crumb...... | *kr* | cupola......... | |
| crumble.... | *krb* | cur............ | *kr kua* |
| crumple.... | *krp Kp* | curate......... | *Kua* |
| crupper..... | | curator......... | *krb* |
| crusade..... | *ksd* | curb.......... | *k/ ku* |
| cruse....... | *kus* | curd.......... | |
| crush....... | *kz k,* | cure.......... | *krfu* |
| crust....... | *kc* | curfew........ | *kys)* |
| crutch...... | *ki* | curiosity....... | |
| cry......... | | curious........ | *kyx krl* |
| crypt....... | *kp* | curl........... | |
| crystal...... | *ksl* | curlew........ | *krlu* |
| crystalline.. | *ksln* | curly......... | *krl* |
| crystallize... | *kslz kb* | currant........ | *kr/* |
| cub........ | *kub kbl* | currency....... | *kr/* |
| cube........ | | current........ | *kr-* |
| cubical..... | *kl, kbl* | curry.......... | *ky* |
| cubist...... | | curse......... | *krs krsy* |
| cubit....... | | cursory........ | |
| cuckoo..... | *kku* | curtail......... | *k/l k/n* |
| cucumber... | *Kkb* | curtain........ | |
| cud........ | *kd* | curtsy......... | *k/s, krvb* |
| cuddle...... | *kdl* | curvature...... | |
| cudgel...... | *kjl* | curve.......... | *krv* |
| cue........ | *ku* | cushion........ | *kj* |
| cuff........ | *kf* | custard........ | *ksd* |
| cuirass..... | *gr'* | custodian...... | *ksdn* |

| | | | | |
|---|---|---|---|---|
| custody..... | *ksd, ks* | cuttlefish...... | *ktlf* | |
| custom...... | | cycle......... | *sk* | |
| customary... | *ksry* | cyclone........ | *skln* | |
| customer.... | *Ks* | cylinder....... | *Sl —* | |
| cut........ | *kt* | cylindrical..... | *Sl —K* | |
| cute........ | *ku* | cymbal........ | *srb* | |
| cuticle...... | *ktik* | cynic.......... | *srnk* | |
| cutlass...... | *ktl'* | cynical........ | *snk* | |
| cutlery...... | *ktly* | cynicism....... | *snsz* | |
| cutlet....... | *ktlt* | cypress........ | *sp'z* | |
| *cutler*....... | *Kt* | czar.......... | *za* | |

## D

| | | | | |
|---|---|---|---|---|
| dab........ | *db* | dandy......... | *d —,* | |
| dad........ | *dd* | danger........ | *Dgx, D1* | |
| daddy..... | *dd,* | dangerous..... | *Dgx* | |
| dado...... | *ddo* | dangle........ | *dgl* | |
| daffodil..... | *dfdl* | dank......... | *dq* | |
| dagger...... | *Dg* | dapper........ | *Dp* | |
| daily...... | *dl* | dapple........ | *dp* | |
| daintiness... | *d-'* | *dare*.......... | *da* | |
| dainty...... | *d-,* | daring........ | *da_* | |
| dairy....... | *dy* | *dark*......... | *drk* | |
| daisy....... | *dz,* | darken....... | *drkn, Drk* | |
| dale........ | *dal* | *darker*........ | *Drk* | |
| dalliance.... | *dl* | *darkly*........ | *drkl* | |
| dally....... | *dl* | darkness....... | *drk'* | |
| dam........ | *d* | darling....... | *drlg* | |
| damage..... | *dy* | darn......... | *drn* | |
| damageable. | *dyb* | dart......... | *d/* | |
| damask..... | *drsk* | dash......... | *dz, Dz* | |
| dame....... | *da* | dasher........ | | |
| damn....... | *d* | dastard....... | *dSd* | |
| damnable... | *dmb* | data.......... | *dta* | |
| damnation... | *dmy* | date.......... | *da* | |
| damp....... | *drp* | daub......... | *dab* | |
| dampness... | *drp'* | *daughter*...... | *Da* | |
| damper..... | *Drp* | daunt........ | *d-* | |
| damsel...... | *drsl* | dauntless...... | *d-l'* | |
| damson..... | *drsn* | dauntlessness.. | *d-"* | |
| *dance*....... | *d* | davenport..... | *dvnp/* | |
| *dancer*....... | *D* | davit......... | *dvt* | |
| dandelion.... | *d — ln* | daw.......... | *da* | |
| dandle...... | *d — l* | dawdle....... | *ddl* | |
| dandruff..... | *d — rf* | dawn........ | *dan* | |

# DAY

| | | | |
|---|---|---|---|
| day | *d* | decant | *dk-* |
| daybreak | *dbk* | decanter | *Dk-* |
| daylight | *dli* | decapitate | *dkpla* |
| dayspring | *dspg* | decay | *dka* |
| daytime | *dli* | decease | *dss* |
| daze | *dz* | deceit | *dse* |
| dazzle | *dzl* | deceitful | *dsef* |
| deacon | *dkn* | deceivable | *dseb* |
| dead | *dd* | deceive | *dse* |
| deaden | *ddn* | deceiver | *Dse* |
| deadliness | *ddl'* | December | *dc* |
| deadly | *ddl* | decent | *ds-* |
| deaf | *df* | decency | *ds/* |
| deafen | *dfn* | deception | *dspj* |
| deafness | *df'* | deceptive | *dspv* |
| deal | *dl* | decide | *dsd* |
| dealer | *Dl* | decidedly | *dsd* |
| dealing | *dl* | deciduous | *dsdx* |
| dean | *dn* | decimal (dec) | *dsrl* |
| deanery | *dny* | decipher | *dsf* |
| dear | *de* | decision | *dsy* |
| dearer | *De* | decisive | *dssv* |
| dearly | *del* | deck | *dk* |
| dearth | *drl* | declaim | *dc* |
| death | *dl* | declaimer | *Dc* |
| deathbed | *dlbd* | declamation | *dcy* |
| deathless | *dll'* | declamatory | *dcrly* |
| debar | *dba* | declarable | *dcb* |
| debarred | *dbā* | declaration | *dcy* |
| debark | *dbrk* | declarative | *dcv* |
| debase | *dbs* | declaratively | *dcvl* |
| debatable | *dbal* | declaratory | *dcly* |
| debate | *dba* | declare | *dc* |
| debauch | *dbc* | declarer | *Dc* |
| debauchery | *dbcy* | declension | *dcy* |
| debenture | *db-u* | declinable | *dcnb* |
| debilitate | *dbla* | declination | *dcny* |
| debit | *dbl* | declinatory | *dcnly* |
| debouch | *dbz* | decline | *dcn* |
| debris | *dbe* | decliner | *Dcn* |
| debt | *dl* | declinometer | *dcnre* |
| debtor | *Dl* | declinous | *dcnx* |
| decade | *dkd* | declivity | *dcv)* |
| decadence | *dkd* | declivous | *dcvt* |
| decagon | *dkgn* | decoction | *dkkj* |
| decamp | *dkrp* | decompose | *dkpz* |

**DECOMPOSE**

## DECOMPOSITION

| | | | |
|---|---|---|---|
| decomposition... | *dkpz* | defender...... | *Df* |
| decorate........ | *dka* | defense........ | *df* |
| decoration...... | *dky* | defenseless... | *dfl'* |
| decorative...... | *dkev* | defensible..... | *dfv* |
| decorator....... | *Dka* | defensive..... | *dfv* |
| decorous........ | *dkx* | defer......... | *df* |
| decorum........ | *dk* | deference..... | *df* |
| decoy.......... | *dky* | deferential.... | *dfx* |
| decrease........ | *dks* | defiance...... | *df* |
| decree......... | *dke* | defiant....... | *df* |
| decrement...... | *dk* | deficiency..... | *dfz* |
| decrepit........ | *dkpl* | deficient..... | *dfj* |
| decrepitude..... | *dkpld* | deficit........ | *dfsl* |
| decry.......... | *dke* | defile........ | *dfl* |
| decumbent...... | *dkb* | definable...... | *dfl* |
| dedicate........ | *ddka* | define...... | *dfe* |
| dedication...... | *ddky* | definite....... | *dfn* |
| deduce......... | *dds* | definition..... | *dfny* |
| deduct........ | *ddk* | definitive..... | *dfnv* |
| deductive...... | *ddkv* | deflect....... | *dflk* |
| deed.......... | *dd* | deflower...... | *d* |
| deem.......... | *de* | deforce....... | *dfs* |
| deep.......... | *dep* | deform........ | *df* |
| deepen........ | *dpn* | deformity..... | *df* |
| deeper......... | *Dp* | defraud....... | *dfd* |
| deeply......... | *dpl* | defray........ | *dfa* |
| deepness....... | *dp'* | deft.......... | *df* |
| deer.......... | *de* | defunct....... | *dfq* |
| deface......... | *dfs* | defy.......... | *df* |
| defacement..... | *dfs* | degenerate..... | *dJna* |
| defalcate....... | *dflka* | degeneration... | *dJny* |
| defalcation..... | *dflky* | degradation.... | *Dgd* |
| defamation..... | *dfy* | degrade....... | *Dgd* |
| defamatory..... | *dfdy* | degree........ | *Dg* |
| defame........ | *dfa* | deification.... | *df* |
| default........ | *dfll* | deify......... | *df* |
| defeasibility.... | *dfzl)* | deign......... | *dn* |
| defeasible...... | *dfzb* | deity......... | *d)* |
| defeasibleness... | *dfzb* | dejected...... | *djk* |
| defeat......... | *dfe* | dejection...... | *djky* |
| defect......... | *dfk* | delay......... | *dla* |
| defection...... | *dfky* | delectable..... | *dlkb* |
| defective....... | *dfkv* | delegate....... | *dlga* |
| defence........ | *df* | delegation..... | *dlgy* |
| defend........ | *df* | delete........ | *dle* |
| **defendant**....... | *df* | deleterious..... | *dllyx* |

## DELETION

| | |
|---|---|
| deletion | *dley* |
| delf | *dlf* |
| deliberate | *dLba* |
| deliberation | *dLby* |
| deliberative | *dLbv* |
| delicacy | *dlks,* |
| delicate | *dlka* |
| delicious | *dlx* |
| *delight* | *dle* |
| delightful | *dlef* |
| delightsome | *dles* |
| delineate | *dlna* |
| delineation | *dlny* |
| delineator | *Dlna* |
| delinquency | *dlq* |
| delinquent | *dlq-* |
| delirious | *dlyx* |
| delirium | *dly* |
| deliver | *dl* |
| deliverance | *dl* |
| deliverer | *Dl* |
| delivery | *dl* |
| dell | *dl* |
| delta | *dlla* |
| delude | *dld* |
| deluge | *dlg* |
| delusion | *dly* |
| delusive | *dlsv* |
| delve | *dlv* |
| demagog | *d gg* |
| *demand* | *d —* |
| demarcation | *d vrky* |
| demean | *d m* |
| demeanor | *D m* |
| dement | *d -* |
| demerit | *d vrt* |
| demise | *d z* |
| demission | *d y* |
| demit | *d l* |
| demobilization | *d vbzy* |
| demobilize | *d vbz* |
| democracy | *d vks,* |
| democrat | *d vkt* |
| democratic | *d vkt* |
| demolish | *d vlz* |
| demolition | *d vly* |

| | |
|---|---|
| demon | *d m* |
| demoniac | *d mk* |
| demoniacal | *d ml* |
| demonstrable | *d mSb* |
| demonstrate | *d mSa* |
| demonstration | *d mSy* |
| demonstrative | *d mSv* |
| demoralization | *d vlzy* |
| demoralize | *d vlz* |
| demur | *d vr* |
| demure | *d vu* |
| demureness | *d vu'* |
| demurrage | *d vy* |
| demurring | *d vr* |
| den | *dn* |
| denial | *dnel* |
| denizen | *dnzn* |
| denominate | *dn ma* |
| denomination | *dn my* |
| denominator | *Dn ma* |
| denotation | *dnly* |
| denote | *dnl* |
| denouement | *dn m,* |
| denounce | *dn* |
| denouncement | *dn-* |
| dense | *d '* |
| denseness | *d; d* |
| density | *d;* |
| dent | *d-* |
| dental | *d-l* |
| dentist | *d-,* |
| dentistry | *d-S,* |
| denudation | *dndy* |
| denude | *dnd* |
| denunciate | *dn'a* |
| denunciation | *dnly* |
| deny | *dnu* |
| depart | *dp/* |
| department (dpt) | *dp/-* |
| departure | *dp/u* |
| depauperize | *dppz* |
| depend | *dp —* |
| dependant | *dp — -* |
| dependence | *dp —/* |
| dependency | *dp —* |
| dependent | *dp — -* |

**DEPENDENT**

DEPICT

| | |
|---|---|
| depict......... | *dpk* |
| deplete........ | *dpe* |
| depletion...... | *dpej* |
| deplorable..... | *dpób* |
| deplore........ | *dpo* |
| deploy......... | *dpy* |
| depone........ | *dpm* |
| deponent...... | *dpm-* |
| depopulate..... | *dppla* |
| depopulation... | *dpply* |
| deport......... | *dp/* |
| deportation..... | *dp/j* |
| deportment.... | *dp/-* |
| depose........ | *dpz* |
| deposit........ | *dpzl* |
| depositary...... | *dpzly* |
| depositor...... | *Dpz* |
| depot.......... | *dpo* |
| depravation.... | *dpzy* |
| deprave........ | *dpa* |
| depravity...... | *dpv)* |
| deprecate...... | *dpka* |
| deprecatory.... | *dpkly* |
| depreciate..... | *dpza* |
| depreciation.... | *dpzj* |
| depreciative.... | *dpzv* |
| depreciatory.... | *dpzly* |
| depredate...... | *dpda* |
| depredation.... | *dpdj* |
| depress........ | *dp'* |
| depression..... | *dpj* |
| deprivation..... | *dpvy* |
| deprive........ | *dpv* |
| depth.......... | *dpl* |
| deputation..... | *dpuy* |
| depute......... | *dpu* |
| deputy......... | *dpl,* |
| derange....... | *dry* |
| derangement... | *dry-* |
| derelict........ | *dylk* |
| deride......... | *drd* |
| derision........ | *dry* |
| derisive........ | *drsv* |
| derisory....... | *drsy* |
| derivation...... | *dyvy* |
| derivative...... | *drvr* |

| | |
|---|---|
| derive........ | *dru* |
| derogate...... | *drga* |
| derogatory.... | *drgly* |
| derrick...... | *drk* |
| dervish....... | *drv?* |
| descant...... | *dsk-* |
| descend...... | *ds—* |
| descendant... | *ds—-* |
| descent....... | *ds-* |
| describe..... | *des* |
| description.... | *des* |
| descriptive... | *desv* |
| descry........ | *dsku* |
| desecrate..... | *dska* |
| desecration.... | *dskj* |
| desert........ | *do/* |
| desertion..... | *dsj* |
| deserve....... | *dsv* |
| desiccate...... | *dska* |
| desiderate.... | *Dsa* |
| desideratum... | *Dsa* |
| design........ | *dzm* |
| designate..... | *dzgna* |
| designation... | *dzgnj* |
| designer...... | *Dzm* |
| desirable..... | *dzb* |
| desire........ | *dze* |
| desirous...... | *dzx* |
| desist........ | *ds,* |
| desk......... | *dsk* |
| desolate...... | *dsla* |
| desolation..... | *dslj* |
| despair....... | *dsa* |
| despatch...... | *dsc* |
| desperado..... | *dsdo* |
| desperate..... | *dsa* |
| desperation.... | *dsj* |
| despicable..... | *dskb* |
| despise....... | *dsz* |
| despite........ | *dsu* |
| despoil....... | *dsyl* |
| despoliation.... | *dslj* |
| despond...... | *ds—* |
| despondency... | *ds—/* |
| despondent.... | *ds—-* |
| despot........ | *dsl* |

DESPOT

DESPOTISM.

despotism....... *dstz dz/*
dessert......... *dsny*
destination...... *dsn*
destine......... *dsn*
destiny......... *dsn,*
destitute........ *dstu*
destitution...... *dsly*
destroy......... *dsy*
destroyer....... *dsyr*
destructible..... *dskb*
destruction...... *dsky*
destructive...... *dskv*
desultoriness.... *dslly*
desultory....... *dslly*
detach.......... *dlc*
detachment..... *dlc-*
detail.......... *dll*
detain......... *dln*
detect......... *dlk*
detection....... *dlkf*
detective........ *dlkv*
detector........ *Dlk*
detention....... *dly*
deter......... *Dra D*
deteriorate...... *Dry*
deterioration.... *D ma*
determinate..... *D my*
determination... *D m*
determine....... *D m*
determined...... *dl,*
deterrent....... *D-*
detest.......... *dslb*
detestable...... *dlsf*
detestation...... *dlm*
dethrone........ *dlm-*
dethronement... *dlna*
detonate........ *dlu*
detour......... *Dk*
detract......... *D-l D-*
detriment....... *D-l*
detrimental..... *dus*
deuce.......... *dvsa*
devastate....... *dvsf*
devastation..... *dvlp*
develop........ *dvlp-*
development....

deviate....... *dwa dvs*
device........ *dvl*
devil........ *dvl dvlz*
deviiish....... *dvx*
devious....... *dvz*
devise........ *Dvz*
deviser....... *dvyd*
devoid........ *dvlf*
devolution... *dolv*
devolve....... *dvo*
devote........ *dvy*
devotion....... *dvvr*
devour....... *dvl*
devout....... *du*
dew.......... *dudp*
dewdrop....... *du,*
dewy......... *Dx)*
dexterity....... *Dxx*
dexterous..... *dblk*
diabolic........ *dd*
diadem........ *dgnss*
diagnosis...... *dgml*
diagonal...... *dg*
diagram....... *dil*
dial......... *dlk*
dialect........ *dlkt*
dialectic....... *dlktl*
dialectical..... *dlg*
dialogue...... *d se*
diameter...... *d sekl*
diametrically... *d -*
diamond....... *Dp*
diaper........ *dfvx*
diaphanous..... *df*
diaphragm..... *dy*
diary......... *dlnk*
diatonic....... *dlrb*
diatribe....... *des*
dice.......... *dkla*
dictate......... *dkly*
dictation....... *Dkla*
dictator........ *dklyl*
dictatorial...... *dkf*
diction......... *dkfy dk*
dictionary.....
dictum........

DICTUM

## DID

|  | |
|---|---|
| did | dd |
| didn't | dd– |
| die | du |
| diet | dil |
| differ | df |
| difference | df |
| different | df– |
| difficult | dfk |
| difficulties | dfks |
| difficulty | dfk |
| diffident | dfd– |
| diffuse | dfz |
| diffusible | dfzl |
| diffusive | dfsv |
| dig | dg |
| digest | dj |
| digestible | dysl |
| digestion | dysy |
| digestive | dysv |
| digger | Dg |
| dignify | dgnf |
| dignitary | dgnly |
| dignity | dgn) |
| digress | Dg' |
| digression | Dgy |
| digressive | Dgsv |
| dike | dik |
| dilapidate | dlpda |
| dilapidated | dlpdā |
| dilapidation | dlpdy |
| dilatable | dlab |
| dilatation | dlly |
| dilate | dla |
| dilatory | dlly |
| dilemma | dlra |
| dilettante | dll– |
| diligence | dly |
| diligent | dlg– |
| dilute | dlu |
| dilution | dly |
| diluvial | dlvl |
| dim | d |
| dime | du |
| dimension | dy |
| diminish | dmy |
| diminution | dmy |

|  | |
|---|---|
| diminutive | dmv |
| dimly | dl |
| dimple | dp |
| din | dn |
| dine | din |
| dingle | dgl |
| dingy | dy |
| dinner | Dn |
| diocese | dss |
| dip | dp |
| diphtheria | aflya |
| diphthong | aflg |
| diploma | dpra |
| diplomacy | dprs |
| diplomat | dprl |
| diplomatic | dprt |
| diplomatist | dprl |
| dipper | Dp |
| dipsomania | dpsma |
| dire | du |
| direct | drk |
| direction | drky |
| directive | drkv |
| directly | drkl |
| director | Drk |
| dirge | dry |
| dirigible | dryl |
| dirk | drk |
| dirt | d |
| dirty | d |
| disable | dsb |
| disabuse | dsbz |
| disadvantage | dsav |
| disadvantageous | dsavx |
| disaffect | dsfk |
| disaffection | dsfky |
| disagree | dsdg |
| disagreeable | dsdgl |
| disagreement | dsdg– |
| disallow | dsl |
| disallowance | dsl |
| disannul | dsnl |
| disappear | dsap |
| disappearance | dsap |
| disappoint | dspy– |
| disappointment | dspy– |

**DISAPPOINTMENT**

## DISAPPROBATION

| | |
|---|---|
| disapprobation. *dspby* | discord.......... *dsk/* |
| disapprove...... *dspv* | discordant....... *dsk/-* |
| disarm........ *dsa* | discount........ *dis* |
| disarmament... *dsa-* | discountenance... *dskl/* |
| disarrange..... *dsry* | discourage....... *dskry* |
| disarray....... *dsra* | discouragement.. *dskry-* |
| disassociate.... *dsza* | discourse........ *dskrs* |
| disassociation.. *dszj* | discourteous..... *dsk/x* |
| disaster....... *ds* | discover........ *dskv* |
| disastrous...... *dsse* | discoverer....... *dskvr* |
| disavow....... *dsv* | discovery....... *dskv,* |
| disband........ *dsb —* | discredit........ *dscr* |
| disbelief....... *dsblf* | discreditable....... *dscrb* |
| disburden..... *dsb/m* | discreet.......... *dske* |
| disburse....... *dsbrs* | discrepancy..... *dskp/* |
| disc........... *dsk* | discrepant...... *dskp-* |
| discard........ *dsk/* | discretion........ *dsky* |
| discern........ *dsn* | discretionary..... *dskyy* |
| discernible..... *dsnb* | discriminate...... *dsk na* |
| discerning..... *dsn* | discrimination.... *dsk ny* |
| discernment.... *dsn-* | discriminative.... *dsk nv* |
| discharge...... *dscg* | discursive........ *dskrsv* |
| disciple........ *dsp* | discuss.......... *dsk* |
| disciplinarian.. *dspnyn* | discussion........ *dsky* |
| disciplinary.... *dspny* | disdain.......... *dsdn* |
| discipline...... *dspn* | disdainful........ *dsdnf* |
| disclaim....... *dskla* | disease.......... *dzz* |
| disclose....... *dsklz* | disembark....... *ds brk* |
| disclosure...... *dsklz/* | disembarrass..... *ds br* |
| discolor........ *dstl* | disembody....... *ds bd,* |
| discoloration... *dstly* | disembogue...... *ds bg* |
| discomfit....... *dskft* | disenchant....... *dsnc* |
| discomfiture.... *dskflu* | disenchantment.. *dsnc --* |
| discompose.... *dskpz* | disencumber..... *dsnkb* |
| discomposure.. *dskpz* | disendow........ *ds — v* |
| disconcert...... *dsks/* | disengage........ *dsngj* |
| disconnect..... *dsknk* | disengagement... *dsngj -* |
| disconnection.. *dsknkj* | disentail. ...... *ds - l* |
| disconsolate.... *dsksla* | disentangle...... *ds - gl* |
| discontent..... *dskl -* | disentanglement.. *ds - gl -* |
| discontentment. *dskl --* | disenthral....... *dsnll* |
| discontinuance. *dsku* | disenthrone...... *dsnln* |
| discontinuation. *dsky* | disentitle........ *dsnttl* |
| discontinue.... *dsku* | disentomb....... *dsnlu* |
| discontinuity... *dsku)* | disestablish...... *dsesl* |
| discontinuous.. *dskux* | disesteem........ *dsse* |

**DISESTEEM**

DISFAVOR

| | | | |
|---|---|---|---|
| disfavor... ... | *dsdv* | dismissal...... | *dsrsl* |
| disfigure........ | *dsfg* | dismount....... | *ds r-* |
| disfigurement... | *dsfg-* | disobedience.... | *dsbd* |
| disfranchise..... | *dsfez* | disobedient..... | *dsbd-* |
| disfranchisement | *dsfcz-* | disobey........ | *dsba* |
| disgorge........ | *dsgy* | disoblige....... | *dsby* |
| disgrace... | *dsgs* | disorder....... | *dsO* |
| disgraceful...... | *dsgsf* | disorganization.. | *dsoq* |
| disguise........ | *dsgz* | disorganize..... | *dsoq* |
| disgust......... | *dsq,* | disown........ | *dson* |
| dish........... | *d? * | disparage...... | *dsfq* |
| dishearten...... | *dsh/m* | disparagement.. | *dsfq-* |
| dishevel........ | *dzvl* | disparity........ | *ds)* |
| dishonest....... | *dson,* | dispassionate... | *dsja* |
| dishonesty...... | *dsons,* | dispatch........ | *dsc* |
| dishonor........ | *dsOn* | dispel.......... | *dsl* |
| dishonorable.... | *dsOnb* | dispensable..... | *dslb* |
| disillusion....... | *dsly* | dispensary...... | *dsly* |
| disillusionment.. | *dsly-* | dispensation.... | *dslf* |
| disincline....... | *dsncn* | dispense........ | *ds* |
| disinfect........ | *dsnfk* | disperse........ | *dss* |
| disinfection..... | *dsnfky* | dispersion...... | *dsf* |
| disingenuous... | *dsngnu* | dispirit......... | *dsrl* |
| disinherit....... | *dsnrl* | displace........ | *dspl* |
| disintegrate..... | *ds-ga* | displant........ | *ds-* |
| disintegration... | *ds-gy* | display. ....... | *dsa* |
| disinter........ | *dsN* | displease....... | *dsz* |
| disinterested.... | *dsNo* | displeasure...... | *dsf* |
| disjoin.......... | *dsyyn* | disport......... | *ds/* |
| disjoint........ | *dsyy-* | disposal........ | *dszl* |
| disjunction...... | *dsygy* | dispose........ | *dsz* |
| disjunctive...... | *dsygv* | disposition...... | *dszy* |
| disk........... | *dsk* | dispossess...... | *dspz* |
| dislike.......... | *dslk* | disproportion.... | *dspf* |
| dislocate........ | *dslka* | disproportionate. | *dspfa* |
| dislocation...... | *dslkf* | disprove........ | *dsv* |
| dislodge........ | *dsly* | disputant....... | *dsu-* |
| disloyal......... | *dslyl* | disputation...... | *dsuy* |
| disloyalty...... | *dslyll,* | dispute......... | *dsu* |
| dismal......... | *dz rl* | disqualification.. | *dsqlf* |
| dismantle....... | *ds r-l* | disqualify....... | *dsqlf* |
| dismast......... | *ds,* | disquiet........ | *dsql* |
| dismay......... | *ds ra* | disquietude..... | *dsqld* |
| dismember..... | *ds rb* | disquisition..... | *dsqz* |
| dismemberment. | *ds rb-* | disregard....... | *dsrg/* |
| dismiss......... | *ds ,* | disrelish....... | *dsrlz* |

DISRELISH

**DISREPAIR**

| | | | |
|---|---|---|---|
| disrepair | *dsrpa* | distinction | *dsq* |
| disreputable | *dsrpub* | distinctive | *dsqr* |
| disrepute | *dskpu* | distinguish | *dsqz* |
| disrespect | *dsrsk* | distinguished | *dsqz* |
| disrespectful | *dsrskf* | distort | *dsf* |
| disrobe | *dsrb* | distortion | *dsf* |
| disruption | *dsrpy* | distract | *dsk* |
| disruptive | *dsrpv* | distraction | *dsky* |
| dissatisfaction | *dsal* | distrain | *dsn* |
| dissatisfy | *dsal* | distraught | *dsl* |
| dissect | *dsk* | distress | *ds'* |
| dissemble | *dsrb* | distressful | *dssf* |
| dissembler | *Dsrb* | distribute | *dsbu* |
| disseminate | *dsrna* | distribution | *dsby* |
| dissemination | *dsrny* | distributive | *dsbv* |
| dissension | *dsy* | district | *dsk* |
| dissent | *ds-* | distrust | *ds,* |
| dissertation | *ds/q* | distrustful | *dssf* |
| disservice | *dsvs* | disturb | *dsb* |
| dissimilar | *dsrl* | disturbance | *dsb* |
| dissimilarity | *dsrl)* | disunion | *dsun* |
| dissimilitude | *dsrlld* | disuse | *dsus* |
| dissimulation | *dsrly* | disyllable | *dslb* |
| dissipate | *dspa* | ditch | *dc* |
| dissipation | *dspy* | ditto | *dlo* |
| dissociate | *dsza* | ditty | *d)* |
| dissoluble | *dslb* | diurnal | *drnl* |
| dissolute | *dslu* | divan | *dvn* |
| dissolution | *dsly* | divaricate | *dvyka* |
| dissolve | *dzlv* | dive | *dc* |
| dissonant | *dsn-* | diver | *Dc* |
| dissuade | *dsrd* | diverge | *dvry* |
| dissuasion | *dsy* | divergent | *dvry-* |
| dissuasive | *dsrsv* | diverse | *dvrs* |
| distaff | *dsf* | diversity | *dvrs)* |
| distance | *ds* | divert | *dv/* |
| distant | *ds-* | divest | *dv,* |
| distaste | *ds,* | divestment | *dvs-* |
| distasteful | *dssf* | divide | *dvd* |
| distemper | *dsIrp* | dividend | *dvd-* |
| distend | *ds-* | dividends | *dvd--* |
| distil | *dsl* | divider | *Dvd* |
| distillation | *dsly* | dividing | *dvd* |
| distiller | *Dsl* | divination | *dvnj* |
| distillery | *dsly* | divine | *dvn* |
| distinct | *dsq* | divinity | *dvn)* |

**DIVINITY**

DIVISIBILITY

| | | | |
|---|---|---|---|
| divisibility..... | *dvzb* | domicile......... | *dnsl* |
| divisible....... | *dvzb* | dominant........ | *d m-* |
| division....... | *dv Dvz* | dominate........ | *d ma* |
| divisor........ | | domination...... | *d my* |
| divorce........ | *dvrs* | domineer........ | *d me* |
| divulge........ | *divlg* | dominical........ | *d mk* |
| dizzy.......... | *dz,* | dominion (dom).. | *d mn* |
| *do*............ | *du* | domino.......... | *d mo* |
| docile......... | *dsl* | don.............. | *dn* |
| dock.......... | *dk* | donation......... | *dny* |
| docket......... | *dkl* | done............. | *dn* |
| *doctor*........ | *dr* | donkey.......... | *dq,* |
| doctrinaire..... | *Dkna* | donor........... | *Dn* |
| doctrine...... | *Dkn* | *don't*........... | *do-* |
| document...... | *dk-* | doom........... | *du* |
| documentary... | *dk-y* | *door*........... | *do* |
| dodder........ | *Dd* | doorstep........ | *dosp* |
| dodge........ | *dy* | doorway........ | *do a* |
| dodo......... | *dao* | dormant........ | *do-* |
| doe.......... | *do* | dormitory....... | *do-ly* |
| *doer*......... | *Du* | dorsal.......... | *dosl* |
| *does*........ | *dz* | dory........... | *dy* |
| doesn't....... | *dz-* | dose........... | *dos* |
| doff.......... | *df* | dost........... | *d,* |
| *dog*.......... | *dy* | dot........... | *dl* |
| doge......... | *doy* | dotage......... | *dy dl/* |
| doggerel...... | *Dgl* | dotard......... | |
| dogma....... | *dgra* | dote.......... | *do* |
| dogmatic..... | *dgr* | doth.......... | *dl* |
| dogmatism.... | *dg-lz* | double......... | *db* |
| dogmatize..... | *dg-lz* | doublet........ | *dbl* |
| doily......... | *dyl* | doubt......... | *d l* |
| doings........ | *du* | *doubter*....... | *Dl* |
| doldrums...... | *Drs* | doubtful....... | *d Y* |
| doleful....... | *dlf* | .doubtless....... | *d ll* |
| doll.......... | *dl* | douche........ | *duz* |
| dollar (d)..... | *Dl* | dough......... | *do* |
| dolly........ | *dl,* | doughnut...... | *donl* |
| dolmen....... | *dl m* | doughty....... | *d l,* |
| dolorous...... | *dlrx* | dove.......... | *dv* |
| dolphin....... | *dlfn* | dower......... | *D* |
| dolt......... | *dll* | *down*......... | *d m* |
| domain....... | *d m* | downcast...... | *d mk,* |
| dome........ | *do* | downright...... | *d mu* |
| *domestic*..... | *d S* | downstairs...... | *d msas* |
| domesticate.... | *drska* | *downward*...... | *d m/* |

DOWNWARD

## DOWNWARDS

| | |
|---|---|
| downwards.... | *shorthand* |
| downy........ | *shorthand* |
| dowry........ | *shorthand* |
| doxology...... | *shorthand* |
| doze......... | *shorthand* |
| dozen (doz)... | *shorthand* |
| drab......... | *shorthand* |
| drachm....... | *shorthand* |
| draft........ | *shorthand* |
| drag......... | *shorthand* |
| dragoman..... | *shorthand* |
| dragon........ | *shorthand* |
| dragoon....... | *shorthand* |
| drain........ | *shorthand* |
| drainage..... | *shorthand* |
| drake........ | *shorthand* |
| dram........ | *shorthand* |
| drama........ | *shorthand* |
| dramatic...... | *shorthand* |
| drank........ | *shorthand* |
| drape......... | *shorthand* |
| drapery....... | *shorthand* |
| drastic........ | *shorthand* |
| draught....... | *shorthand* |
| draughtsman.. | *shorthand* |
| *draw*........ | *shorthand* |
| drawback..... | *shorthand* |
| drawbridge.... | *shorthand* |
| *drawer*....... | *shorthand* |
| drawl........ | *shorthand* |
| drawn........ | *shorthand* |
| dray......... | *shorthand* |
| dread........ | *shorthand* |
| dreadful...... | *shorthand* |
| *dream*........ | *shorthand* |
| *dreamer*...... | *shorthand* |
| dreamland.... | *shorthand* |
| dreary........ | *shorthand* |
| dreg.......... | *shorthand* |
| drench........ | *shorthand* |
| *dress*......... | *shorthand* |
| *dresser*....... | *shorthand* |
| dressmaker.... | *shorthand* |
| drew......... | *shorthand* |
| dribble....... | *shorthand* |
| driblet........ | *shorthand* |

| | |
|---|---|
| dried............ | *shorthand* |
| drier............ | *shorthand* |
| drift............. | *shorthand* |
| driftwood........ | *shorthand* |
| *drill*............ | *shorthand* |
| *drink*........... | *shorthand* |
| *drinker*.......... | *shorthand* |
| drip............. | *shorthand* |
| *drive*............ | *shorthand* |
| drivel........... | *shorthand* |
| *driver*........... | *shorthand* |
| drizzle........... | *shorthand* |
| droll............. | *shorthand* |
| dromedary........ | *shorthand* |
| drone............ | *shorthand* |
| droop............ | *shorthand* |
| *drop*............. | *shorthand* |
| dropsy........... | *shorthand* |
| droshky (drosky)... | *shorthand* |
| dross............ | *shorthand* |
| drought........... | *shorthand* |
| drove............ | *shorthand* |
| drown............ | *shorthand* |
| drowsiness......... | *shorthand* |
| drowsy........... | *shorthand* |
| drub............. | *shorthand* |
| drudge........... | *shorthand* |
| drudgery......... | *shorthand* |
| drug............. | *shorthand* |
| drugget........... | *shorthand* |
| druggist.......... | *shorthand* |
| drum............. | *shorthand* |
| drunk............ | *shorthand* |
| drunkard.......... | *shorthand* |
| drunken.......... | *shorthand* |
| drunkenness....... | *shorthand* |
| drupe............ | *shorthand* |
| *dry*............. | *shorthand* |
| dryad............ | *shorthand* |
| dryer............ | *shorthand* |
| dryly............ | *shorthand* |
| dual............. | *shorthand* |
| dub............. | *shorthand* |
| dubiety........... | *shorthand* |
| dubious........... | *shorthand* |
| ducat............ | *shorthand* |

**DUCAT**

DUCHESS

duchess........ *dc'*
duck.......... *dk*
duckling....... *dklg*
duct.......... *dk*
ductile........ *dkl*
dudgeon....... *djn*
due........... *du*
duel.......... *dul*
duellist........ *dul,*
duet.......... *dul*
dug........... *dg*
duke.......... *duk*
dulcet........ *dlsl*
dull.......... *dl*
dulness........ *dl'*
duly.......... *dul*
dumb......... *d,*
dump......... *dsp*
dun........... *dn*
dunce......... *d*
dung.......... *dg*
dungeon....... *djn*
duo........... *duo*
dupe.......... *dup*
duplicate (dup). *dpka*
duplication..... *dpkj*
duplicity....... *dps)*
durable........ *dub*

duration..... *diy*
durbar...... *drba*
dure........ *du*
during....... *du*
durst........ *dr,*
dusk........ *dsk*
dusky....... *dsk,*
dust........ *d,*
duster....... *dS*
dusty....... *ds,*
dutiable..... *dtb.*
dutifully..... *dly*
duty........ *dl,*
dwarf....... *drf*
dwell....... *dl*
dweller..... *Dl*
dwelling.... *dl*
dwelt....... *dll*
dwindle.... *d—l*
dye........ *du*
dying....... *du*
dynamic..... *dnsk*
dynamite.... *dnn*
dynamo..... *dno*
dynasty..... *dns,*
dysentery.... *ds-y*
dyspepsia.... *dspps*
dyspeptic.... *dsppt*

E

each.......... *ec*
eager.......... *Eg*
eagerness...... *Eg'*
eagle.......... *egl*
eaglet......... *eglt*
ear........... *er*
earl.......... *El*
earldom...... *Eld*
earlier........ *El*
early......... *El*
earn.......... *En*
earnest........ *En,*
earnestness.... *Ens'*
earning........ *En*

earth........ *El*
earthen...... *Eln*
earthly...... *Ell*
earthward.... *El/*
ease........ *ez*
easel....... *ezl*
easier....... *Eg*
easily....... *ezl*
east......... *eS*
Easter....... *eS*
easterly..... *eSl*
eastern...... *Ern*
eastward..... *E/*
easy........ *ez*

EASY

| | | | |
|---|---|---|---|
| eat........... | *el* | effacement....... | *efs-* |
| eatable....... | *elb* | effect............ | *efk* |
| eater......... | *El* | effective......... | *efkv* |
| eaves......... | *evs* | effectual......... | *efkl* |
| ebb.......... | *eb* | effeminacy....... | *ef vs,* |
| ebony........ | *ebn,* | effeminate....... | *ef ma* |
| ebullition..... | *ebl* | effervesce........ | *efvs* |
| ecarté........ | *ek/a* | effete............ | *efe* |
| eccentric...... | *X-k* | efficacious....... | *efkv* |
| eccentrical.... | *X-K* | efficiency........ | *efʒ* |
| eccentricity... | *X-ʃ* | efficient......... | *efʒ-* |
| ecclesiastic.... | *eklzS* | effort............ | *efl* |
| echo......... | *eko* | effrontery....... | *ef-y* |
| eclat......... | *ekla* | effulgent........ | *efly-* |
| eclectic....... | *eklkT* | effusion......... | *efl* |
| eclipse........ | *eklps* | effusive.......... | *efsv* |
| ecliptic....... | *eklpT* | egg.............. | *eg* |
| eclogue....... | *eklg* | egoism........... | *egz* |
| economic..... | *ek-k* | egoist........... | *eg,* |
| economical... | *ek-l* | egotist.......... | *egl,* |
| economist.... | *ek-,* | egotistical........ | *eglsk* |
| economy...... | *ek-,* | egregious......... | *egx* |
| ecstasy....... | *xs,* | egress............ | *eg'* |
| ecstatic....... | *xT* | eider............. | *d* |
| eczema....... | *x-a* | eiderdown........ | *ld-* |
| eddy......... | *ed,* | eider-duck....... | *ldk* |
| edge......... | *ey* | eidograph........ | *dgf* |
| edging....... | *ey-* | eight (8).......... | *8* |
| edible........ | *edb* | eighteen (18)...... | *18* |
| edict........ | *edk* | eighteenth (18t)... | *18l* |
| edification.... | *edf* | eighth (8t)........ | *8l* |
| edifice........ | *edfs* | eighty (80)........ | *80* |
| edify......... | *edf* | either............ | *E* |
| edit.......... | *edl* | ejaculate.......... | *eykla* |
| edition....... | *edy* | ejaculation........ | *eykly* |
| editor........ | *Ed* | ejaculatory........ | *eyklly* |
| editorial...... | *Edl* | eject............. | *eyk* |
| educate....... | *edka* | ejection.......... | *eykf* |
| education..... | *edky* | ejectment........ | *eyk-* |
| educational... | *edkjl* | eke............... | *ek* |
| educe........ | *eds* | elaborate......... | *eLba* |
| eel.......... | *el* | elaborately....... | *eLbal* |
| e'er.......... | *er* | elaboration....... | *eLby* |
| eerie......... | *er,* | elapse............ | *elps* |
| efface........ | *efs* | elastic............ | *elS* |
| effaceable.... | *efsb* | elasticity......... | *elssʃ* |

**ELATE**

| | |
|---|---|
| elate.......... | elevate........ |
| elation......... | elevation....... |
| elbow.......... | elevator....... |
| elder.......... | eleven (11)..... |
| elderberry..... | eleventh (11t).. |
| eldest......... | elf............ |
| elect.......... | elicit......... |
| election........ | elide.......... |
| elector........ | eligibility..... |
| electric........ | eligible........ |
| electrical....... | eliminate...... |
| electrically..... | elimination..... |
| electrician..... | elision......... |
| electricity...... | ell............ |
| electrifiable.... | ellipse......... |
| electrification... | elm........... |
| electrified...... | elocution...... |
| electrify....... | elocutionist..... |
| electrifying..... | elongate....... |
| electro......... | elope......... |
| electrocute..... | eloquence...... |
| electrocution... | eloquent...... |
| electrode...... | else.......... |
| electrolier...... | elsewhere...... |
| electrology..... | elucidate....... |
| electrolysis..... | elucidation..... |
| electrolyte...... | elude.......... |
| electrolyzable... | elusion........ |
| electrolyze..... | elusive........ |
| electrolyzing... | elusory........ |
| electro-magnet.. | elves......... |
| electro-magnetism | elysian........ |
| electrometer.... | elysium........ |
| electromotor... | emaciate....... |
| electroplate..... | emaciation..... |
| electroscope.... | emanate....... |
| electrotype..... | emanation..... |
| electrotyper.... | emancipation... |
| eleemosynary... | emancipator.... |
| elegance....... | emasculate..... |
| elegant........ | embalm....... |
| elegy.......... | embank....... |
| element....... | embankment... |
| elementary..... | embargo....... |
| elephant....... | embark........ |
| elephantine.... | embarkation... |

**EMBARKATION**

## EMBARRASS

| | |
|---|---|
| embarrass...... | *ibr* |
| embarrassment.. | *ibrs-* |
| embassy........ | *ibo,* |
| embattle........ | *ibll* |
| embattled....... | *ibll* |
| embellish....... | *iblz* |
| embellishment .. | *iblz-* |
| ember.......... | *ib* |
| embezzle....... | *ibzl* |
| embitter........ | *ibl* |
| emblazon........ | *iblzn* |
| emblazonment... | *iblzn-* |
| emblazonry..... | *iblznr,* |
| emblem........ | *ib* |
| emblematic...... | *ib-* |
| embodiment..... | *ibd-* |
| embody......... | *ibd,* |
| embolden....... | *ibdln* |
| embosom........ | *ibz* |
| emboss........ | *ib'* |
| embossment.... | *ibs-* |
| embowel........ | *ibl* |
| embower....... | *ib-* |
| embrace........ | *ibs* |
| embrasure...... | *ibz* |
| embrocate...... | *ibka* |
| embrocation..... | *ibkj* |
| embroider...... | *iBy* |
| embroidery..... | *iBy,* |
| embroil........ | *ibyl* |
| embryo......... | *ibo* |
| embryonic...... | *ibnk* |
| emend.......... | *is* |
| emendation..... | *is—j* |
| emendator...... | *is—d* |
| emerald........ | *ild.* |
| emerge........ | *isj* |
| emergency...... | *isj* |
| emeritus........ | *islk* |
| emersion....... | *isj* |
| emery.......... | *is* |
| emetic.......... | *ist* |
| emigrant........ | *iq-* |
| emigrate........ | *iga* |
| emigration...... | *igj* |
| eminence....... | *im* |

| | |
|---|---|
| eminent......... | *im-* |
| emission........ | *isj* |
| emit............ | *ist* |
| emollient........ | *isl-* |
| emolument....... | *islu-* |
| emotion........ | *isj* |
| emperor........ | *ip* |
| emphasize....... | *ifz* |
| emphatic........ | *ift* |
| empire......... | *ipi* |
| empiric......... | *ipik* |
| empiricism...... | *ipiz* |
| employ........ | *ipy* |
| employee....... | *ipye* |
| employer....... | *ipy* |
| employment..... | *ipy-ipy* |
| emporium....... | *ip'* |
| empress........ | *ip'* |
| emptiness....... | *i'* |
| empty.......... | *il,* |
| empyreal........ | *ipyl* |
| emulate......... | *ila* |
| emulation....... | *ij* |
| emulsion........ | *ilj* |
| enable.......... | *nb* |
| enact.......... | *nak* |
| enactment...... | *nak-* |
| enamel.......... | *nl* |
| enamor......... | *nl* |
| enamored....... | *nl* |
| encage......... | *nkj* |
| encamp........ | *nkjp* |
| encase........ | *nks* |
| encaustic....... | *nkS* |
| enchant........ | *nc-* |
| enchantment..... | *nc--* |
| enchantress...... | *nc-'* |
| encircle........ | *nCl* |
| enclitic......... | *ncT* |
| enclose......... | *ncz* |
| enclosure........ | *ncz* |
| encomiast........ | *nks,* |
| encomium....... | *nk* |
| encompass........ | *nkp'* |
| encompassment... | *nkps-* |
| encore.......... | *nks* |

**ENCORE**

## ENCOUNTER

| | | | |
|---|---|---|---|
| encounter | *nk* | engross | *ng'* |
| encourage | *nkry* | engrossment | *ngs-* |
| encouragement | *nkry-* | engulf | *nglf* |
| encroach | *nkc* | enhance | *nh* |
| encroachment | *nkc-* | enhancement | *nh-* |
| encrust | *nk,* | enigma | *ngra* |
| encrustation | *nksy* | enigmatic | *ngr* |
| encumber | *nKb* | enjoin | *nyyn* |
| encumbrance | *nKbl* | enjoy | *nyy* |
| encyclical | *nsklk* | enjoyable | *nyyb* |
| encyclopaedia | *nsklpd* | enjoyment | *nyy-* |
| end | *e —* | enkindle | *nk—l* |
| endanger | *ndy* | enlarge | *nly* |
| endear | *nde* | enlargement | *nly-* |
| endearment | *nde-* | enlighten | *nlin* |
| endeavor | *nDv* | enlightenment | *nlin-* |
| endemic | *ndrk* | enlist | *nl,* |
| ending | *e —* | enlistment | *nls-* |
| endless | *e — l'* | enliven | *nlin* |
| endogen | *ndyn* | enmity | *n,)* |
| endorse | *ndrs* | ennoble | *nnb* |
| endorsement | *ndrs-* | ennui | *n-e* |
| endow | *nd* | enormous | *nr-x* |
| endowment | *nd-* | enough | *nf* |
| endue | *ndu* | enquire | *nqu* |
| endurance | *ndu* | enrage | *nry* |
| endure | *ndu* | enrapture | *nrpu* |
| enema | *nra* | enrich | *nrc* |
| enemy | *n,)* | enroll | *nrl* |
| energetic | *nyt* | enrollment | *nrl-* |
| energy | *ny,* | ensample | *ns-p* |
| enervate | *nva* | ensconce | *nsk* |
| enfeeble | *nfb* | enshrine | *nzin* |
| enfilade | *nfld* | enshroud | *nzrd* |
| enfold | *nfol* | ensign | *nsn* |
| enforce | *nfs* | ensilage | *nsly* |
| engage | *ngy* | enslave | *nsla* |
| engagement | *ngy-* | enslavement | *nsla-* |
| engender | *nj—* | ensnare | *nsna* |
| engine | *ngn* | ensue | *nsu* |
| engineer | *nynr* | ensure | *nzu* |
| English | *eglz* | entablature | *nlblu* |
| engraft | *ngf* | entail | *nll* |
| engrain | *ngn* | entangle | *nlgl* |
| engrave | *nga* | entanglement | *nlgl-* |
| engraver | *nga* | enter | *n* |

**ENTER**

ENTERIC

| | | | |
|---|---|---|---|
| enteric | | envy | |
| enterprise | | enwind | |
| enterprising | | enwrap | |
| entertain | | epaulet | |
| *entertainment* | | ephemeral | |
| enthrall | | epic | |
| enthrone | | epicure | |
| enthusiasm | | epicycle | |
| enthusiast | | epidemic | |
| enthusiastic | | epidermis | |
| entice | | epiglottis | |
| *entire* | | epigram | |
| *entirely* | | epigrammatic | |
| entitle | | epigrammatical | |
| entity | | epigraph | |
| entomb | | epilepsy | |
| entomologist | | epileptic | |
| entomology | | epilog | |
| entrails | | episcopal | |
| entrance | | episcopate | |
| entrancement | | *episode* | |
| entrap | | epistle | |
| entreat | | epitaph | |
| entreaty | | epithet | |
| entree | | epitome | |
| entrench | | epitomize | |
| entrenchment | | epoch | |
| entrust | | epode | |
| entry | | equability | |
| entwine | | equable | |
| enumerate | | equableness | |
| enumeration | | equal | |
| enumerator | | equality | |
| enunciate | | *equalization* | |
| enunciation | | equanimity | |
| envelop | | equate | |
| envelope | | equation | |
| envelopment | | equator | |
| envenom | | equatorial | |
| enviable | | equestrian | |
| envious | | equiangular | |
| environ | | equidistant | |
| environment | | equilateral | |
| environs | | equilibrium | |
| envisage | | equimultiple | |
| envoy | | equine | |

EQUINE

| | | | |
|---|---|---|---|
| equinoctial..... | *egnx* | esculent........ | *eskl-* |
| equinox........ | *egnx* | escutcheon...... | *esken* |
| equip.......... | *egp* | esk............ | *esk* |
| equipage....... | *egpy* | esophagus...... | *esfgx* |
| equipment...... | *egp-* | esoteric......... | *Esk* |
| equipoise...... | *egpyz* | esparto......... | *es/o* |
| equitable...... | *eglt* | especial......... | *esx* |
| equity......... | *eg)* | especially....... | *esx* |
| equivalent..... | *eqvl-* | espionage....... | *esny* |
| equivocal...... | *egvi* | esplanade....... | *espnd* |
| equivocate..... | *egvka* | espousal........ | *es zl* |
| equivocation.... | *egvky* | espouse......... | *es s* |
| era............ | *era* | espy........... | *ese* |
| eradicate....... | *erdka* | esquire......... | *esq* |
| erase.......... | *ers* | essay.......... | *esa* |
| eraser......... | *Ers* | essayist......... | *esa,* |
| ere............ | *Ɛ* | essence......... | *es* |
| erect.......... | *erk* | essential........ | *esx* |
| erection....... | *erky* | establish........ | *esl* |
| ermine........ | *Ɛm* | establishment... | *esl-* |
| erode.......... | *erd* | estate.......... | *esa* |
| erosion........ | *ery* | esteem......... | *ese* |
| erosive........ | *ersv* | esthetic........ | *est* |
| erotic.......... | *ert* | estimable....... | *es-b* |
| err............ | *Ɛ* | estimate........ | *es-a* |
| errand......... | *Ɛ-* | estimation...... | *es-y* |
| errant......... | *Ɛ-* | estrange........ | *esS* |
| errantry....... | *Ɛ-r,* | estrangement.... | *esy-* |
| erratic......... | *erT* | estuary......... | *esy* |
| erroneous...... | *Ɛnx* | et cetera........ | *etc* |
| error.......... | *Ɛ* | etch........... | *ec* |
| erst........... | *Ɛ,* | eternal......... | *Enl* |
| erubescent..... | *Ɛbs-* | eternity......... | *En) Ɛ* |
| eructation...... | *erky* | ether.......... | *El* |
| erudite........ | *Ɛde* | ethereal........ | *Elz* |
| eruption....... | *erpy* | etherealize...... | *elk* |
| eruptive....... | *erpv* | ethic.......... | *elt* |
| erysipelas...... | *Ɛsplss* | ethical......... | *elnk* |
| escalade....... | *eskld* | ethnic......... | *elngs* |
| escapade....... | *eskpd* | ethnography..... | *etkl* |
| escape......... | *eskp* | etiquette........ | *et-ol* |
| escapement.... | *eskp-* | etymology....... | *uklpx* |
| escarp......... | *eskrp* | eucalyptus...... | *uynk* |
| escheat........ | *escl* | eugenic......... | *ul,* |
| eschew........ | *escu* | eulogist......... | *ulyz* |
| escort.........*esk/* | | eulogize........ | |

| | | | |
|---|---|---|---|
| eulogy | *ulg,* | exact | *xk* |
| eunuch | *unk* | exaction | *xkj* |
| euphonical | *ufnk* | exactitude | *xkld* |
| euphonious | *ufnx* | exactly | *xkl* |
| euphony | *ufn,* | exactness | *xk'* |
| euphuism | *ufz,* | exactor | *xk* |
| Europe | *urp* | exaggerate | *xja* |
| euthanasia | *ulnz* | exaggerative | *xjv* |
| evacuate | *evka* | exalt | *xll* |
| evade | *evd* | exaltation | *xlly* |
| evaporate | *evpa* | examination | *x mj* |
| evasion | *evj* | examine | *x m* |
| evasive | *evsv* | examiner | *x m* |
| eve | *ev* | example | *x p* |
| even | *vn* | exasperate | *xsa* |
| evening | *vn eve* | exasperation | *xsj* |
| evenly | *vnl* | excavate | *xkva* |
| evenness | *vn'* | excavation | *xkvj* |
| event | *ev-* | exceed | *xd* |
| eventide | *vnld* | exceeding | *xd* |
| eventual | *ev-l* | excel | *xl* |
| ever | *Ev* | excellence | *xl* |
| evergreen | *Evgn* | excellency | *xl* |
| everlasting | *Evls* | excellent | *xl-* |
| evermore | *Evro* | except | *xp* |
| every | *Ev,* | exception | *xpj* |
| everybody | *Ev, bd,* | exceptional | *xpjl* |
| everyday | *Ev, d* | excerpt | *xsp* |
| everyone | *Ev, 1* | excess | *x'* |
| everything | *Ev,* | excessive | *xsv* |
| everywhere | *Ev, r* | exchange | *xcj* |
| evict | *evk* | exchangeability | *xcjb,)* |
| evidence | *evd* | excise | *xz* |
| evident | *evd-* | excision | *xy* |
| evil | *evl* | excite | *xu* |
| evildoer | *evlDu* | excitement | *xu-* |
| evince | *evsa* | exclaim | *xc* |
| eviscerate | *evsa* | exclamation | *xcj* |
| evoke | *evk* | exclamatory | *xcrly* |
| evolution | *evlj* | exclude | *xcd* |
| evolve | *evlv* | exclusive | *xcsv* |
| evulsion | *evlj* | excogitate | *xkjta* |
| ewe | *u* | excommunicate | *xkuka* |
| ewer | *U* | excoriate | *xka* |
| exacerbate | *xsba* | excrement | *xk-* |
| exacerbation | *xsbj* | excrescence | *xks* |

EXCRUCIATE

| | |
|---|---|
| excruciate | *xksa* |
| exculpate | *xklpa* |
| excursion | *xkry* |
| excursionist | *xkry,* |
| excursive | *xkrsv* |
| excusable | *xkzb* |
| excuse | *xkz* *xkb* |
| execrable | *xkb* |
| execrate | *xka* |
| execration | *xkj* |
| execute | *xku* |
| execution | *xkj* |
| executioner | *Xkj* |
| executive | *xkv* |
| executor | *Xk* |
| executrix | *Xkx* |
| exegesis | *xyss* |
| exemplar | *Xrp* |
| exemplary | *xrpy* |
| exemplification | *xrpf* |
| exempt | *x* |
| exemption | *xy* |
| exercise | *Xsz* |
| exert | *x/y* |
| exertion | *xy* |
| exhalation | *xhly* |
| exhale | *xhl* |
| exhaust | *x,* |
| exhaustion | *xsy* |
| exhaustive | *xsv* |
| exhibit | *xbl* |
| exhibition | *xby* |
| exhibitor | *Xbl* |
| exhilarate | *xlra* |
| exhilaration | *xly* |
| exhort | *x/* |
| exhortation | *x/y* |
| exhume | *xu* |
| exigency | *xy* |
| exigent | *xy-* |
| exile | *xl* |
| exist | *x,* |
| existed | *xŏ* |
| existence | *xs* |
| exit | *xl* |
| exodus | *xdx* |

| | |
|---|---|
| exogen | *xyn* |
| exonerate | *xona* |
| exorbitant | *xobl-* |
| exorcise | *ksy* |
| exordium | *x/~* |
| exoteric | *xok* |
| exotic | *x* |
| expand | *xp* |
| expanse | *xp* |
| expansion | *xpy* |
| expansive | *xpv* |
| expatiate | *xpza* |
| expatriate | *Paa* |
| expect | *xpk* |
| expectancy | *xpk* |
| expectant | *xpk-* |
| expectation | *xpky* |
| expectorate | *xpkra* |
| expedient | *xpd-* |
| expedite | *xpdu* |
| expedition | *xpdy* |
| expel | *xpl* |
| expend | *xp-* |
| expenditure | *xp-lu* |
| expense | *xp* |
| expensive | *xpv* |
| experience | *xp-* |
| experiment | *xp-* |
| expert | *xp/* |
| expiable | *xpb* |
| expiate | *xpa* |
| expiration | *xpy* |
| expire | *xpu* |
| expiscate | *xpska* |
| explain | *xpn* |
| explanation | *xpny* |
| expletive | *xpv* |
| explicate | *xpka* |
| explicit | *xpsl* |
| explode | *xpd* |
| exploit | *xpyl* |
| exploitation | *xpyy* |
| exploration | *xpoy* |
| exploratory | *xpoly* |
| explore | *xpo* |
| explorer | *Xpo* |

EXPLORER

# EXPLOSION

| | | | |
|---|---|---|---|
| explosion...... | | extinct......... | |
| exponent....... | | extinction...... | |
| export......... | | extinguish..... | |
| exportation..... | | extinguisher.... | |
| expose......... | | extirpate....... | |
| exposition...... | | extol.......... | |
| expostulate..... | | extort......... | |
| exposure........ | | extortion....... | |
| expound....... | | extortionate.... | |
| *express*........ | | extra.......... | |
| expression...... | | extract........ | |
| expressive...... | | extraction...... | |
| *expressly*....... | | extradite....... | |
| expulsion...... | | extradition..... | |
| expunge....... | | extraneous..... | |
| expurgate....... | | extraordinary... | |
| exquisite....... | | extravagance... | |
| exscind......... | | extravagant.... | |
| extant........... | | extreme....... | |
| extasy......... | | extremity...... | |
| extemporaneous | | extricable...... | |
| extempore..... | | extricate....... | |
| extemporize.... | | exuberance.... | |
| *extend*.......... | | exuberant...... | |
| *extendable*..... | | exude......... | |
| extension...... | | exult.......... | |
| extensive...... | | exultant....... | |
| extent.......... | | exultation...... | |
| extenuate...... | | *eye*........... | |
| exterior........ | | eyeball........ | |
| exterminate.... | | eyebrow....... | |
| exterminatory... | | eyelet......... | |
| external....... | | eyelid......... | |
| externality..... | | eyesight....... | |

**F**

| | | | |
|---|---|---|---|
| fable.......... | | facial.......... | |
| fabric......... | | facile......... | |
| fabricate....... | | facilitate....... | |
| fabrication..... | | facility........ | |
| fabulous....... | | facsimile....... | |
| facade......... | | *fact*.......... | |
| *face*........... | | faction........ | |
| facet.......... | | factious........ | |
| facetious....... | | factiousness.... | |

FACTIOUSNESS

## FACTOR

factor  
factory  
faculty  
fad  
fade  
fadeless  
fag  
faggot  
fail  
failure  
fain  
faint  
fair  
fairer  
fairness  
fairy  
faith  
faithful  
faithfulness  
faithless  
fake  
falcon  
fall  
fallacious  
fallacy  
fallen  
fallible  
fallow  
false  
falsetto  
falsify  
falsity  
falter  
fame  
familiar  
familiarize  
family  
famine  
famish  
famous  
famously  
fan  
fanatic  
fanaticism  
fancy  
fane  

fang  
fantastic  
fantasy  
far  
far-away  
farce  
farcical  
fare  
farewell  
farm  
farmer  
farmhouse  
farmyard  
far-off  
farrier  
farrow  
farther  
farthest  
farthing  
fascinate  
fascination  
fashion  
fashionable  
fast  
fasten  
fastening  
faster  
fastidious  
fat  
fatal  
fatalism  
fatalistic  
fate  
father  
fatherland  
fatherless  
fathom  
fathomable  
fathomless  
fatigue  
fatness  
fatter  
fatuous  
faucet  
fault  
faultless  

**FAULTLESS**

## FAULTY

| | |
|---|---|
| faulty...... | |
| favor....... | |
| favorable... | |
| favorite..... | |
| favoritism... | |
| fawn....... | |
| fay........ | |
| fealty...... | |
| fear........ | |
| fearful...... | |
| fearless..... | |
| feasibility... | |
| feasible..... | |
| feast....... | |
| feat........ | |
| feather..... | |
| feature..... | |
| February.... | |
| fecund...... | |
| fecundity... | |
| fed........ | |
| federal...... | |
| federation... | |
| fee........ | |
| feeble...... | |
| feed........ | |
| feeder...... | |
| feel........ | |
| feeling...... | |
| feet........ | |
| feign...... | |
| feint....... | |
| felicitate.... | |
| felicitous.... | |
| felicity...... | |
| feline....... | |
| fell........ | |
| fellow...... | |
| fellowship... | |
| felon....... | |
| felonious.... | |
| felony...... | |
| felt........ | |
| female...... | |
| feminine..... | |
| femoral..... | |

| | |
|---|---|
| fen........... | |
| fence......... | |
| fencible........ | |
| fend.......... | |
| fender........ | |
| fennel........ | |
| ferment....... | |
| fermentation... | |
| fern.......... | |
| ferocious...... | |
| ferocity....... | |
| ferret......... | |
| ferric......... | |
| ferrule........ | |
| ferry......... | |
| fertile........ | |
| fertility....... | |
| fertilization.... | |
| fertilize........ | |
| fertilizer....... | |
| ferule......... | |
| fervent........ | |
| fervor........ | |
| festal......... | |
| fester......... | |
| festival........ | |
| festive......... | |
| festivity....... | |
| festoon........ | |
| fetch.......... | |
| fete........... | |
| fetid.......... | |
| fetish......... | |
| fetlock........ | |
| fetter......... | |
| feud.......... | |
| feudalism.. .... | |
| feudatory...... | |
| fever......... | |
| feverish........ | |
| feverishly....... | |
| feverishness..... | |
| few.......... | |
| fewer......... | |
| fey........... | |
| fez........... | |

## FIASCO

| | | | |
|---|---|---|---|
| fiasco | | filly | |
| fib | | film | |
| fiber | | filmy | |
| fibrous | | filter | |
| fickle | | filth | |
| fiction | | filthiness | |
| fictitious | | filthy | |
| fiddle | | filtrate | |
| fidelity | | filtration | |
| fidget | | fimbriate | |
| fiducial | | fin | |
| fiduciary | | final | |
| fie | | finally | |
| fief | | finance | |
| *field* | | financial | |
| *fielder* | | financier | |
| fiend | | finch | |
| fiendish | | *find* | |
| fierce | | *finder* | |
| fierceness | | *fine* | |
| fiery | | *fineness* | |
| fife | | *finer* | |
| fifteen (15) | | finery | |
| fifteenth (15t) | | *finger* | |
| fifth (5t) | | finial | |
| fiftieth (50t) | | finical | |
| fifty (50) | | *finish* | |
| fig | | finite | |
| *fight* | | fir | |
| *fighter* | | fire | |
| figment | | firearms | |
| figurative | | firebrand | |
| *figure* | | firefly | |
| figurehead | | fireman | |
| filament | | fireplace | |
| filbert | | fireproof | |
| filch | | fireside | |
| file | | firkin | |
| filer | | *firm* | |
| filial | | firmament | |
| filibuster | | *firmer* | |
| filgree | | firmly | |
| *fill* | | firmness | |
| *filler* | | *first* | |
| fillet | | first-born | |
| fillip | | firth | |

FISCAL

| | | | |
|---|---|---|---|
| fiscal | | flatterer | |
| fish | | flattery | |
| fisher | | flatulent | |
| fisherman | | flaunt | |
| fishhook | | flavor | |
| fissile | | flaw | |
| fissure | | flax | |
| fist | | flaxen | |
| fistula | | flay | |
| fit | | flea | |
| fitful | | flecked | |
| fitly | | fled | |
| fitness | | fledge | |
| five (5) | | flee | |
| fix | | fleece | |
| fixed | | fleecy | |
| fixture | | fleet | |
| fizz | | flesh | |
| flabby | | fleshy | |
| flaccid | | flew | |
| flag | | flexibility | |
| flagellant | | flexible | |
| flagellate | | flick | |
| flageolet | | flicker | |
| flagitious | | flies | |
| flagon | | flight | |
| flagrant | | flimsy | |
| flail | | flinch | |
| flake | | fling | |
| flambeau | | flint | |
| flamboyant | | flinty | |
| flame | | flip | |
| flamingo | | flippant | |
| flange | | flirt | |
| flank | | flirtation | |
| flannel | | flit | |
| flannelette | | flitch | |
| flap | | float | |
| flapper | | flock | |
| flare | | floe | |
| flash | | flog | |
| flashy | | flood | |
| flask | | floor | |
| flat | | flooring | |
| flatten | | flop | |
| flatter | | floral | |

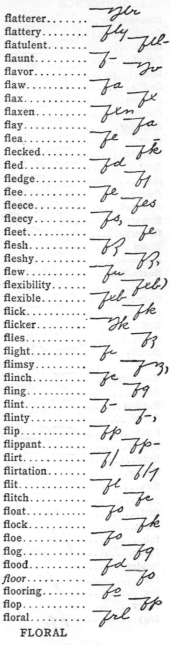

FLORAL

## FLORESCENCE

| | | | | |
|---|---|---|---|---|
| florescence | | foible | | |
| floret | | foil | | |
| florid | | foist | | |
| florist | | fold | | |
| floss | | folder | | |
| flotilla | | foliage | | |
| flotsam | | foliate | | |
| flounce | | foliation | | |
| flounder | | folio | | |
| flour | | folk | | |
| flourish | | follicle | | |
| flout | | follow | | |
| flow | | follower | | |
| flower | | following | | |
| floweret | | folly | | |
| flowerpot | | foment | | |
| flowery | | fomentation | | |
| flown | | fond | | |
| fluctuate | | fondle | | |
| fluctuation | | fondness | | |
| flue | | food | | |
| fluency | | fool | | |
| fluent | | foolish | | |
| fluff | | foolishness | | |
| fluid | | foolscap | | |
| fluidity | | foot | | |
| fluke | | football | | |
| flummery | | footman | | |
| flung | | footprint | | |
| flunkey | | footsteps | | |
| flurry | | footstool | | |
| flush | | fop | | |
| fluster | | for | | |
| flute | | forage | | |
| flutter | | forbade | | |
| flux | | forbear | | |
| fly | | forbearance | | |
| foal | | forbid | | |
| foam | | forbidden | | |
| fob | | force | | |
| focus | | forceful | | |
| fodder | | forcefully | | |
| foe | | forcible | | |
| fog | | ford | | |
| foggy | | fore | | |
| fogy | | forearm | | |

FOREBODE

| | | | |
|---|---|---|---|
| forebode....... | | forgetfulness... | |
| forecast........ | | *forgettable*..... | |
| forecastle...... | | forgive........ | |
| foreclose....... | | forgiveness.... | |
| foreclosure..... | | forgo.......... | |
| forefather...... | | forgot......... | |
| forefinger...... | | forgotten....... | |
| forego ........ | | fork........... | |
| foregone....... | | forlorn......... | |
| foreground..... | | *form*.......... | |
| forehead....... | | formal......... | |
| foreign........ | | *formation*...... | |
| foreigner....... | | *formative*..... | |
| forejudge...... | | *former*........ | |
| foreknow...... | | *formerly*....... | |
| foreland....... | | *formidable*..... | |
| forelock........ | | formula........ | |
| foreman....... | | formulate...... | |
| foremast....... | | fornication..... | |
| forementioned.. | | forsake........ | |
| foremost....... | | forsook........ | |
| forenoon....... | | forsooth....... | |
| forensic........ | | forswear....... | |
| forerunner..... | | forsworn....... | |
| foresail........ | | fort........... | |
| foresee........ | | forte.......... | |
| foreshadow..... | | *forth*.......... | |
| foreshorten..... | | forthcoming.... | |
| foreshow....... | | forthwith...... | |
| foresight....... | | fortieth (40t)... | |
| *forest*......... | | fortification.... | |
| forestall........ | | fortify......... | |
| foretaste....... | | fortissimo. .... | |
| foretell........ | | fortitude....... | |
| forethought..... | | fortnight....... | |
| foretoken...... | | fortress........ | |
| foretold........ | | fortuitous...... | |
| forever........ | | fortunate...... | |
| forewarn....... | | fortune........ | |
| forfeit......... | | forty(40) ...... | |
| forfeiture....... | | forum......... | |
| forgave........ | | forward........ | |
| forge........... | | *forwardness*.... | |
| forgery......... | | fossil.......... | |
| *forget*......... | | foster......... | |
| *forgetful*....... | | fought........ | |

FOUGHT

## FOUL

| | |
|---|---|
| foul | |
| *found* | |
| *foundation* | |
| *founder* | |
| foundling | |
| fount | |
| fountain | |
| four (4) | |
| fourfold (4fol) | |
| fourscore (4sko) | |
| fourteen (14) | |
| *fourteenth* (14t) | |
| fourth (4t) | |
| fowl | |
| fowler | |
| *fox* | |
| foxglove | |
| foxhound | |
| fracas | |
| fraction | |
| fractional | |
| fractious | |
| fracture | |
| fragile | |
| fragility | |
| fragment | |
| fragmentary | |
| fragrance | |
| fragrant | |
| frail | |
| frailty | |
| frame | |
| framework | |
| franc | |
| *France* | |
| franchise | |
| frank | |
| frankincense | |
| franklin | |
| frantic | |
| fraternal | |
| fraternity | |
| fraternize | |
| fratricide | |
| fraud | |
| fraudulent | |

| | |
|---|---|
| fraught | |
| fray | |
| freak | |
| freakish | |
| freckle | |
| *free* | |
| freebooter | |
| freedman | |
| *freedom* | |
| freehand | |
| freehold | |
| freeman | |
| *freer* | |
| freethinker | |
| freeze | |
| freight (fgt) | |
| *French* | |
| frenzy | |
| frequency | |
| frequent | |
| *fresh* | |
| *fresher* | |
| freshet | |
| freshman | |
| freshness | |
| fret | |
| fretful | |
| friable | |
| friar | |
| fricassee | |
| friction | |
| Friday | |
| fried | |
| *friend* | |
| friendly | |
| friendship | |
| frieze | |
| frigate | |
| fright | |
| frighten | |
| frightful | |
| frigid | |
| frigidity | |
| frill | |
| fringe | |
| frisk | |

**FRISKY**

| | |
|---|---|
| frisky | |
| fritter | |
| frivolous | |
| frizz | |
| fro | |
| frock | |
| frog | |
| frolic | |
| frolicsome | |
| *from* | |
| frond | |
| frondescence | |
| *front* | |
| frontage | |
| frontal | |
| frontier | |
| frontispiece | |
| frontlet | |
| frost | |
| frostbitten | |
| frosty | |
| froth | |
| froward | |
| frown | |
| froze | |
| frozen | |
| fructescence | |
| fructification | |
| tructify | |
| frugal | |
| frugality | |
| frugiferous | |
| frugivorous | |
| *fruit* | |
| *fruitful* | |
| fruition | |
| fruitless | |
| frustrate | |
| frustration | |
| frustum | |
| frutescent | |
| fruticose | |
| fry | |
| fuchsia | |
| fudge | |
| fuel | |

| | |
|---|---|
| fugacious | |
| fugitive | |
| fugleman | |
| *fugue* | |
| fulcrum | |
| fulfil | |
| fulgent | |
| fuliginous | |
| *full* | |
| *fully* | |
| fulminate | |
| fulness | |
| fulsome | |
| fumble | |
| fume | |
| fumigate | |
| fun | |
| function | |
| functionary | |
| fund | |
| *fundamental* | |
| funeral | |
| fungus | |
| funicle | |
| funnel | |
| funny | |
| fur | |
| furbelow | |
| furbish | |
| furious | |
| furl | |
| furlong | |
| furlough | |
| furnace | |
| furnish | |
| furniture | |
| furrow | |
| furry | |
| further | |
| furtherance | |
| furthermore | |
| furthermost | |
| furthest | |
| furtive | |
| fury | |
| fuse | |

**FUSE**

**FUSIBLE**

| | | | |
|---|---|---|---|
| fusible | | futile | |
| fusil | | future | |
| fusilade | | futurist | |
| fusion | | futuristic | |
| fuss | | futurity | |
| fustian | | fuzz | |

## G

| | | | |
|---|---|---|---|
| gab | | gamboge | |
| gabardine | | gambol | |
| gabble | | game | |
| gabion | | gammer | |
| gable | | gammon | |
| gad | | gamut | |
| gadfly | | gander | |
| gaff | | gang | |
| gag | | ganglion | |
| gage | | gangrene | |
| gaiety | | gangway | |
| gaily | | gantlet | |
| gain | | gaol | |
| gainer | | gap | |
| gaiter | | gape | |
| gale | | garage | |
| gall | | garb | |
| gallant | | garbage | |
| gallantry | | garble | |
| galleon | | garden | |
| gallery | | gardener | |
| galley | | gargle | |
| galliard | | gargoyle | |
| gallinaceous | | gerish | |
| galliot | | garland | |
| gallon | | garlic | |
| galloon | | garment | |
| gallop | | garner | |
| galloway | | garnet | |
| gallows | | garnish | |
| galop | | garnishment | |
| galvanic | | garniture | |
| galvanism | | garret | |
| galvanize | | garrison | |
| galvanometer | | garrulous | |
| gamble | | garter | |
| gambler | | garth | |

**GARTH**

## GAS

gas............
gasconade......
gaselier........
gaseous........
gash..........
gasoline........
gasometer......
gasp..........
gastric........
gastronomy.....
gate..........
gateway.......
gather........
gaudy.........
gauge.........
gaunt.........
gauntlet........
gauze.........
gave..........
gavel.........
gavotte........
gawk.........
gay...........
gaze..........
gazelle........
gazette........
gazetteer.......
gear..........
geese..........
gelatin........
gelatinous......
geld..........
gelid.........
gem..........
gender........
genealogist.....
genealogy......
general........
generality......
generalization...
generalize......
generalship.....
generate.......
generation.....
generative......
generator......

generic.........
generosity......
generous.......
genesis.........
genial..........
genitive.........
genius..........
genteel.........
gentian.........
gentility.........
gentile.........
gentle.........
gentleman ....
gentlemanly.....
gentlemen ..
gentleness......
gentlewoman....
gentlewomen....
gently.........
gentry.........
genuflexion....
genuine........
genus..........
geographer......
geographical....
geography......
geologist........
geology.........
geometrical.....
geometrician....
geometry.......
georgette.......
georgic.........
geranium.......
gerfalcon.......
germ...........
German........
germinate......
germination.....
germinative....
gerund.........
gesticulate......
gesticulation....
gesticulatory....
gesture.........
get.............

## GEWGAW

| | |
|---|---|
| gewgaw....... | *gga* |
| geyser........ | |
| ghastliness.... | *gsl* |
| ghastly....... | *gsl* |
| ghaut......... | *gal* |
| gherkin....... | *grkn* |
| ghost......... | *go,* |
| ghostly....... | *gsl* |
| ghoul......... | *gul* |
| ghoulish...... | *glʒ* |
| giant......... | *ju-* |
| giantess...... | *ju-'* |
| gibber........ | *gb* |
| gibberish..... | *gbʒ* |
| gibbet........ | *jbl* |
| gibbous....... | *gbx* |
| gibe.......... | *jeb* |
| giber......... | *jb* |
| giblet........ | *jbl* |
| giddy......... | *gd,* |
| *gift*........... | *gf* |
| zig........... | *gg* |
| gigantic...... | *jg-k* |
| giggle........ | *ggl* |
| giggler....... | *ggl* |
| gigot........ | *jgi* |
| gild......... | *gld* |
| gilder....... | *gld* |
| gill......... | *gl* |
| gill......... | *jl* |
| gillie....... | *gl,* |
| gillyflower.... | *jl je* |
| gilt......... | *gll* |
| gimbal....... | *jrb* |
| gimcrack..... | *jrkk* |
| gimlet....... | *grll* |
| gimp........ | *grp* |
| gin......... | *jn* |
| ginger...... | *Ji* |
| gingerbread... | *jjbd* |
| gingham...... | *gg* |
| gipsy........ | *jps* |
| giraffe....... | *jf* |
| gird........ | *ji* |
| girdle....... | *gjl* |
| *girl*.......... | *g* |

| | |
|---|---|
| girlhood...... | *ghd* |
| girlish...... | *gz* |
| girt........ | *gl* |
| gist........ | *,* |
| girth....... | *grl* |
| *give*........ | *ge* |
| *given*....... | *ge* |
| *giver*....... | *ge* |
| gizzard...... | *gzl* *gbx* |
| glabrous..... | *gx* |
| glacial...... | *gx* |
| glacier...... | *gz* |
| glacis..... | *gss* |
| *glad*........ | *gd* |
| gladden..... | *gdn* |
| glade....... | *gd* |
| gladiator.... | *gda* |
| gladiolus..... | *gdle* |
| *gladly*...... | *gdl* |
| *gladness*..... | *gd'* |
| gladsome..... | *gds* |
| glaive...... | *ga* |
| glamour..... | *g* |
| glance...... | *gl* |
| gland...... | *g* |
| glanders..... | *g* |
| glandiferous.. | *gdfx* |
| glandular.... | *g—l* |
| glare....... | *ga* |
| *glass*....... | *g'* |
| glassful..... | *gsf* |
| glassware.... | *gs a* |
| glassy...... | *gs,* |
| glaucous..... | *gkx* |
| glaze...... | *gz* |
| glazer...... | *gz* |
| glazier...... | *gz ge* |
| gleam...... | *gn ge* |
| glean...... | *gn* |
| glebe...... | *geb* |
| glee....... | *ge gef* |
| gleeful...... | *gef* |
| gleeman..... | *g—gn* |
| glen...... | *g—gn* |
| glib....... | *gb gn* |
| glide....... | *gd* |

## GLIMMER

| | |
|---|---|
| glimmer | |
| glimpse | |
| glint | |
| glisten | |
| glitter | |
| gloaming | |
| gloat | |
| globe | |
| globose | |
| globular | |
| globule | |
| glomerate | |
| gloom | |
| gloomy | |
| glorification | |
| glorify | |
| glorious | |
| glory | |
| gloss | |
| glossary | |
| glossology | |
| glossy | |
| glove | |
| glow | |
| glowworm | |
| glucose | |
| glue | |
| glum | |
| glume | |
| glut | |
| gluten | |
| glutinous | |
| glutton | |
| gluttonous | |
| gluttony | |
| glycerin | |
| gnarl | |
| gnash | |
| gnat | |
| gnaw | |
| gnome | |
| gnomon | |
| go | |
| goad | |
| goal | |
| goat | |

| | |
|---|---|
| gobble | |
| gobbler | |
| goblet | |
| goblin | |
| gocart | |
| God | |
| goddess | |
| godfather | |
| godhead | |
| godlike | |
| godly | |
| godmother | |
| goes | |
| goggle | |
| going | |
| gold | |
| golden | |
| goldfinch | |
| goldfish | |
| goldsmith | |
| golf | |
| gondola | |
| gondolier | |
| gonfalon | |
| gone | |
| gong | |
| good | |
| good-by | |
| goodliness | |
| goodly | |
| goodman | |
| goodness | |
| goodwill | |
| goody | |
| goose | |
| gooseberry | |
| gore | |
| gorge | |
| gorgeous | |
| gorget | |
| gorilla | |
| gormandize | |
| gorse | |
| gospel | |
| gossamer | |
| gossip | |

GOSSIP

GOT

| got | grange |
|---|---|
| gotten | granite |
| gouge | grant |
| gourd | granulate |
| gourmand | granulation |
| gout | granule |
| govern | granulous |
| governess | grape |
| government | grapefruit |
| governor | graph |
| gown | graphic |
| gownsman | graphite |
| grab | graphology |
| grace | grapnel |
| graceful | grapple |
| gracious | grasp |
| gradation | grass |
| gradient | grasshopper |
| grade | grassy |
| gradual | grate |
| gradually | grateful |
| graduate | gratification |
| graduation | gratify |
| graft | gratis |
| grail | gratitude |
| grain | gratuitous |
| graminivorous | gratuity |
| grammar | gratulate |
| grammarschool | gratulation |
| grammatical | gratulatory |
| gramophone | grave |
| granary | gravel |
| grand | gravely |
| grandchild | graven |
| grandchildren | gravestone |
| granddaughter | gravimeter |
| grandeur | gravitate |
| grandfather | gravitation |
| grandiloquent | gravity |
| grandma | gravy |
| grandmaster | gray |
| grandmother | grayer |
| grandpa | grayheaded |
| grandparents | grayness |
| grandsire | graze |
| grandson | grease |

GREASE

| | |
|---|---|
| greasiness...... | grisly......... |
| great.......... | grist......... |
| greater....... | gristle........ |
| greathearted... | grit.......... |
| greatness...... | grizzly........ |
| greediness..... | groan......... |
| greedy......... | groat......... |
| green.......... | grocer........ |
| greencrop...... | grocery....... |
| greener........ | grog.......... |
| greenery....... | grogram....... |
| greengage...... | groin......... |
| greengrocer.... | groom......... |
| greenhorn...... | groove........ |
| greenhouse.... | grope......... |
| greenness...... | gross......... |
| greenroom..... | grossest...... |
| greenstone..... | grot.......... |
| greensward.... | grotesque..... |
| greenwood..... | grotto........ |
| greet.......... | ground........ |
| gregarious..... | groundhog.... |
| grenade....... | groundless.... |
| grenadier...... | groundplan.... |
| grew.......... | groundwork... |
| grey.......... | group......... |
| greybeard...... | grouse........ |
| greyhound..... | grout......... |
| griddle........ | grove......... |
| gridiron........ | grovel........ |
| grief.......... | grow.......... |
| grievance...... | grower........ |
| grieve......... | growl......... |
| grievous....... | growth........ |
| griffin........ | grub.......... |
| grill.......... | grubby........ |
| grilse......... | grudge........ |
| grim.......... | gruel......... |
| grimace........ | gruesome..... |
| grimalkin...... | gruff......... |
| grin.......... | grumble...... |
| grind.......... | grumous...... |
| grinder........ | grumpy....... |
| grindstone..... | grunt........ |
| grip.......... | guano........ |
| gripe.......... | guarantee.... |

## GUARANTOR

guarantor......
guard.......
guardhouse....
guardian.......
guardroom.....
guardsman.....
guava.........
gubernatorial...
gudgeon.......
guerdon.......
guerilla.......
guess.........
guesser........
guest..........
guidance.......
guide.........
guidebook.....
guidepost......
guild.........
guilder........
guile.........
guileful.......
guileless.......
guilelessness...
guillotine......
guilt..........
guiltless......
guilty.........
guinea.........
guise..........
guitar.........
gulf...........
gull...........

gullibility.........
gullible...........
gully.............
gulp.............
gum.............
gun.............
gunboat.........
gunnel...........
gunner..........
gunnery.........
gunpowder.......
gunwale.........
gurgle...........
gurnet...........
gush.............
gusset...........
gust.............
gut.............
gutta-percha......
gutter...........
guttural..........
guy.............
guzzle...........
gymnasium (jm)...
gymnast..........
gymnastics........
gypsum..........
gypsy...........
gyrate...........
gyration.........
gyroscope........
gyve.............
gyves............

## H

ha............
habeas corpus..
haberdasher....
habiliment.....
habit..........
habitable......
habitat........
habitation......
habitual.......

habituate........
habitude.........
hack.............
hackney.........
had..............
haddock.........
hadn't...........
hadst...........
hag..............

**HAG**

# HAGGARD

haggard.......
haggle.........
hail...........
*hair*...........
hairy..........
hake..........
halberd........
halcyon........
hale...........
*half*...........
halibut........
*hall*...........
halloo.........
hallow.........
hallucination...
halo..........
halt...........
halter.........
halve.........
halyard.......
ham...........
hamlet........
hammer.......
hammock......
hamper........
hamstring......
*hand*..........
handbill.......
handbook......
handcuff.......
handful........
handglass......
handicap.......
handiwork.....
handkerchief...
handle.........
handmade.....
handsome......
handwriting....
handy.........
*hang*..........
*hanger*........
hangman......
hanker........
hansom........
hap...........

haphazard....
hapless.......
haply.........
*happen*.......
*happier*.......
happily.......
*happiness*.....
*happy*.........
harangue.....
harass........
harbinger.....
harbor........
harborage.....
*hard*.........
harden........
*harder*........
hardhearted...
*hardihood*.....
*hardly*.........
*hardness*.......
hardship......
hardware......
hardy.........
hare..........
harem.........
haricot........
hark..........
harlequin......
harlequinade..
harlot.........
harm..........
harmless......
harmonica....
harmonious...
harmony......
harness.......
harp..........
harpoon.......
harpsichord ...
harpy.........
harrow........
harry.........
harsh.........
harshness......
hart..........
hartshorn......

**HARTSHORN**

**HARVEST**

| | |
|---|---|
| harvest | heal |
| has | health |
| hash | healthful |
| hasn't | healthier |
| hasp | healthy |
| hassock | heap |
| hast | hear |
| haste | heard |
| hasten | hearer |
| hastily | hearken |
| hasty | hearsay |
| hat | hearse |
| hatch | heart |
| hatchet | hearted |
| hatchway | heartfelt |
| hate | hearth |
| hateful | heartily |
| hater | heartless |
| hath | heartlessness |
| hatred | hearty |
| haughty | heat |
| haul | heater |
| haulage | heath |
| haunch | heathen |
| haunt | heathenish |
| have | heather |
| haven | heave |
| haversack | heaven |
| havoc | heavenly |
| hawk | heavenward |
| hawser | heaver |
| hawthorn | heavier |
| hay | heavily |
| haycock | heaviness |
| hazard | heavy |
| hazardous | hecatomb |
| haze | heckle |
| hazel | hectic |
| hazy | hector |
| he | he'd |
| head | hedge |
| headache | hedgehog |
| headlight | hedgerow |
| headlong | heed |
| headquarters | heedless |
| headstrong | heel |

**HEEL**

**HEIFER**

| | |
|---|---|
| heifer........ | *hf* |
| *height*........ | *hu* |
| heinous........ | *hne* |
| heir.......... | *a'* *a* |
| heiress........ | *a'* |
| heirloom....... | *alu* |
| *held*.......... | *hl* |
| hell.......... | *hl* |
| he'll.......... | *h'l* |
| hellish........ | *hlg* |
| hello.......... | *hlo* |
| helm.......... | *hl* |
| helmet........ | *hlnt* |
| helot.......... | *hll* |
| *help*.......... | *hp* *hfp* |
| *helper*........ | |
| *helpful*....... | *hpf* |
| helpless....... | *hpl'* |
| hem.......... | *hn* |
| hemisphere.... | *hnsf* |
| hemlock....... | *hnlk* |
| hemp......... | *hnp* |
| hemstitch...... | *hnsc* |
| hen.......... | *hn* |
| hence........ | *h* *hfl* |
| henceforth..... | *hfl* |
| henceforward... | *hfl* |
| henchman..... | *hcn* |
| hepatic....... | *hpt* |
| heptagon...... | *hpgn* |
| heptarchy..... | *hprk,* |
| *her*.......... | *h* |
| herald........ | *hrld* |
| heraldic....... | *hrldk* |
| heraldry....... | *hrldr,* |
| herb......... | *hrb* |
| herbaceous .... | *hrbc* |
| herbage....... | *hrby* |
| herd.......... | *h/* |
| herdsman...... | *h//* |
| *here*.......... | *he* |
| hereafter...... | *heaf* |
| hereby....... | *heb* |
| hereditary..... | *hrdly* |
| heredity....... | *hrd)* |
| herein........ | *hen* |

| | |
|---|---|
| here's...... | *he's* |
| heresy...... | *hrs,* |
| heretic...... | *hrt* |
| heretofore... | *helf* |
| herewith.... | *he* |
| heritage.... | *hrly* |
| hermetic.... | *hrt* |
| hermit...... | *hrd* |
| hermitage... | *hrdy* |
| hero......... | *hro* |
| heroic...... | *hrtk* |
| heroine..... | *hrn* |
| heroism..... | *hrz* |
| herring...... | *hrg* |
| hers........ | *hs* |
| herself...... | *hs'* |
| he's........ | *h's* |
| hesitate..... | *hzta* |
| *hesitation*... | *hzly* |
| hew......... | *hu* |
| hewer....... | *Hu* |
| hexagon..... | *hegn* |
| hexameter... | *he le* |
| hey......... | *ha* |
| hiatus...... | *hlx* |
| hibernal..... | *Hbnl* |
| hiccup....... | *hkp* |
| hickory...... | *hky* |
| hid......... | *hd* |
| hidden...... | *hdn* |
| *hide*........ | *hd* |
| hideous..... | *hdx* |
| hie......... | *hu* |
| hierarchy.... | *Hrk,* |
| hieratic...... | *HT* |
| higgle...... | *hgl* |
| *high*........ | *hu* |
| *higher*....... | *Hu* |
| highland..... | *hul—* |
| highness..... | *hu'* |
| highroad..... | *hrd* |
| highway..... | *hua* |
| *hill*.......... | *hl* |
| hillock....... | *hlk* |
| hillside...... | *hlsd* |
| hilltop....... | *hltp* |

**HILLTOP**

HILLY

| | | | |
|---|---|---|---|
| hilly | *hl,* | holder | *Hol* |
| hilt | *hll* | hole | *hl* |
| him | | holiday | *hld* |
| himself | *hu* | holiness | *hl'* |
| hind | *hu* | holland | *hl* |
| hinder | *H* | hollow | *hlo* |
| hinge | *hy* | hollowness | *hlo'* |
| hint | *h-* | holly | *hl* |
| hip | *hp* | hollyhock | *hlhk* |
| hippodrome | *hpdo* | holm | *ho* |
| hippopotamus | *hppl* | holocaust | *hlk,* |
| hire | *hu* | holograph | *hlgf* |
| hireling | *hulg* | holster | *hlf* |
| hirsute | *hrsu* | holt | *hll hl,* |
| his | *s* | holy | |
| hiss | *h'* | homage | *hy ho* |
| histology | *hsol* | home | |
| historian | *hsn* | homeless | *hol'* |
| historic | *hsk* | homeliness | *hol'* |
| historical | *hSk* | homely | *hol* |
| history | *hS,* | homesick | *hosk* |
| hit | *hl* | homeward | *ho/* |
| hitch | *hc* | homicide | *hosd* |
| hither | *H* | homily | *hl* |
| hithermost | *Hro,* | hominy | *hm,* |
| hitherto | *Hl* | homoepathy | *hopl,* |
| hitherward | *Hl* | homologous | *hlgx* |
| hive | *hu* | homologue | *hlg* |
| ho | *ho* | homonym | *hm* |
| hoar | *ho* | hone | *hn* |
| hoard | *ho/* | honest | *on,* |
| hoarse | *hrs* | honesty | *ons,* |
| hoary | *hy* | honey | *hn,* |
| hoax | *hox* | honeycomb | *hnko* |
| hobble | *hb* | honeymoon | *hn* |
| hobby | *hb,* | honeysuckle | *hnsk* |
| hobgoblin | *hbgbn* | honor | *On On* |
| hock | *hk* | honorable | *Onb* |
| hockey | *hk,* | honorary | *Ony* |
| hocus | *hkx* | hood | *hd* |
| hod | *hd* | hoodwink | *hd-g* |
| hoe | *ho* | hoof | *hf* |
| hog | *hg* | hook | *hke* |
| hogshead | *hgshd* | hookah | *hka* |
| hoist | *hy,* | hoop | *hp* |
| hold | *hol* | hoot | *hul* |

**HOOT**

## HOP

| Word | Shorthand |
|------|-----------|
| hop | hp |
| hope | hop |
| hopeful | hopf |
| hopeless | hopl |
| hopelessness | hop" |
| hopper | Hp |
| horde | ho/ |
| horehound | hoh— |
| horizon | hrzn |
| horizontal | hrz-l |
| horn | hrn |
| hornbook | hrnbk |
| hornet | hrnt |
| hornpipe.,. | hrnpp |
| horologe | hrl/ |
| horoscope | hrskp |
| horrible | hrb |
| horrid | hrd |
| horrific | hrfk |
| horror | Hr |
| horse | hrs |
| horseback | hrsbk |
| horsehair | hrsha |
| horseman | hrs— |
| horseshoe | hrszu |
| horseshoer | hrszur |
| hortative | h/v |
| horticulture | h/kllu |
| horticulturist | h/kllu, |
| hose | hz |
| hosiery | hzy |
| hospice | hss |
| hospitable | hslb |
| hospital | hsll |
| hospitality | hsll) |
| host | ho, |
| hostage | hsy |
| hostel | hsl |
| hostelry | hslr, |
| hostess | ho' |
| hostile | hsl |
| hostility | hsl) |
| hostler | Hsl |
| hot | hl |
| hotel | hll |
| hothouse | hlhs |

| Word | Shorthand |
|------|-----------|
| hotter | Hl |
| hound | hr— |
| hour | r |
| hourly | rl |
| house | hs |
| household | hshl |
| housekeeper | hslp |
| housetop | hslp |
| housewife | hsf |
| housework | hsk |
| hovel | hvl |
| hover | Hv |
| how | h |
| howbeit | hbl |
| howdah | hda |
| howe'er | hr |
| however | hv |
| howitzer | Hlz |
| howl | hl |
| howsoever | hsv |
| hoyden | hydn |
| hub | hb |
| hubbub | hbb |
| huckleberry | hkby |
| huckster | hks |
| huddle | hdl |
| hue | hu |
| huff | hf |
| hug | hg |
| huge | huy |
| hulk | hlk |
| hull | hl |
| hum | h |
| human | hm |
| humane | han |
| humanism | hmz |
| humanity | hm) |
| humankind | hmke |
| humble | hb |
| humbleness | hb' |
| humbug | hbg |
| humdrum | hd |
| humid | hd |
| humidity | hd) |
| humiliate | hla |
| humiliation | hly |

**HUMILIATION**

## HUMILITY

| | | | |
|---|---|---|---|
| humility | | hustle | |
| hummock | | hut | |
| humor | | hutch | |
| humorist | | hydrant | |
| humorous | | hydrate | |
| hump | | hydraulic | |
| hunch | | hydrocarbon | |
| *hundred* | | hydrocephalus | |
| hundredfold | | hydrogen | |
| hundredth | | hydrometer | |
| hundredweight | | hydropathic | |
| hung | | hydrophobia | |
| hunger | | hydroplane | |
| hungers | | hydrostatics | |
| hungry | | hydroxide | |
| hunk | | hyena | |
| *hunt* | | hygiene | |
| *hunter* | | hygienic | |
| huntsman | | hymen | |
| hurdle | | hymeneal | |
| hurdy-gurdy | | hymn | |
| hurl | | hyperbola | |
| hurrah | | hyperbole | |
| hurray | | hyphen | |
| hurricane | | hypnosis | |
| *hurry* | | hypnotic | |
| *hurt* | | hypnotism | |
| hurtful | | hypnotize | |
| hurtle | | hypochondria | |
| *husband* | | hypocrisy | |
| husbandry | | hypocrite | |
| hush | | hypodermic | |
| husk | | hypotenuse | |
| hussar | | hypothesis | |
| hussy | | hyssop | |
| hustings | | hysteria | |

## I

| | | | |
|---|---|---|---|
| iambic | | icicle | |
| iambus | | iconoclasm | |
| ibex | | iconoclast | |
| ibis | | icy | |
| *ice* | | I'd | |
| iceberg | | idea | |
| ice-cream | | ideal | |

## IDEAL

## IDEALISM

| | | | |
|---|---|---|---|
| idealism........ | *idlz* | illness......... | *il* |
| idealist........ | *idl,* | illogical....... | *lgk* |
| idealize......... | *idlz* | illuminate...... | *lma* |
| identical........ | *id-K* | illumination.... | *lmy* |
| identically...... | *id-K* | illumine........ | *lm* |
| identifiable...... | *id-fb* | illusion........ | *ilj* |
| identification.... | *id-f* | illustrate...... | *ilsa* |
| identify........ | *id-f* | illustration.... | *ilsj* |
| identity........ | *id-)* | illustrative..... | *ilsv* |
| idiograph....... | *idgf* | illustrious...... | *ilsi* |
| idiom........... | *id* | I'm........... | *i* |
| idiosyncrasy..... | *idsqs,* | image......... | *ij* |
| idiot............ | *idl* | imagery........ | *yy* |
| idiotic.......... | *idT* | imaginable..... | *jnb* |
| idle............ | *idl* | imaginary...... | *yny* |
| idleness........ | *idl* | imagination.... | *jny* |
| idler........... | *Idl* | imaginative.... | *jnv* |
| idol............ | *Idl* | imagine........ | *yjn* |
| idolatress....... | *Idl* | imbecile....... | *ibsl* |
| idolatrous....... | *Idlx* | imbecility...... | *ibsl)* |
| idolatry........ | *Idl,* | imbibe........ | *ibb* |
| idolize.......... | *idlz* | imbricate...... | *ibka* |
| idyl............ | *idl* | imbroglio...... | *iblo* |
| idyllic.......... | *idlk* | imbrue........ | *ibu* |
| if.............. | *f* | imbue........ | *ibu* |
| igneous......... | *Igx* | imitable....... | *ilb* |
| ignite........... | *Igl* | imitate........ | *ila* |
| ignoble......... | *Igb* | imitation...... | *ilj* |
| ignominious..... | *Igmx* | imitative...... | *ilv* |
| ignominy....... | *Igm,* | imitator....... | *Ila* |
| ignoramus...... | *Igx* | immaculate.... | *ikla* |
| ignorance....... | *Igf* | immanent...... | *im-* |
| ignorant........ | *Ig-* | immaterial..... | *ival* |
| ignore.......... | *Ig* | immature...... | *imu* |
| ilex............ | *ilx* | immeasurable.. | *izb* |
| ill............. | *il* | immediate..... | *ida* |
| I'll........... | *il* | immemorial... | *nyl* |
| illegal.......... | *ilgl* | immense...... | *i)* |
| illegality........ | *ilgl)* | immensity..... | *i)* |
| illegible ........ | *ilgb* | immerge...... | *ivy* |
| illegitimacy..... | *ilyvs,* | immerse..... | *ivs* |
| illegitimate...... | *ilyva* | immersion..... | *ivy* |
| illiberal......... | *ilbl* | immigrate..... | *iga* |
| illicit. ......... | *ilsl* | immigrant.... | *ig-* |
| illimitable....... | *ilmb* | immigration... | *igy* |
| illiterate........ | *ilsa* | imminence.... | *in* |

## IMMINENT

imminent......
immobile......
immobility......
immoderate.....
immodest......
immolate......
immoral......
immorality......
immortal......
immortality.....
immortalize.....
immovable......
immunity......
immure......
immutability....
immutable......
imp............
impact..........
impair..........
impale.........
impalement.....
impalpable......
impanel........
impart.........
impartial.......
impartiality......
impassability....
impassable......
impassible......
impassion......
impassionate....
impassive.......
impatience......
impatient.......
impeach........
impeccable......
impecunious.....
impede.........
impediment.....
impel..........
impellent.......
impend........
impenetrability..
impenetrable....
impenitent......
imperative......

imperceptible....
imperfect.......
imperfection.....
imperforate.....
imperforation....
imperial........
imperialism......
imperialist......
imperil.........
imperious.......
imperishable....
impermeable....
impersonal......
impersonate.....
impersonation...
impertinent.....
imperturbability..
imperturbable...
imperviable.....
impervious......
impetuous......
impiety.........
impinge.........
impingement....
impious.........
impiousness......
impish..........
implacability....
implacable......
implant.........
implead.........
implement......
implicate........
implicit.........
implicitness......
implore.........
imploringly......
imply...........
impolite........
impoliteness.....
impolitic........
imponderability..
imponderable....
import..........
importance......
*important*.......

## IMPORTANT

# IMPORTANTLY

| | | | |
|---|---|---|---|
| importantly | *ypl* | improvisation | *ypvzy* |
| importation | *p, yp/y* | improvise | *ypvz* |
| importer | *yp,* | imprudent | *ypd-* |
| importunate | *yp/na* | impudence | *ypd* |
| importune | *yp/m* | impudent | *ypd-* |
| importunity | *yp/m)* | impugn | *ypn* |
| impose | *ypz* | impulse | *ypls* |
| imposition | *ypzy* | impulsive | *yplsv* |
| impossibility | *ypsb)* | impunity | *ypn,* |
| impossible | *yps, ypsb* | impure | *ypu* |
| imposter | *yps* | impureness | *ypu'* |
| imposture | *ypsu* | impurity | *ypu)* |
| impotency | *ypt* | imputation | *ypuy* |
| impotent | *ypt-* | impute | *ypu* |
| impound | *ypo-* | in | *n* |
| impoverish | *pov* | inability | *nb)* |
| impoverishment | *pov-* | inaccessibility | *nesb)* |
| impracticable | *ypkkb* | inaccessible | *nesb* |
| imprecate | *ypko* | inaccuracy | *nkus,* |
| imprecation | *ypky* | inaccurate | *nkua* |
| imprecatory | *ypkly* | inaction | *naky* |
| impregnable | *ypgnb* | inactivity | *naku)* |
| impregnate | *ypgna* | inadequacy | *ndgs,* |
| impregnation | *ypgny* | inadequate | *ndga* |
| impress | *yp'* | inadequateness | *ndga'* |
| impressibility | *ypsb)* | inadmissibility | *narsb)* |
| impressibleness | *ypsb'* | inadmissible | *narsb* |
| impression | *ypy* | inadvertent | *nav/-* |
| impressionable | *ypyb* | inalienable | *nalnb* |
| impressive | *yp'a, ypsv* | inane | *nan* |
| imprimatur | *yp'a* | inanimate | *nara* |
| imprint | *yp-* | inanition | *nny* |
| imprison | *ypzn* | inanity | *nn)* |
| imprisonment | *ypzn-* | inapplicability | *npkb)* |
| improbability | *ypbb)* | inapplicable | *npkb* |
| improbable | *ypbb* | inappreciable | *npzb* |
| improbity | *ypb)* | inapproachable | *npcb* |
| impromptu | *yplu* | inappropriate | *nppa* |
| improper | *yp'p* | inapt | *nap* |
| impropriate | *yppa* | inaptitude | *npld* |
| impropriety | *yppi)* | inarticulate | *n/kla* |
| improvable | *ypvb* | inartificial | *na/f'* |
| improve | *ypv* | inasmuch | *ns rc* |
| improvement | *ypv-* | inattention | *naly* |
| improvidence | *ypvd* | inattentive | *nal-v* |
| improvident | *ypvd-* | inaudible | *nadb* |

INAUDIBLY

| | | | |
|---|---|---|---|
| inaudibly | *nadb* | incitement | *nsc-* |
| inaugural | *nagul* | incivility | *nsvl)* |
| inaugurate | *nagua* | inclemency | *nc* |
| inauguration | *naguy* | inclement | *nc-* |
| inauspicious | *nasx* | inclination | *neny* |
| inborn | *nbrn* | incline | *nen* |
| inbred | *nbd* | inclined | *nen* |
| incalculable | *nklkll* | inclose | *nez* |
| incandescent | *nk—s-* | include | *ned* |
| incantation | *nk-1* | inclusion | *ncy* |
| incapability | *nkpb)* | inclusive | *ncsv* |
| incapable | *nkpb* | inclusively | *ncsvl* |
| incapacious | *nkpx* | incognito | *nkgnlo* |
| incapacitate | *nkpsla* | incognizable | *nkgnzb* |
| incapacity | *nkps)* | incoherent | *nkh-* |
| incarcerate | *nkasa* | incombustible | *nkbsb* |
| incarceration | *nkasy* | income | *nk* |
| incarnate | *nkrna* | incommensurable | *nk'ub* |
| incarnation | *nkrny* | incommensurate | *nk'ua* |
| incase | *nkes* | incommode | *nkd* |
| incasement | *nkes-* | incommodious | *nkdx* |
| incautious | *nkx* | incommunicable | *nknkb* |
| incendiarism | *ns—yy* | incommutable | *nkub* |
| incendiary | *ns—y* | incomparable | *nkb* |
| incense | *ns* | incompatibility | *nkplb)* |
| incentive | *ns-v* | incompatible | *nkplb* |
| inception | *nspy* | incompatibleness | *nkplb'* |
| inceptive | *nspv* | incompatibly | *nkplb* |
| incertitude | *ns/ld* | incompetence | *nkpl* |
| incessant | *nss-* | incompetency | *nkpl* |
| incest | *ns,* | incompetent | *nkpl-* |
| incestuous | *nssx* | incomplete | *nkpe* |
| inch | *in nc* | incompleteness | *nkpe'* |
| inchoate | *nka* | incomprehensibility | *nkph'b)* |
| incident | *nsd-* | incomprehensible | *nkph'b* |
| incidental | *nsd-l* | incomprehensive | *nkph'v* |
| incinerate | *nsna* | incompressible | *nkpsb* |
| incinerator | *nsnar* | incomputable | *nkpub* |
| incipient | *nsp-* | inconceivable | *nkseb* |
| incise | *nsz* | inconclusive | *nkcsv* |
| incision | *nsy* | incondensable | *nkd'b* |
| incisive | *nssv* | incongruity | *nkgu)* |
| incisively | *nssvl* | incongruous | *nkgx* |
| incisor | *nSo* | inconsequent | *nksg-* |
| incitation | *nsiy* | inconsiderable | *ntsb* |
| incite | *nsc* | inconsiderate | *nksa* |

**INCONSIDERATE**

## INCONSIDERATENESS

| | | | |
|---|---|---|---|
| inconsiderateness | *nksa* | incumbency | *nkb* |
| inconsideration.. | *nksy* | incumbent | *nkb-* |
| inconsistence.... | *nkss* | incumbrance | *nkb* |
| inconsistency.... | *nkss* | incur | *nkr* |
| inconsistent..... | *nkss-* | incurable | *nkub* |
| inconsolable..... | *nkslb* | incursion | *nkry* |
| inconsonant..... | *nksn-* | incursive | *nkrsv* |
| inconspicuous.... | *rikskx* | incurvate | *nkrva* |
| inconstant....... | *nks-* | incurvation | *nkrcy* |
| inconsumable... | *nksrb* | incurvity | *nkrw)* |
| incontestable.... | *nkslsb* | indebted | *ndt* |
| incontinent...... | *nt'-* | indebtedness | *ndld'* |
| incontinently.... | *nt'-l* | indecency | *nds* |
| incontrovertible.. | *nkv/b* | indecent | *nds-* |
| inconvenience... | *nkv* | indecipherable | *ndsfb* |
| inconvertibility.. | *nkv/b)* | indecision | *ndsy* |
| inconvertible.... | *nkv/b* | indecisive | *ndssv* |
| inconvincible.... | *nkv b* | indeclinable | *ndcnb* |
| incorporate...... | *nkpa* | indecomposable | *ndkpzb* |
| incorporation.... | *nkpy* | indecorum | *ndk* |
| incorporeal...... | *nkepel* | indecorous | *ndkx* |
| *incorrect*........ | *nkrk* | *indeed* | *ndd* |
| incorrigibility.... | *nkyb)* | indefatigable | *ndflgb* |
| incorrigible...... | *nkyb* | indefatigably | *ndflgl* |
| incorrodible..... | *nkdb* | indefatigableness.. | *ndflgb'* |
| incorrupt........ | *nkrp* | indefeasible | *ndfzb* |
| incorruptibility... | *nkrpb)* | indefensible | *ndf b* |
| incorruptible.... | *nkrpb,* | indefinable | *ndfb* |
| incorruptibleness. | *nkrpb'* | indefinite | *ndfn* |
| incorruption..... | *nkrpy* | indefiniteness | *ndfn'* |
| incorruptness.... | *nkrp'* | indelible | *ndlb* |
| *increase*........ | *nks* | indelicacy | *ndlks,* |
| incredible....... | *nkdb* | indelicate | *ndlka* |
| incredulity...... | *nkdl)* | indemnification | *nd mf* |
| incredulous..... | *nkdlx* | indemnify | *nd my* |
| incriminate...... | *nk ma* | indemnity | *nd m)* |
| incrust.......... | *nk,* | indemonstrable.... | *nd mSb* |
| incrustation..... | *nksy* | indent | *nd-* |
| incubate........ | *nkba* | indentation | *nd-y* |
| incubation...... | *nkby* | indenture | *nd-u* |
| incubator....... | *Nkba* | independence | *ndp* |
| incubus......... | *nkbx* | independency | *ndp* |
| inculcate........ | *nklka* | independent | *ndp* |
| inculcation...... | *nklky* | indescribable | *ndesb* |
| inculpable...... | *nklpb* | indestructible | *ndSkb* |
| inculpate........ | *nklpa* | indeterminable | *nD mb* |

## INDETERMINATE

| | |
|---|---|
| indeterminate.... | *nⱭma* |
| indetermination.. | *nⱭny* |
| indeterminateness | *nⱭma* |
| index........... | *ndx* |
| *Indian*.......... | *ndn* |
| *indicate*........ | *ndka* |
| indication...... | *ndky* |
| indicative...... | *ndkv* |
| indicator....... | *ndka* |
| indict.......... | *ndc* |
| indictable...... | *ndcb* |
| indictment..... | *ndc-* |
| indifference.. . | *ndf* |
| *indifferent*...... | *ndf-* |
| indigenous..... | *ndynx* |
| indigent....... | *ndy-* |
| indigested..... | *ndjⱭ* |
| indigestible.... | *ndjsb* |
| indigestion...... | *ndjsn* |
| indignant....... | *ndgn-* |
| indignation...... | *ndgny* |
| indignity........ | *ndgn)* |
| indigo.......... | *ndg* |
| *indirect*........ | *ndrk* |
| indirection...... | *ndrky* |
| indiscernible.... | *ndsnb* |
| indiscoverable.. | *ndskvb* |
| indiscreet....... | *ndske* |
| indiscretion.... | *ndsky* |
| indiscriminate .. | *ndsk ma* |
| indiscrimination | *ndsk ny* |
| indiscriminative. | *ndsk v* |
| indispensable.... | *nds b* |
| indispose....... | *ndsz* |
| indisposition.... | *ndszy* |
| indisputable..... | *ndsub* |
| indissoluble..... | *ndsllb* |
| indistinct....... | *ndsq* |
| indistinguishable | *ndsqzb* |
| indite.......... | *ndc* |
| individual....... | *ndvdl* |
| individualism.... | *ndvdlz* |
| individuality..... | *ndvdl )* |
| individualize.... | *ndvdlz* |
| *indivisible*...... | *ndvzb* |
| indocile......... | *ndsl* |
| indocility....... | *ndsl )* |
| indoctrinate..... | *nⱭkna* |
| indolence....... | *ndl* |
| indolent........ | *ndl-* |
| indomitable.... | *ndvb* |
| indoors......... | *ndos* |
| indubitable..... | *ndbll* |
| induce.......... | *nds* |
| inducement.... | *nds-* |
| induct.......... | *ndk* |
| induction....... | *ndky* |
| inductive....... | *ndkv* |
| indulge........ | *ndly* |
| indulgence..... | *ndly* |
| indurate....... | *ndua* |
| industrial...... | *ndSl* |
| industrious..... | *ndSv* |
| *industry*....... | *ndⱭ,* |
| inebriate....... | *nba* |
| inebriation..... | *nby* |
| ineffable....... | *nfb* |
| ineffaceable.... | *nfsb* |
| ineffective..... | *nfkv* |
| ineffectual..... | *nfkl* |
| inefficacious... | *nfkx* |
| inefficacy...... | *nfks,* |
| inefficiency..... | *nfy* |
| inefficient...... | *nfy-* |
| inelegant...... | *nlg-* |
| ineligible...... | *nljb* |
| ineloquent..... | *nlz-* |
| inept........... | *nep* |
| ineptitude...... | *npld* |
| ineptness...... | *np'* |
| inequality..... | *neg)* |
| inequitable.... | *nzib* |
| ineradicable... | *nrdkb* |
| inert.......... | *n/* |
| inertia......... | *nza* |
| inessential..... | *nsx* |
| inestimable.... | *ns b* |
| inevitable..... | *nvlb* |
| inevitableness. | *nvlb'* |
| inevitably..... | *nvlb* |
| inexact....... | *nxk* |
| inexcusable... | *nxkzb* |

**INEXCUSABLE**

INEXHAUSTIBLE

| | | | |
|---|---|---|---|
| inexhaustible.... | | infirmity....... | |
| inexorable...... | | infix........... | |
| inexpedient..... | | inflame......... | |
| inexperienced... | | inflammable.... | |
| *inexpressibly*.... | | inflammation.... | |
| inexpensive..... | | inflammatory... | |
| inexpiable...... | | inflate......... | |
| inexplicable..... | | inflect......... | |
| inexplicit........ | | inflection....... | |
| inexpressible.... | | inflective...... | |
| inexpressive..... | | inflexibility...... | |
| inextinguishable. | | inflexible....... | |
| inextricable..... | | inflexibleness... | |
| infallibility...... | | inflict.......... | |
| infallible........ | | infliction....... | |
| infamous....... | | inflorescence.... | |
| infamy.......... | | influence....... | |
| infancy......... | | influential...... | |
| infant.......... | | influenza....... | |
| infanticide...... | | influx.......... | |
| infantile........ | | *inform*......... | |
| infantry......... | | informal....... | |
| infatuate........ | | informality...... | |
| infatuation...... | | informant....... | |
| infect.......... | | *information*..... | |
| infection........ | | *informer*........ | |
| infectious....... | | infraction....... | |
| infelicitous...... | | infranchise...... | |
| infelicity........ | | infrangible...... | |
| infer........... | | infrequent...... | |
| inference....... | | infringe.... .... | |
| inferior......... | | infringement.... | |
| inferiority....... | | infuriate........ | |
| infernal......... | | infuse.......... | |
| infest.......... | | infusible........ | |
| infidel.......... | | infusion........ | |
| infidelity........ | | ingather........ | |
| infiltrate........ | | ingathering...... | |
| infiltration...... | | ingenious....... | |
| infinite......... | | ingenuity....... | |
| infinitesimal..... | | ingenuous....... | |
| infinitive........ | | ingenuousness... | |
| infinitude....... | | ingle........... | |
| infinity......... | | inglorious....... | |
| *infirm*.......... | | ingot........... | |
| infirmary....... | | ingrain......... | |

INGRAIN

| | | | |
|---|---|---|---|
| ingrained | *ngn* | inkwell | *igl* |
| ingrate | *nga* | inlaid | *nld* |
| ingratiate | *ngza* | inland | *nl—* |
| ingratitude | *ngttd* | inlay | *nla* |
| ingredient | *ngd-* | inlet | *nll* |
| ingress | *ng'* | inly | *nl* |
| inhabit | *nhbl* | inmate | *n ra* |
| inhabitable | *nhblb* | inmost | *n ro,* |
| inhabitant | *nhbl-* | inn | *n* |
| inhalation | *nhly* | innate | *nna* |
| inhale | *nhl* | innavigable | *nnvgb* |
| inharmonious | *nhr mx* | inner | *n* |
| inhere | *nhe* | innermost | *n ro,* |
| inherence | *nhe/* | innervate | *nva* |
| inherent | *nhe-* | innervation | *nvy* |
| inherit | *nhrl/* | innerve | *nnrw* |
| inheritance | *nhrl/* | inning | *n* |
| inheritor | *nhrl* | innkeeper | *nkp* |
| inhibit | *nhbl* | innocence | *nns* |
| inhibition | *nhly* | innocent | *nns-* |
| inhibitory | *nhbly* | innocuous | *nnk* |
| inhospitable | *nhslb-* | innovate | *nnva* |
| inhuman | *nh m* | innovation | *nnvy* |
| inhumanity | *nh m)* | innovator | *nnva* |
| inhumation | *nhuy* | innuendo | *nn—o* |
| inhume | *nhu* | innumerable | *nN b* |
| inimical | *n rl* | innutritious | *n Vuk* |
| inimitable | *n lb* | inobservant | *nbsv—* |
| iniquitous | *nglr* | inobtrusive | *nblsv* |
| iniquity | *ng)* | inoculate | *nkla* |
| initial | *u* | inoculation | *nkly* |
| initiate | *n za* | inodorous | *nOdr* |
| initiation | *n zy* | inoffensive | *nf v* |
| initiative | *n zv* | inofficial | *nf* |
| initiatory | *n zly* | inoperative | *npv* |
| inject | *nyk* | inopportune | *np/n* |
| injection | *nyky* | inordinate | *nodna* |
| injector | *Nyk* | inorganic | *nognk* |
| injudicious | *nydx* | inquietude | *ngld* |
| injunction | *ngy* | inquest | *ng,* |
| injure | *nyu* | inquire | *ngu* |
| injurious | *nyyx* | inquiry | *ngy* |
| injury | *nyy* | inquisition | *ngzy* |
| injustice | *nyss* | inquisitive | *ngsv* |
| ink | *ig* | inquisitor | *Ngs* |
| inkling | *igly* | inquisitorial | *ngstyl* |

### INROAD

| | |
|---|---|
| inroad | *nrd* |
| insalubrious | *nslbr* |
| insane | *nsn* |
| insanitary | *nsnly* |
| insatiable | *nszb* |
| insatiate | *nsza* |
| inscribe | *nskb* |
| inscription | *nskpj* |
| inscriptive | *nskpv* |
| inscrutable | *nsklb* |
| insect | *nsk* |
| insecure | *nsku* |
| insecurity | *nsku)* |
| insensate | *nsa* |
| insensibility | *ns/b)* |
| insensible | *ns/b* |
| insensitive | *nsv* |
| insentient | *nsnz-* |
| inseparability | *nspb)* |
| inseparable | *nspb* |
| inseparableness | *nspb'* |
| insert | *ns/* |
| insertion | *nsj* |
| inseverable | *nsvb* |
| inshore | *nzo* |
| inshrine | *nzn* |
| inside | *nsd* |
| insidious | *nsdt* |
| insidiousness | *nsdt'* |
| insight | *nsu* |
| insignia | *nsga* |
| insignificance | *nsgfk* |
| insignificant | *nsgfk-* |
| insincere | *nse* |
| insincerity | *ns)* |
| insinuate | *nsna* |
| insinuation | *nsnuj* |
| insinuative | *nsnuv* |
| insipid | *nspd* |
| insipidity | *nspd)* |
| insipidness | *nspd'* |
| insist | *ns,* |
| insistence | *nss* |
| insobriety | *nsbr)* |
| insole | *nsl* |
| insolence | *nsl* |

| | |
|---|---|
| insolent | *nsl-* |
| insoluble | *nslb* |
| insolvable | *nslvb* |
| insolvency | *nslv* |
| insolvent | *nslv-* |
| insomnia | *ns-ma* |
| insomuch | *ns-c* |
| inspect | *nsk* |
| inspection | *nskj* |
| inspector | *nSk* |
| inspiration | *nsj* |
| inspiratory | *nsuly* |
| inspire | *nsu* |
| instability | *nsb)* |
| install | *nsl* |
| installation | *nslj* |
| installment | *nsl-* |
| instance | *ns/* |
| instant | *ns-* |
| instantaneous | *ns-nc* |
| instantly | *ns-l* |
| instate | *nsa* |
| instead | *nsd* |
| instep | *nsp* |
| instigate | *nsga* |
| instigator | *nsga* |
| instillation | *nslj* |
| instinct | *nsg* |
| instinctive | *nsgv* |
| institute | *nslu* |
| institution | *nslj* |
| instruct | *nSk* |
| instruction | *nSkj* |
| instructive | *nSkv* |
| instructor | *nSkr* |
| instrument | *nS-* |
| instrumental | *nS-l* |
| instrumentalist | *nS-l,* |
| instruments | *nS--* |
| insubordinate | *nsodna* |
| insubordination | *nsodnj* |
| insufferable | *nsfb* |
| insufficiency | *nsfz* |
| insufficient | *nsfz* |
| insular | *Nsl* |
| insulate | *nsla* |

### INSULATE

## INSULATION

| | | | |
|---|---|---|---|
| insulation | _nsly_ | intercede | _Nsd_ |
| insulator | _nsLa_ | intercept | _Nsp_ |
| insult | _nsll_ | intercession | _Nsy_ |
| insuperable | _nspb_ | intercessory | _Nosy_ |
| insupportable | _nsp/b_ | interchange | _Ncy_ |
| insuppressible | _nspsb_ | interchangeable | _Ncyb_ |
| insurable | _nzub_ | interclude | _Nkld_ |
| insurance | _nzu_ | intercollegiate | _Nklya_ |
| insure | _nzu_ | intercommune | _Nkn_ |
| insurgent | _nsy-_ | intercommunicate | _Nkuka_ |
| insurmountable | _ns-b_ | intercommunication | _Nkuky_ |
| insurrection | _nsky_ | intercommunion | _Nknn_ |
| insurrectionary | _nskyy_ | intercommunity | _Nkn)_ |
| insusceptibility | _nsspb)_ | intercostal | _Nksl_ |
| insusceptible | _nsspb_ | intercourse | _Nkrs_ |
| insusceptive | _nsspv_ | interdict | _Ndk_ |
| intact | _nlk_ | interdictory | _Ndky_ |
| intaglio | _nllo_ | interest | _N,_ |
| intangibility | _nlyb)_ | interfere | _Nf. Nf_ |
| intangible | _nlyb_ | interference | _Nfz_ |
| intangibleness | _nlyb'_ | interfuse | _Nfz N_ |
| integer | _Nly_ | interim | _Nr_ |
| integral | _nlgl_ | interior | _Nr Nys-_ |
| integrate | _nlga_ | interjacent | _Nyk_ |
| integrity | _nlg)_ | interject | _Nyk Nyky_ |
| integument | _nlg-_ | interjection | _Nnl_ |
| intellect | _nllk_ | interknit | _Nnl Nls_ |
| intellectual | _nllkl_ | interlace | _Nl/_ |
| intelligence | _Ny_ | interlard | _Nl/ Nle_ |
| intelligent | _Nyb Ny_ | interleave | _Nle_ |
| intelligible | _Nyb_ | interline | _NSk_ |
| intelligibleness | _Nyb'_ | interlocutor | _Nlp NLd_ |
| intemperance | _nlrp_ | interlope | _Nlp_ |
| intemperate | _nlrpa_ | interlude | _Ndn_ |
| intend | _nl-_ | interlunar | _Nry_ |
| intense | _nl_ | intermarriage | _Nry_ |
| intensify | _nlf._ | intermarry | _Nrdl_ |
| intension | _nly._ | intermeddle | _Nrdl_ |
| intensity | _nl)_ | intermedial | _Nrdl_ |
| intensive | _nlv_ | intermediary | _Nrdy_ |
| intent | _nl-_ | intermediate | _Nrda_ |
| intention | _nly_ | interment | _Nr-_ |
| inter | _N_ | intermezzo | _Nrzo_ |
| interact | _Nk_ | interminable | _Nrmb_ |
| intercalary | _Nkly_ | intermingle | _Nrgl_ |
| intercalate | _Nkla_ | intermission | _Nry_ |

**INTERMISSION**

INTERMIT

| | |
|---|---|
| intermit | |
| intermittent | |
| intermix | |
| intermixture | |
| intermundane | |
| intermural | |
| intern | |
| internal | |
| international | |
| internationalize | |
| internecine | |
| internuncio | |
| interpellate | |
| interpellation | |
| interpellator | |
| interpolate | |
| interpolation | |
| interpose | |
| interposition | |
| interpret | |
| interpretation | |
| interpreter | |
| interregnum | |
| interrogate | |
| interrogation | |
| interrogative | |
| interrogatory | |
| interrupt | |
| interruption | |
| intersperse | |
| interspersion | |
| interstate | |
| interstice | |
| interstitial | |
| intertropical | |
| intertwine | |
| intertwist | |
| interval | |
| intervene | |
| intervention | |
| interview | |
| interweave | |
| interwoven | |
| intestacy | |
| intestate | |
| intestine | |

| | |
|---|---|
| intimacy | |
| intimate | |
| intimation | |
| intimidate | |
| intimidation | |
| into | |
| intolerable | |
| intolerance | |
| intonate | |
| intonation | |
| intoxicate | |
| intoxicant | |
| intractable | |
| intramural | |
| intransitive | |
| intransmissible | |
| intransmutable | |
| intrench | |
| intrepid | |
| intrepidity | |
| intricacy | |
| intricate | |
| intrigue | |
| intrinsic | |
| introduce | |
| introduction | |
| introductory | |
| intromission | |
| intromit | |
| introspection | |
| introspective | |
| introversion | |
| introvert | |
| intrude | |
| intrusion | |
| intrusive | |
| intrust | |
| intuition | |
| intuitional | |
| intuitive | |
| inundate | |
| inundation | |
| inure | |
| inurn | |
| inutility | |
| invade | |

INVADE

INVADER

| | | | |
|---|---|---|---|
| invader | *Nod* | invulnerability | |
| invalid | | invulnerable | |
| invalidate | | inward | |
| invalidity | | inweave | |
| invaluable | | inwrought | |
| invariable | | iodine | |
| invasion | | iota | |
| invective | | irascible | |
| inveigle | | ire | |
| inveiglement | | ireful | |
| invent | | iris | |
| invention | | irksome | |
| inventor | | iron | |
| inventory | | ironmonger | |
| inversion | | irradiance | |
| invert | | irradiate | |
| invertebral | | irrational | |
| invest | | irreclaimable | |
| investigate | | irreconcilable | |
| investigation | | irrecoverable | |
| investiture | | irredeemable | |
| investment | | irreducible | |
| inveteracy | | irrefragable | |
| inveterate | | irrefutable | |
| inveterateness | | irregular | |
| invidious | | irregularity | |
| invigorate | | irrelevancy | |
| invigoration | | irrelevant | |
| invincibility | | irreligion | |
| invincible | | irremediable | |
| inviolable | | irremovable | |
| inviolableness | | irreparable | |
| inviolability | | irrepealable | |
| inviolate | | irreprehensible | |
| invisibility | | irrepressible | |
| invisible | | irreproachable | |
| invisibleness | | irreprovable | |
| invitation | | irresistible | |
| invite | | irresolute | |
| invocation | | irresolution | |
| invoice | | irrespective | |
| invoke | | irresponsible | |
| involuntary | | irretrievable | |
| involute | | irreverent | |
| involution | | irreversible | |
| involve | | irrevocable | |

**IRREVOCABLE**

IRRIGATE

| | | | | |
|---|---|---|---|
| irrigate | | issuance | |
| irrigation | | issue | |
| irritable | | isthmus | |
| irritant | | it | |
| irritate | | itch | |
| irritation | | item | |
| irritative | | iterate | |
| irruption | | iteration | |
| irruptive | | itinerant | |
| is | | itinerary | |
| isinglass | | itinerate | |
| island | | its | |
| isle | | it's | |
| isn't | | itself | |
| isolate | | I've | |
| isolation | | ivory | |
| isosceles | | ivy | |

## J

| | | | |
|---|---|---|
| jab | jasper | |
| jabber | jaundice | |
| jacinth | jaunt | |
| jack | javelin | |
| jackal | jaw | |
| jackanapes | jay | |
| jackass | jealous | |
| jacket | jealousy | |
| jade | jean | |
| jag | jeer | |
| jagged | jeerer | |
| jaggedness | jejune | |
| jaguar | jelly | |
| jail | jenny | |
| jailer | jeopardize | |
| jailor | jeopardy | |
| jam | jerk | |
| jamb | jerkin | |
| jangle | jersey | |
| jangler | jest | |
| janitor | jet | |
| January | jewel | |
| jar | jeweler | |
| jargon | jewelry | |
| jargonelle | jib | |
| jasmine | jig | |

| | |
|---|---|
| jilt | |
| jingle | |
| jingo | |
| jitney | |
| job | |
| jockey | |
| jocose | |
| jocular | |
| jocularity | |
| jocularly | |
| jocund | |
| jog | |
| join | |
| joint | |
| jointure | |
| joist | |
| joke | |
| jollification | |
| jollity | |
| jolly | |
| jolt | |
| jostle | |
| jot | |
| journal | |
| journalism | |
| journalist | |
| journalistic | |
| journey | |
| journeyman | |
| joust | |
| jovial | |
| joviality | |
| jovialness | |
| jowl | |
| joy | |
| joyful | |
| joyless | |
| joyous | |
| jubilant | |
| jubilation | |
| jubilee | |
| judge | |
| judgment | |
| judicable | |
| judicative | |
| judicatory | |

| | |
|---|---|
| judicature | |
| judicial | |
| judiciary | |
| judicious | |
| judiciousness | |
| jug | |
| juggle | |
| juggler | |
| jugular | |
| juice | |
| juicy | |
| jujube | |
| julep | |
| July | |
| jumble | |
| jumbler | |
| jump | |
| jumper | |
| junction | |
| juncture | |
| June | |
| jungle | |
| junior | |
| juniority | |
| juniper | |
| junk | |
| junket | |
| juridical | |
| jurisdiction | |
| jurisprudence | |
| jurist | |
| juror | |
| jury | |
| juryman | |
| just | |
| justice | |
| justiciable | |
| justiciary | |
| justifiable | |
| justification | |
| justify | |
| justness | |
| jut | |
| jute | |
| juvenile | |
| juxtaposition | |

# K

kackle..........

kail............

kangaroo.......

karoo...........

kayak..........

kedge..........

keel............

keelage........

keen...........

keenness.......

*keep*...........

*keeper*..........

keepsake.......

keg............

kelp............

kelpie..........

kelson.........

kelt............

ken............

kennel.........

*kept*...........

kerchief........

kern...........

kernel.........

kerosene........

kerseymere.....

kestrell.........

ketchup.........

kettle..........

key............

keystone........

khaki..........

khan...........

Khedive........

kick...........

kid............

kidder.........

kidnap.........

kidnapper.......

kidney..........

*kill*...........

kiln...........

kilo...........

kilogram........

kilometer.......

kilt............

kimono........

kin............

*kind*..........

*kinder*.........

kindergarten...

kindle.........

kindling.......

*kindly*.........

*kindness*.......

kindred... .....

kine...........

*king*...........

kingdom.......

kingly.........

kinsfolk.......

kinsman.......

kinship........

kipper........

kirk...........

*kiss*...........

kit............

kitchen........

kite...........

kith...........

kitten.........

kitty..........

kleptomania....

knack.........

knag..........

knap..........

knapsack......

knave.........

knavery.......

knavish........

knead.........

*knee*.........

kneel..........

knell..........

knelt..........

knew..........

knickerbocker..

knife..........

knight.........

knighthood.....

**KNIGHTHOOD**

knightly........
knit............
knives..........
knob...........
knock..........
knoil..........
knop...........
knot...........

knout........
know.........
knowing......
knowledge....
known.......
knuckle......
kodak........
kosher........

## L

label..........
labial..........
labiate.........
labor...........
laboratory.......
laborer.........
laborious.......
labyrinth........
lace............
lacerate........
laceration.......
lacerative.......
lachrymal.......
lachrimary......
lachrymose.....
lack...........
lackadaisical....
lackey.........
laconic........
lacquer.........
lacrosse.. .....
lactation........
lacteal..........
lactic..........
lactiferous......
lacuna.........
lad............
ladder.........
lade...........
ladies..........
lading.........
ladle...........
lady.........
lag............
laggard........

lagoon.......
laic.........
laid........
lain.......
lair..........
laird.........
laity.........
lake.........
lamb........
lambent......
lambkin.....
lamblike.....
lame........
lament.......
lamentable...
lamentation..
lamina.......
laminate.....
lamination...
lamp........
lampoon.....
lamprey......
lance........
lancet.......
land.........
landau......
landlord.....
landmark....
landscape....
landward.....
lane.........
language.....
languid......
languish......
laniferous....

LANK

| | | | |
|---|---|---|---|
| lank | | laughter | |
| lantern | | launch | |
| lanyard | | launder | |
| lap | | laundress | |
| lapidary | | laundry | |
| lapse | | laureate | |
| larcenist | | laureateship | |
| larceny | | laureation | |
| larch | | laurel | |
| lard | | lava | |
| large | | lavatory | |
| largeness | | lave | |
| larger | | lavender | |
| largess | | lavish | |
| lark | | lavishment | |
| larkspur | | lavishness | |
| larva | | law | |
| lascivious | | lawful | |
| lash | | lawgiver | |
| lass | | lawless | |
| lassitude | | lawmaker | |
| lasso | | lawn | |
| last | | lawyer | |
| latch | | laxation | |
| latchet | | laxative | |
| late | | laxity | |
| lately | | laxness | |
| lateness | | lay | |
| latent | | layer | |
| later | | layette | |
| lateral | | layman | |
| lath | | lazy | |
| lathe | | lea | |
| lather | | lead | |
| latitude | | leaden | |
| latitudinal | | leader | |
| latitudinarian | | leadership | |
| latter | | leaf | |
| lattice | | leafage | |
| laud | | leafless | |
| laudable | | leafy | |
| laudanum | | league | |
| laudation | | leaguer | |
| laudatory | | leak | |
| laugh | | leakage | |
| laughable | | leal | |

LEAL

| | | | |
|---|---|---|---|
| lean | *ln* | legislate | *lgsla* |
| leap | *lep* | legislation | *lgsly* |
| learn | *ln* | legislative | *lgslv* |
| learner | *ln* | legislature | *lgslau* |
| lease | *les* | legitimacy | *lgtns,* |
| leash | *lef* | legitimate | *lgtra* |
| least | *le,* | legitimation | *lgty* |
| leather | *Le* | legitimist | *lgtn,* |
| leathern | *i'vn* | leisure | *lz* |
| leave | *le* | lemon | *lm* |
| leaven | *lvn* | lemonade | *lmd* |
| leaves | *les* | lend | *l—* |
| lecherous | *Lcx* | lender | *L—* |
| lectern | *lkrn* | length | *lnl* |
| lection | *lkj* | lengthen | *lnln* |
| lectionary | *lkjy* | lengthier | *lnl* |
| lecture | *lku* | lengthways | *lnl as* |
| lecturer | *Lku* | lengthwise | *lnl Z* |
| lectureship | *lkuz* | leniency | *ln* |
| led | *ld* | lenient | *ln—* |
| ledge | *lg* | lenitive | *lnv* |
| ledger | *lg* | lenity | *ln)* |
| lee | *le* | lens | *lnz* |
| leech | *lec* | lent | *l—* |
| leek | *lek* | lenticular | *L—kl* |
| leer | *le* | lentil | *l—l* |
| lees | *lz* | leonine | *lenn* |
| leet | *le* | leopard | *lpl* |
| leeway | *lra* | leper | *Lp* |
| left | *lf* | leprosy | *lps, lpx* |
| leg | *lg* | leprous | |
| legacy | *lgs,* | lesion | *lg l'* |
| legal | *lgl* | less | |
| legality | *lgl)* | lessen | *L' lsn* |
| legalization | *lglj* | lesser | *L'* |
| legalize | *lglz* | lesson | *l, lsn* |
| legate | *lga* | lest | *l,* |
| legatee | *lgle* | let | *ll* |
| legation | *lgj* | lethal | *lll* |
| legend | *lg—* | lethargic | *lgk* |
| legendary | *lg—y* | lethargical | *lgl lgk* |
| leggings | *lg=* | lethargy | |
| legibility | *lgb)* | let's | *lls lj,* |
| legible | *lgb* | letter | *L* |
| legion | *lgn* | letterhead | *Lhd* |
| legionary | *lgny* | letterpress | *Lp'* |

**LETTUCE**

lettuce.........
levant.........
levee...........
level...........
lever...........
leverage.......
leveret.........
leviaole........
leviathan.......
levity..........
levy...........
lewd...........
lewdness.......
lexicographer....
lexicography.....
lexicologist......
lexicology......
lexicon.........
liability.........
liable...........
liaison..........
liar............
libation.........
libel...........
libellous........
liberal..........
liberality........
liberalize........
liberate.........
libertine........
*liberty*..........
libidinous......
librarian........
library..........
librate..........
libration........
libratory........
libretto.........
lice............
license..........
licentiate.......
licentious.......
lichen. ........
lick...........
licker..........
lickerish...:....

licorice........
lictor..........
lid.............
*lie*.............
lief............
liege..........
liegeman......
lien...........
lieu...........
lieutenant (lt)..
*life*............
lifeless........
lifelong........
lifetime........
*lift*............
lifter..........
lifting.........
ligament.......
ligature........
*light*..........
lighten.........
*lighter*.........
lighthouse.....
*lightly*........
lightness.......
lightning.......
lightship.......
ligneous.......
lignify.........
ligulate........
ligule.........
*like*...........
likeable........
likely.........
liken.........
likeness.......
likewise.......
lilac...........
lilt............
lily...........
limb..........
limber.........
limbo.........
lime..........
limekiln.......
limelight.......

## LIMESTONE

| | | | |
|---|---|---|---|
| limestone | *lesn* | liquor | *lk* |
| limit | *lrl* | lisle | *lil* |
| limitation | *lry* | lisp | *ls* |
| limitless | *lrll'* | lissom | *ls* |
| limn | *ln* | *list* | *l,* |
| limousine | *lgn* | *listen* | *lsn* |
| limp | *lrp* | *listener* | *Lsn* |
| limpet | *lrpl* | listerine | *lSn* |
| limpid | *lrpd* | listless | *lsl'* |
| linch-pin | *lspn* | lit | *ll* |
| linden | *l—n* | litany | *lln,* |
| *line* | *li* | liter | *Le* |
| lineage | *lry* | literacy | *Lo,* |
| lineal | *lnl* | literal | *Ll* |
| lineament | *ln-* | literally | *Ll* |
| linear | *Lin* | literary | *Ly* |
| linen | *lnn* | literate | *La* |
| *liner* | *Le* | literati | *Ll;* |
| linger | *Lg* | literatim | *Le* |
| lingerie | *lnzy* | literature | *Llu* |
| lingo | *lgo* | lithe | *lil* |
| lingual | *lgl* | lithesome | *lls* |
| linguist | *lg,* | lithograph | *llgf* |
| linguistic | *lg5* | lithographer | *llgf* |
| liniment | *ln-* | lithographic | *llgfk* |
| lining | *li* | lithography | *llgf,* |
| link | *lg* | litigant | *llg-* |
| linnet | *lnl* | litigate | *llga* |
| linoleum | *lnl* | litigation | *llgf* |
| linotype | *lllp* | litigious | *llgx* |
| linseed | *lnsd* | litmus | *llx* |
| linstock | *lnsk* | litter | *L* |
| lint | *l—* | *little* | *ll* |
| lintel | *l-l* | littoral | *Ll* |
| *lion* | *lin* | liturgy | *Lj,* |
| lioness | *lin'* | *live* | *lv* |
| lionize | *lnz* | livelihood | *lilhd* |
| lip | *lp* | livelong | *lvlg* |
| liquation | *lgf* | lively | *lil* |
| liquefaction | *lgfkf* | *liver* | *Lv* |
| liquefy | *lgf* | livery | *lvy* |
| liquescent | *lgs-* | livestock | *lisk* |
| liquid | *lgd* | livid | *lvd* |
| liquidate | *lgda* | lizard | *lz/* |
| liquidation | *lgdf* | llama | *lra* |
| liquidator | *Lgda* | lo | *lo* |

## LOAD

| Word | Shorthand |
|------|-----------|
| load | |
| loadline | |
| loadstone | |
| loaf | |
| loam | |
| loan | |
| loath | |
| loathe | |
| loathsome | |
| loaves | |
| lobby | |
| lobe | |
| lobster | |
| local | |
| locality | |
| localization | |
| localize | |
| locate | |
| location | |
| locative | |
| loch | |
| lock | |
| locket | |
| lock-jaw | |
| locksmith | |
| locomotive | |
| locus | |
| locust | |
| lode | |
| lodestar | |
| lodestone | |
| lodge | |
| lodging | |
| lodgment | |
| loft | |
| lofty | |
| log | |
| logarithm | |
| loggerhead | |
| logic | |
| logical | |
| logician | |
| loin | |
| loiter | |
| loll | |
| lone | |

| Word | Shorthand |
|------|-----------|
| loneliness | |
| lonely | |
| lonesome | |
| long | |
| longevity | |
| longhand | |
| longitude | |
| longitudinal | |
| look | |
| lookout | |
| loom | |
| loon | |
| loop | |
| loose | |
| loosen | |
| loot | |
| lop | |
| loquacious | |
| loquacity | |
| lord | |
| lordly | |
| lordship | |
| lore | |
| lorn | |
| lorry | |
| lose | |
| loser | |
| losing | |
| loss | |
| lost | |
| lot | |
| lotion | |
| lotus | |
| loud | |
| louder | |
| loudly | |
| lounge | |
| lour | |
| louse | |
| lout | |
| louver | |
| lovable | |
| love | |
| loveliness | |
| lovely | |
| lover | |

**LOVER**

## LOW

| | | | |
|---|---|---|---|
| low | lo | luminosity | l ms) |
| lower | lol — Lo | luminous | l mx |
| lowland | lol — | lump | l p |
| lowliness | lol' | lunacy | lns, |
| lowly | lol | lunar | Ln |
| loyal | lyl | lunate | lna |
| loyalist | lyl, lyll, | lunatic | lnt |
| loyalty | | lunation | lny |
| lozenge | lzj | lunch | lc |
| lubber | Sb | luncheon | lcn |
| lubricant | lbk — | lung | lq |
| lubricate | lbka | lunge | lj |
| lubricator | Lbka | lupine | lpn |
| lubricity | lbs) | lurch | lrc |
| lucent | ls — | lure | lu |
| lucid | lsd | lurid | lud |
| lucidity | lsd) | lurk | lrk |
| lucidness | lsd) | luscious | lc |
| luck | lk | lush | lf |
| luckless | lk, lkl' | lust | l, |
| lucky | lk, | luster | ls, lS |
| lucrative | Skv | lusty | ls, |
| lucre | Sk | luxuriant | lxy — |
| ludicrous | ldkx | luxuriate | lxya |
| luff | lf | luxurious | lxyx |
| lug | lq | luxury | lxy |
| luggage | lgj | lye | li |
| lugubrious | lgbx | lying | li |
| lukewarm | lkvr | lymph | lmf |
| lull | ll | lymphatic | lmft |
| lullaby | llb | lynch | lc |
| lumbago | l bgo | lynx | lnx |
| lumber | L rb | lyre | Li |
| lumberman | L b — | lyric | lrk |
| luminary | l my | lyrical | lrl |

## M

| | | | |
|---|---|---|---|
| ma | ra | machine | Zn |
| macadamize | rkd rz | machinery | Zny |
| macaroni | Vkn, | machinist | Zn, |
| macaroon | Vkn | mackerel | Vkl |
| macaw | rka | mad | rd |
| mace | ras | madam | rd |
| macerate | rsa | madcap | rdkp |
| machination | rkny | madden | rdn |

## MADE

| | |
|---|---|
| made | maker |
| mademoiselle | maladministration |
| madness | malady |
| madrigal | malapert |
| maelstrom | malaria |
| magazine | malcontent |
| magenta | male |
| maggot | malediction |
| magic | malefactor |
| magical | malevolent |
| magician | malformation |
| magisterial | malice |
| magistracy | malicious |
| magistrate | malign |
| magnanimity | malignant |
| magnanimous | malignity |
| magnate | malison |
| magnesia | mall |
| magnet | mallard |
| magnetism | malleable |
| magnetize | mallet |
| magneto | mallow |
| magnificence | malmsey |
| magnificent | malpractice |
| magnify | malt |
| magniloquent | maltreat |
| magnitude | malversation |
| magnolia | mama |
| magpie | mamma |
| mahogany | mammal |
| maid | mammoth |
| maiden | mammy |
| maidenhood | man |
| mail | manacle |
| maim | manage |
| main | management |
| mainland | manager |
| maintain | mandamus |
| maintenance | mandarin |
| maize | mandate |
| majestic | mandatory |
| majesty | mandible |
| majolica | mandolin |
| major | mandrake |
| majority | mane |
| make | manful |

MANGE

| | |
|---|---|
| mange......... | |
| manger........ | |
| mangle........ | |
| mango......... | |
| mangrove...... | |
| mangy......... | |
| manhood...... | |
| mania......... | |
| maniac........ | |
| manicure....... | |
| manifest....... | |
| manifestation... | |
| manifold....... | |
| manila......... | |
| maniple........ | |
| manipulate..... | |
| mankind....... | |
| *manly*......... | |
| manna......... | |
| *manner*........ | |
| mannerism..... | |
| manoeuvre..... | |
| manor......... | |
| manse......... | |
| mansion....... | |
| manslaughter... | |
| mansuetude.... | |
| mantel........ | |
| mantle........ | |
| mantlet........ | |
| mantua........ | |
| manual........ | |
| manufacture.... | |
| manufacturer.... | |
| manumit....... | |
| manure........ | |
| manuscript (mss) | |
| *many*.......... | |
| map........... | |
| maple.......... | |
| mar........... | |
| maraud........ | |
| marble........ | |
| *march*......... | |
| marchioness..... | |
| marconigram.... | |

| | |
|---|---|
| mare......... | |
| margarine..... | |
| marge........ | |
| margin....... | |
| marginate..... | |
| margrave..... | |
| marigold...... | |
| marine....... | |
| mariner....... | |
| marionette.... | |
| marital....... | |
| maritime...... | |
| marjoram..... | |
| *mark*........ | |
| *marker*....... | |
| *market*....... | |
| *marketable*.... | |
| marketplace... | |
| marl......... | |
| marline....... | |
| marmalade.... | |
| marmoreal.... | |
| marmoset.... | |
| marmot...... | |
| maroon....... | |
| marquee...... | |
| marquess..... | |
| marriage...... | |
| married....... | |
| marrow....... | |
| marry........ | |
| marsh........ | |
| marshal...... | |
| marshy....... | |
| mart......... | |
| marten....... | |
| martial....... | |
| martin....... | |
| martinet...... | |
| martingale.... | |
| martyr........ | |
| martyrologist.. | |
| martyrology... | |
| marvel....... | |
| marvelous.... | |
| masculine..... | |

MASCULINE

## MASH

| | | | |
|---|---|---|---|
| mash | | maudlin | |
| mask | | maugre | |
| mason | | maul | |
| masonry | | maulstick | |
| masquerade | | maunder | |
| masquerader | | mausoleum | |
| mass | | mauve | |
| massacre | | mavis | |
| massage | | maw | |
| massive | | mawkish | |
| massy | | maxim | |
| mast | | maximum | |
| *master* | | *may* | |
| *masterful* | | *May* | |
| masterpiece | | maybe | |
| mastery | | maybloom | |
| masticate | | mayor | |
| mastication | | mayoralty | |
| mastiff | | mayoress | |
| mastodon | | maypole | |
| mat | | mayst | |
| matador | | maze | |
| match | | mazurka | |
| matchless | | *me* | |
| mate | | mead | |
| material | | meadow | |
| materialism | | meager | |
| materialist | | meal | |
| materiality | | *mean* | |
| maternal | | meander | |
| maternity | | *meaner* | |
| mathematician | | *meanness* | |
| mathematics | | meant | |
| matin | | meantime | |
| matricide | | meanwhile | |
| matriculate | | measles | |
| matriculation | | measurable | |
| matrimonial | | *measure* | |
| matrimony | | *measurement* | |
| matrix | | meat | |
| matron | | mechanic | |
| *matter* | | mechanical | |
| mattock | | mechanism | |
| mattress | | medal | |
| mature | | medalist | |
| maturity | | medallist | |

## MEDALLION

| | |
|---|---|
| medallion | *rdln* |
| meddle | *rdl* |
| meddler | *rdl* |
| meddlesome | *rdls* |
| medial | *rdl* |
| mediate | *rda* |
| mediation | *rdy* |
| mediator | *rda* |
| medical | *rdk* |
| medicate | *rdka* |
| medication | *rdkj* |
| medicative | *rdkv* |
| medicinal | *rdsnl* |
| medicine | *rdsn* |
| mediocre | *rdk* |
| mediocrity | *rdk)* |
| meditate | *rdla* |
| meditation | *rdly* |
| meditative | *rdlv* |
| medium | *rd* |
| medlar | *rdl* |
| medley | *rdl* |
| meed | *rd* |
| meek | *ek* |
| meeker | *rke* |
| meekness | *rk'* |
| meerschaum | *rez* |
| meet | *re* |
| megaphone | *rgfn* |
| melancholy | *lnkl* |
| melee | *rle* |
| meliorate | *lra* |
| mellifluent | *lflu-* |
| mellifluous | *lflx* |
| mellow | *lo* |
| melodious | *ldx* |
| melodrama | *ldra* |
| melodramatic | *ld* |
| melody | *ld,* |
| melon | *rln* |
| melt | *rll* |
| member | *rb* |
| membership | *rb)* |
| membrane | *rbn* |
| membraneous | *rbnx* |
| memento | *r-o* |

| | |
|---|---|
| memoir | *ra* |
| memorable | *rb* |
| memorandum | *rero* |
| memorial | *ryl* |
| memorize | *rrz* |
| memory | *ry* |
| men | *r* |
| menace | *ro* |
| menagerie | *ryy* |
| mend | *r—* |
| mendacious | *r—x* |
| mendacity | *r—s)* |
| mendicancy | *r—k* |
| mendicant | *r—k-* |
| mendicity | *r—s)* |
| menial | *rl* |
| meningitis | *ryx)* |
| mensurable | *rzul* |
| mensuration | *rzy* |
| mental | *r-l* |
| mentality | *r-l)* |
| mention | *ry* |
| mentor | *r-* |
| menu | *ru* |
| meow | |
| mercantile | *rk-l* |
| mercenary | *rsny* |
| mercerize | *rsz* |
| merchandise | *rdse* |
| merchant | *rc-* |
| merchantman | *rc-r-* |
| merciful | *rsf* |
| merciless | *rsl* |
| mercury | *rky* |
| mercy | *rs,* |
| mere | *re* |
| merely | *rel* |
| meretricious | *rylx* |
| merge | *ry* |
| meridian | *rydn* |
| meridional | *rydnl* |
| merino | *ryno* |
| merit | *rl* |
| meritorious | *rylyx* |
| merk | *rke* |
| merle | *rl* |

## MERLIN

| | | | |
|---|---|---|---|
| merlin | | mice | |
| merlon | | microbe | |
| mermaid | | microcosm | |
| merriment | | micrometer | |
| merry | | microphone | |
| mesh | | microscope | |
| mesmeric | | mid | |
| mesmerism | | midday | |
| mesmerist | | *middle* | |
| mesmerize | | middy | |
| mess | | midge | |
| *message* | | midnight | |
| messenger | | midst | |
| messuage | | midsummer | |
| *met* | | midway | |
| metal | | midwinter | |
| metallic | | mien | |
| metalliferous | | *might* | |
| metallurgy | | *mightier* | |
| metamorphic | | mightiest | |
| metamorphose | | *mightily* | |
| metaphor | | *mighty* | |
| metaphysician | | mignonette | |
| metaphysics | | migrate | |
| mete | | migration | |
| metempsychosis | | milch | |
| meteor | | mild | |
| meteorolite | | mildness | |
| meteorologist | | *mile* | |
| meteorology | | mileage | |
| meter | | milestone | |
| methinks | | miliary | |
| method | | military | |
| methodical | | militate | |
| methought | | militia | |
| methylated | | *milk* | |
| metonic | | milkmaid | |
| metric | | milkman | |
| metronome | | milkweed | |
| metropolis | | milky | |
| metropolitan | | *mill* | |
| mettle | | millennial | |
| mettlesome | | millennium | |
| mew | | *miller* | |
| miasma | | millet | |
| mica | | milliard | |

# MILLINERY

| | | | |
|---|---|---|---|
| millinery | | miracle | |
| million | | miraculous | |
| millionaire | | mirage | |
| millions | | mire | |
| millstone | | mirror | |
| milt | | mirth | |
| mimeograph | | misadventure | |
| mimetic | | misadvised | |
| mimic | | misalliance | |
| mimicry | | misanthrope | |
| minaret | | misanthropist | |
| minatory | | misanthropy | |
| mince | | misapply | |
| mind | | misapprehend | |
| mindful | | misapprehension | |
| mine | | misappropriate | |
| miner | | missappropriation | |
| mineral | | misarrange | |
| mineralist | | misarrangement | |
| mineralize | | misbecome | |
| mineralogist | | misbehave | |
| mineralogy | | misbehaviour | |
| mingle | | misbelieve | |
| miniature | | miscalculate | |
| minimize | | miscalculation | |
| minimum | | miscall | |
| minion | | miscarry | |
| minister | | miscellaneous | |
| ministerial | | miscellany | |
| ministration | | mischance | |
| ministry | | mischief | |
| mink | | mischievous | |
| minnow | | misconceive | |
| minor | | misconception | |
| minority | | misconduct | |
| minster | | misconstruction | |
| minstrel | | misconstrue | |
| minstrelsy | | miscount | |
| mint | | miscreant | |
| mintage | | misdate | |
| minuend | | misdeal | |
| minus | | misdeed | |
| minute | | misdemean | |
| minuteness | | misdemeanor | |
| minutiae | | misdirect | |
| minx | | misdirection | |

**MISDIRECTION**

## MISDO

| | |
|---|---|
| misdo | misemploy |
| misemployment | miser |
| miserable | miserly |
| misery | misfit |
| misfortune | misgiving |
| misgovern | misgovernment |
| misguide | mishap |
| misimprove | misimprovement |
| misinform | misinformant |
| misinformation | misinterpret |
| misinterpretation | misjudge |
| misjudgment | mislay |
| mislead | misled |
| mismanage | mismanagement |
| misname | misnomer |
| misogamist | misogynist |
| misplace | misplead |
| mispoint | misprint |
| mispronounce | misproportion |
| misquotation | misread |
| misreckon | misrelate |
| misreport | misrepresent |
| misrepresentation | misrule |

| | |
|---|---|
| miss | missal |
| misshape | missile |
| mission | missionary |
| misspent | misstate |
| mist | mistake |
| mistletoe | mistranslate |
| mistranslation | mistress |
| mistrust | mistrustful |
| misty | misunderstand |
| misuse | mite |
| miter | mitigate |
| mitigation | mitigative |
| mitigator | mitt |
| mitten | mix |
| mixer | mixing |
| mixture | mizzen |
| mizzle | mnemonic |
| moan | moat |
| mob | mobile |
| mobilization | mobilize |
| moccasin | mock |
| mocker | mockery |
| mode | model |

**MODEL**

## MODERATE

| | |
|---|---|
| moderate..... | *(shorthand)* |
| modern....... | *(shorthand)* |
| modernize.... | *(shorthand)* |
| modest....... | *(shorthand)* |
| modesty...... | *(shorthand)* |
| modicum..... | *(shorthand)* |
| modification... | *(shorthand)* |
| modify....... | *(shorthand)* |
| modish....... | *(shorthand)* |
| modiste....... | *(shorthand)* |
| modulate..... | *(shorthand)* |
| modulation.... | *(shorthand)* |
| modulator..... | *(shorthand)* |
| mohair....... | *(shorthand)* |
| moiety........ | *(shorthand)* |
| moil......... | *(shorthand)* |
| moist......... | *(shorthand)* |
| moisten....... | *(shorthand)* |
| moisture...... | *(shorthand)* |
| molar........ | *(shorthand)* |
| molasses...... | *(shorthand)* |
| mold......... | *(shorthand)* |
| molder....... | *(shorthand)* |
| moldy........ | *(shorthand)* |
| mole......... | *(shorthand)* |
| molecular..... | *(shorthand)* |
| molecule...... | *(shorthand)* |
| molest........ | *(shorthand)* |
| molestation... | *(shorthand)* |
| mollient...... | *(shorthand)* |
| mollification... | *(shorthand)* |
| mollify....... | *(shorthand)* |
| mollusk....... | *(shorthand)* |
| molten....... | *(shorthand)* |
| *moment*...... | *(shorthand)* |
| momentarily... | *(shorthand)* |
| momentary.... | *(shorthand)* |
| momentous... | *(shorthand)* |
| momentum.... | *(shorthand)* |
| monad........ | *(shorthand)* |
| monadical..... | *(shorthand)* |
| monarch...... | *(shorthand)* |
| monarchy..... | *(shorthand)* |
| monastery.... | *(shorthand)* |
| monastic...... | *(shorthand)* |
| monastical.... | *(shorthand)* |

| | |
|---|---|
| monasticism... | *(shorthand)* |
| *Monday*....... | *(shorthand)* |
| *money*........ | *(shorthand)* |
| mongrel....... | *(shorthand)* |
| monition....... | *(shorthand)* |
| monitor........ | *(shorthand)* |
| monk.......... | *(shorthand)* |
| monkey........ | *(shorthand)* |
| monochrome... | *(shorthand)* |
| monocule...... | *(shorthand)* |
| monody....... | *(shorthand)* |
| monogamy..... | *(shorthand)* |
| monograph.... | *(shorthand)* |
| monography.... | *(shorthand)* |
| monolith....... | *(shorthand)* |
| monologue..... | *(shorthand)* |
| monomania.... | *(shorthand)* |
| monopetalous.. | *(shorthand)* |
| monoplane..... | *(shorthand)* |
| monopolize..... | *(shorthand)* |
| monopoly...... | *(shorthand)* |
| monosyllable... | *(shorthand)* |
| monotheist..... | *(shorthand)* |
| monotone...... | *(shorthand)* |
| monotonous.... | *(shorthand)* |
| monsoon....... | *(shorthand)* |
| monster....... | *(shorthand)* |
| monstrance.... | *(shorthand)* |
| monstrosity.... | *(shorthand)* |
| monstrous..... | *(shorthand)* |
| *month*......... | *(shorthand)* |
| *monthly*....... | *(shorthand)* |
| monument..... | *(shorthand)* |
| monumental.... | *(shorthand)* |
| mood.......... | *(shorthand)* |
| moody......... | *(shorthand)* |
| *moon*.......... | *(shorthand)* |
| moonbeam..... | *(shorthand)* |
| moonlight...... | *(shorthand)* |
| moonshine..... | *(shorthand)* |
| moor.......... | *(shorthand)* |
| moorage....... | *(shorthand)* |
| moorish....... | *(shorthand)* |
| moorland...... | *(shorthand)* |
| moose......... | *(shorthand)* |
| moot.......... | *(shorthand)* |

## MOOT

## MOP

| | | | |
|---|---|---|---|
| mop | | motherhood | |
| mope | | motif | |
| moral | | motion | |
| moralist | | motionless | |
| morality | | *motive* | |
| moralize | | motley | |
| morass | | motor | |
| morbid | | motorcycle | |
| morbidity | | motorist | |
| morbific | | motorman | |
| mordant | | mottle | |
| *more* | | motto | |
| moreen | | mould | |
| moreover | | moulder | |
| morganatic | | mouldy | |
| morgue | | moult | |
| moribund | | mound | |
| morion | | *mount* | |
| morn | | *mountain* | |
| *morning* | | mountaineer | |
| morocco | | mountainous | |
| moron | | mountebank | |
| morose | | mourn | |
| morphia | | mourner | |
| morphine | | mournful | |
| morris | | mourning | |
| morrow | | mouse | |
| morsel | | moustache | |
| mortal | | *mouth* | |
| mortality | | mouthful | |
| mortar | | *movable* | |
| mortgage | | *move* | |
| mortification | | *movement* | |
| mortify | | mover | |
| mortise | | mow | |
| mortmain | | mow | |
| mortuary | | mower | |
| mosaic | | mown | |
| mosque | | *Mr* | |
| mosquito | | Mrs | |
| moss | | *much* | |
| mossy | | mucilage | |
| *most* | | mucilaginous | |
| mote | | muck | |
| moth | | mucus | |
| *mother* | | mud | |

## MUDDLE

| | | | |
|---|---|---|---|
| muddle | *shorthand* | murmur | *shorthand* |
| muddy | *shorthand* | murrain | *shorthand* |
| muezzin | *shorthand* | muscatel | *shorthand* |
| muff | *shorthand* | muscle | *shorthand* |
| muffin | *shorthand* | muscular | *shorthand* |
| muffle | *shorthand* | muse | *shorthand* |
| muffler | *shorthand* | museum | *shorthand* |
| mufti | *shorthand* | mush | *shorthand* |
| mug | *shorthand* | mushroom | *shorthand* |
| muggy | *shorthand* | music | *shorthand* |
| mulatto | *shorthand* | musical | *shorthand* |
| mulberry | *shorthand* | musician | *shorthand* |
| mulct | *shorthand* | musk | *shorthand* |
| mule | *shorthand* | musket | *shorthand* |
| muleteer | *shorthand* | musketeer | *shorthand* |
| mulish | *shorthand* | musketry | *shorthand* |
| mull | *shorthand* | muskrat | *shorthand* |
| mullet | *shorthand* | muslin | *shorthand* |
| mulligatawny | *shorthand* | mussel | *shorthand* |
| mullion | *shorthand* | must | *shorthand* |
| multifarious | *shorthand* | mustard | *shorthand* |
| multifold | *shorthand* | muster | *shorthand* |
| multiform | *shorthand* | mutability | *shorthand* |
| multigraph | *shorthand* | mutable | *shorthand* |
| multiplane | *shorthand* | mutableness | *shorthand* |
| multiple | *shorthand* | mute | *shorthand* |
| multiplication | *shorthand* | mutilate | *shorthand* |
| multiply | *shorthand* | mutilation | *shorthand* |
| multitude | *shorthand* | mutilator | *shorthand* |
| mum | *shorthand* | mutineer | *shorthand* |
| mumble | *shorthand* | mutinous | *shorthand* |
| mummy | *shorthand* | mutiny | *shorthand* |
| mump | *shorthand* | mutter | *shorthand* |
| mumpish | *shorthand* | mutton | *shorthand* |
| munch | *shorthand* | mutual | *shorthand* |
| mundane | *shorthand* | muzzle | *shorthand* |
| municipal | *shorthand* | my | *shorthand* |
| municipality | *shorthand* | myopia | *shorthand* |
| munificence | *shorthand* | myriad | *shorthand* |
| muniment | *shorthand* | myrmidon | *shorthand* |
| munition | *shorthand* | myrrh | *shorthand* |
| mural | *shorthand* | myrtle | *shorthand* |
| murder | *shorthand* | myself | *shorthand* |
| murderer | *shorthand* | mysterious | *shorthand* |
| murderous | *shorthand* | mystery | *shorthand* |
| murky | *shorthand* | mystic | *shorthand* |

## MYSTICAL

| | | | |
|---|---|---|---|
| mystical | _st | mythical | _th |
| mystification | _sf | mythologic | _tolk |
| mystify | _sf | mythologist | _tol, |
| myth | _th | mythology | _tol |

## N

| | | | |
|---|---|---|---|
| nab | _nb | natural | nal |
| nabob | _nbb | naturalist | nal, |
| nadir | na | naturalization | nalz, |
| nag | _ng | naturalize | nalz |
| naiad | _ned | nature | na |
| nail | _nal | naught | nat |
| nailer | _nl | naughty | _nt, |
| naive | _nav | nausea | _nza |
| naked | _nkd | nauseous | _nzs |
| nakedness | _nkd' | nautical | _ntk |
| name | na | nautilus | _ntls |
| nameless | _nal' | naval | _nal |
| namely | nal | nave | _na |
| namesake | _nask | navigable | _nvgb |
| nap | _np | navigate | _nvga |
| nape | _nap | navigation | _nvgj |
| napery | _npy | navigator | Nvga |
| naphtha | _nfla | navy | _nv, |
| napkin | _npken | nay | _na |
| napless | _npl' | near | ne |
| narcissus | _nrssx | nearby | _neb |
| narcotic | _nrkt | nearly | _nel |
| narrate | _nra | nearness | _ne' |
| narration | _nrj | neat | _ne |
| narrative | _nrv | neatness | _ne' |
| narrow | _nro | nebula | _nbla |
| narrowness | _nro' | nebulous | _nbls |
| nasal | _nzl | necessarily | _nec |
| nasturtium | _nst | necessary | _nec |
| nasty | _ns, | necessitate | _necta |
| natal | _ntl | necessitous | _nects |
| nation | _nj | necessity | _nec) |
| national | _nyl | neck | _nk |
| nationalism | _nylz | necklace | _nkls |
| nationalist | _nyl, | necktie | _nkte |
| nationality | _nyl) | neckwear | _nk ra |
| nationalize | _nylz | necrology | _nkol |
| native | _nav | necromancy | _nkr |
| nativity | _nav) | necropolis | _nkpls |

NECROPOLIS

**NECROSIS**

necrosis....... *nkss*
necrotic........ *nkt*
nectar.......... *nke*
nectarine....... *nkn*
need........... *nd*
needful........ *ndf*
needle.......... *ndl*
needless....... *ndl'*
needlewoman... *ndl*
needy.......... *nd,*
ne'er.......... *ne*
nefarious...... *nfyx*
negate......... *nga*
negative....... *ngv*
neglect........ *nglk*
negligence..... *nglj*
negligent...... *nglj-*
negotiable..... *ngzb*
negotiate...... *ngza*
negotiation..... *ngzj*
negotiator...... *ngza*
negro.......... *ngo*
negroid........ *ngyd*
neigh.......... *na*
neighbor....... *nb*
neighborhood... *nbhd*
neither........ *ne*
neology........ *nol*
neophyte....... *nofe*
nephew........ *nfu*
nepotism....... *nptz*
nereid......... *nyd*
nerve......... *nrv*
nerveless...... *nrvl'*
nervous........ *nrvt*
nervousness.... *nrvt'*
nescience...... *nsj*
nescient....... *nsj-*
nest.......... *n,*
nestle ........ *nsl*
net........... *nt*
nether........ *ne*
nettle.......... *ntl*
network........ *ntwk*
neuralgia...... *nrlj*
neuralgic...... *nrljk*

neuritis....... *nru)*
neurotic...... *nrt*
neuter........ *nu*
neutral........ *nul*
neutrality..... *nul)*
neutralization... *nulz*
neutralize..... *nulz*
never......... *nv*
nevertheless.... *nvtl'*
new........... *nu*
newborn...... *nubrn*
newcomer..... *nuk*
newness....... *nu'*
news.......... *nz*
newspaper..... *nzp*
newt.......... *nu*
next.......... *nx*
New York..... *ny*
nib........... *nb*
nibble......... *nb*
nice.......... *ns*
nicely........ *nsl*
niceness....... *ns'*
nicer......... *ns*
niche......... *nc*
nick.......... *nk*
nickel......... *nkl*
nickname...... *nkna*
nicotine....... *nktn*
nidification..... *ndf*
niece......... *nes*
niggard....... *ngl*
nigh.......... *nu*
night......... *nu*
nightcap...... *nukp*
nightfall...... *nufal*
nightgown..... *nugn*
nightingale.... *nugl*
nightly....... *nul*
nightmare..... *nura*
nightshirt...... *nufl*
nimble........ *nmb*
nimbus....... *nmbs*
nincompoop... *nqppp*
nine (9)....... *9*
nineteen (19)... *19*

**NINETEEN**

NINETEENTH

| | |
|---|---|
| nineteenth (19t). | *19t* |
| ninety (90) | *90* |
| ninny | |
| nip | |
| nipple | |
| nit | |
| niter | |
| nitrate | |
| nitric | |
| nitrogen | |
| nitrous | |
| no | |
| nobility | |
| noble | |
| nobleman | |
| nobleness | |
| nobly | |
| nobody | |
| nocturn | |
| nocturnal | |
| nod | |
| noddle | |
| noddy | |
| node | |
| noggin | |
| *noise* | |
| noiseless | |
| *noisier* | |
| *noisily* | |
| noisome | |
| noisy | |
| nomad | |
| nomenclature | |
| nominal | |
| nominate | |
| nomination | |
| nominator | |
| nonage | |
| nonagenarian | |
| nonagon | |
| nonce | |
| nonchalance | |
| nonchalant | |
| nondescript | |
| *none* | |
| nonentity | |

| | |
|---|---|
| nonesuch | |
| nonpareil | |
| nonplus | |
| nonsense | |
| nonsensical | |
| noodle | |
| nook | |
| noon | |
| noonday | |
| noontide | |
| noose | |
| nor | |
| normal | |
| *north* | |
| northeast | |
| northeastern | |
| northerly | |
| northern | |
| *northward* | |
| northwest | |
| northwestern | |
| nose | |
| nostril | |
| *not* | |
| notable | |
| notably | |
| notary | |
| notation | |
| notch | |
| *note* | |
| noteworthy | |
| *nothing* | |
| *notice* | |
| *noticeable* | |
| notification | |
| *notify* | |
| notion | |
| *notoriety* | |
| *notorious* | |
| notwithstanding | |
| nought | |
| noun | |
| nourish | |
| nourishment | |
| novel | |
| novelette | |

**NOVELETTE**

## NOVELIST

| | | | |
|---|---|---|---|
| novelist | *nvl,* | numerable | |
| novelty | *nvll,* | numeral | |
| November | | numerate | |
| novice | | numeration | |
| novitiate | | numerator | |
| now | | numeric | |
| nowadays | | numerical | |
| nowhere | | numerous | |
| noxiousness | | numskull | |
| nozzle | | nun | |
| nucleus | | nunnery | |
| nude | | nuptial | |
| nudge | | nurse | |
| nudity | | nursery | |
| nugatory | | nursling | |
| nugget | | nurture | |
| nuisance | | nut | |
| null | | nutmeg | |
| nullification | | nutriment | |
| nullify | | nutrition | |
| nullity | | nutritious | |
| numb | | nutritive | |
| number | | nutting | |
| numberless | | nutty | |
| numbness | | nymph | |

## O

| | | | |
|---|---|---|---|
| O | | obesity | |
| oaf | | obey | |
| oak | | obfuscate | |
| oaken | | obit | |
| oakum | | obituary | |
| oar | | object | |
| oasis | | objection | |
| oat | | objectionable | |
| oath | | objective | |
| oatmeal | | objector | |
| obduracy | | objurgation | |
| obdurate | | oblate | |
| obedience | | oblation | |
| obedient | | obligation | |
| obeisance | | obligatory | |
| obelisk | | oblige | |
| obese | | oblique | |
| obeseness | | obliqueness | |

**OBLIQUENESS**

# OBLIQUITY

| | | | | |
|---|---|---|---|---|
| obliquity | *obq)* | occasional | *okjl* | |
| obliterate | *Oba* | occidental | *xd-l* | |
| obliteration | *Oly* | occult | *okll* | |
| oblivion | *obvn* | occultation | *oklly* | |
| oblivious | *obvx* | occupancy | *okp* | |
| obliviousness | *obvi'* | occupant | *okp-* | |
| oblong | *oblq* | occupation | *okpy* | |
| obloquy | *obz,* | occupy | *okr okpe* | |
| obnoxious | *obnx* | occur | *okr* | |
| obscene | *obsn* | occurrence | *okr/* | |
| obsceneness | *obsn'* | ocean | *oj* | |
| obscenity | *obsn)* | ocelot | *osll* | |
| obscuration | *obskuy* | ocher | *Ok* | |
| obscure | *obsku* | o'clock..(°) | *oklk* | |
| obscurity | *obsku)* | octagon | *okgn* | |
| obsequies | *obsqz* | octangular | *okdgl* | |
| obsequious | *obsqx* | octant | *ok-* | |
| obsequiousness | *obsqx'* | octave | *okv* | |
| observance | *obsv/* | October | *oc* | |
| observant | *obsv-* | octodecimo | *okdsro* | |
| observation | *obsvy* | octogenarian | *okjnyn* | |
| observe | *obsv* | octopod | *okpd* | |
| observer | *Obsv* | octopus | *okpx* | |
| obsolescent | *obsls-* | octoroon | *Okl Okn* | |
| obsolete | *obsle* | ocular | *Okl* | |
| obsoleteness | *obsle'* | oculist | *okl,* | |
| obstacle | *obsK* | odd | *od* | |
| obstetric | *obstk* | oddity | *od' od)* | |
| obstinacy | *obsns,* | oddness | *od'* | |
| obstinate | *obsna* | odds | *od ods* | |
| obstinateness | *obsna'* | ode | *od* | |
| obstreperous | *obSpx* | odious | *odx* | |
| obstruct | *obSk* | odontology | *od-ol* | |
| obstruction | *obSkj* | odor | *Od* | |
| obstructive | *obSkv* | odorous | *Odx* | |
| obtain | *obtn* | o'er | *-o* | |
| obtainable | *oblnb* | of | *v* | |
| obtrude | *obld* | off | *of* | |
| obtrusion | *obly* | offal | *ofl* | |
| obtrusive | *oblsv* | offend | *Of of-* | |
| obtuse | *obls* | offender | *Of-* | |
| obtuseness | *obls'* | offense | *of/v of* | |
| obverse | *obvrs* | offensive | *of/v* | |
| obviate | *obva* | offer | *ofly of* | |
| obvious | *obvx* | offertory | *ofly* | |
| occasion | *okj* | office | *ofs* | |

OFFICE

## OFFICER

| | | | |
|---|---|---|---|
| officer | | one | |
| official | | oneness | |
| officiate | | onerous | |
| officious | | oneself | |
| offing | | onion | |
| offset | | onlooker | |
| offspring | | only | |
| oft | | onset | |
| often | | onslaught | |
| oftener | | onward | |
| oftentimes | | onyx | |
| ofttimes | | ooze | |
| ogle | | opacity | |
| ogre | | opal | |
| oh | | opalescent | |
| ohm | | opaque | |
| oil | | opaqueness | |
| oilcloth | | ope | |
| oilskin | | open | |
| oily. : | | openly | |
| ointment | | opera | |
| old | | operate | |
| olden | | operatic | |
| older | | operation | |
| oleaginous | | operative | |
| oleander | | operator | |
| oleograph | | operetta | |
| olfactory | | ophthalmia | |
| oligarch | | opiate | |
| oligarchical | | opine | |
| olive | | opinion | |
| omega | | opinionated | |
| omelet | | opiniouative | |
| omen | | opium | |
| ominous | | opossum | |
| omission | | opponent | |
| omit | | opportune | |
| omnibus | | opportunism | |
| omnifarious | | opportunist | |
| omnipotent | | opportunity | |
| omnipresent | | oppose | |
| omniscience | | opposite | |
| omniscient | | opposition | |
| omnivorous | | oppress | |
| on | | oppression | |
| once | | oppressive | |

OPPRESSIVE

OPPRESSOR

| | |
|---|---|
| oppressor | orifice |
| opprobrious | origin |
| opprobrium | original |
| oppugn | originality |
| optative | originate |
| optic | origination |
| optical | originator |
| optician | oriole |
| optimism | orison |
| optimist | orlop |
| option | ormolu |
| opulent | ornament |
| or | ornamentation |
| oracle | ornate |
| oracular | ornithology |
| oral | orography |
| orange | orphan |
| orangeade | orphanage |
| oration | orpine |
| orator | orrery |
| oratory | orthodox |
| orb | orthography |
| orbit | orthopter |
| orchard | ortolan |
| orchestra | oscillate |
| orchid | oscillation |
| ordain | oscillatory |
| ordeal | osculate |
| order | osculatory |
| ordinal | osier |
| ordinance | osmium |
| ordinarily | osprey |
| ordinary | osseous |
| ordination | ossification |
| ore | ossify |
| organ | ossifrage |
| organic | ossivorous |
| organism | ostensible |
| organist | ostentation |
| organization | ostentatious |
| organize | osteopathy |
| orgasm | ostler |
| orgies | ostracism |
| oriel | ostracise |
| orient | ostrich |
| oriental | other |

OTHER

OTHERWISE

| | |
|---|---|
| otherwise....... | *O-3* *O* |
| otter.......... | |
| ouch.......... | *ouc* |
| ought.......... | *ol* |
| ounce ..... | *oz* |
| *our*............. | *r* |
| ours............. | *rs* |
| ourself......... | *rs* |
| ourselves....... | *rs* |
| oust............ | *ou,* |
| ouster.......... | *ouS* |
| out............. | *ou* |
| outbalance...... | *oubal* |
| outbreak........ | *oubk* |
| outburst........ | *oubr,* |
| outcast......... | *ouk,* |
| outcome........ | *ouk* |
| outcry.......... | *ouki* |
| outdoor........ | *ou oudo* |
| outer.......... | *Ou* |
| outermost....... | *Ouro,* |
| outfit.......... | *oufl* |
| outfitter........ | *ouH* |
| outgo.......... | *oug* |
| outgrown....... | *ougn* |
| outhouse........ | *ouh-s* |
| outing.......... | *ou* |
| outlandish...... | *oul—?* |
| outlast.......... | *oul,* |
| outlaw.......... | *oula* |
| outlay.......... | *oula* |
| outlet.......... | *oull* |
| outline......... | *ouli* |
| outlive.......... | *oulv* |
| outlook......... | *oulo* |
| outlying...... . | *ouli* |
| outmost........ | *ouro,* |
| outnumber...... | *ouno* |
| outnumbered.... | *ounō* |
| outrage........ | *oury* |
| outrageous...... | *ouryx* |
| outreach........ | *ourc* |
| outrigger........ | *ouRg* |
| outright......... | *ouri* |
| outrun.......... | *ourn* |
| outset.......... | *ousl* |

| | |
|---|---|
| outshine...... | *ouʒn* |
| outside........ | *ousd* |
| outsider....... | *ouSd* |
| outskirt...... | *ousk/* |
| outspread..... | *ousd* |
| outstand...... | *ous—* |
| outstretch..... | *ouSc* |
| outstrip....... | *oulp* |
| outvote....... | *ouvo* |
| outward...... | *ou/* |
| outweigh..... | *oura* |
| outwit........ | *ourl* |
| outwork...... | *our-k* |
| oval.......... | *ovl* |
| ovary......... | *ovy* |
| ovation........ | *ovy* |
| oven......... | *ovn* |
| over.......... | *V* |
| overalls....... | *Vls* |
| overawe...... | *Va* |
| overbalance... | *Vbal* |
| overbear...... | *Vba* *Vb/* |
| overboard..... | *Vb/m* |
| overburden... | *Vk* |
| overcame..... | *Vk,* |
| overcast...... | *Vcq* |
| overcharge.... | *Vklod* |
| overcloud..... | *Vko* |
| overcoat...... | *Vk* |
| overcome..... | *Vdu* |
| overdo........ | *Vda* |
| overdraw...... | *Vdi* |
| overdrive..... | *Vdu* |
| overdue..... | *Vesra* |
| overestimate... | *Vflo* |
| overflow...... | *Vgo* |
| overgrow..... | *Vgn* |
| overgrown.... | *Vhq* *Vhl* |
| overhang...... | *Vhd* *Vhe* |
| overhaul...... | |
| overhead..... | *Vjy* |
| overhear...... | *Vld* |
| overjoy....... | *Vl* *Vlp* |
| overlaid...... | |
| overland...... | |
| overlap....... | |

OVERLAP

## OVERLAY

| | | | |
|---|---|---|---|
| overlay | *Vla* | overtook | *Vlk* |
| overleap | *Vlp* | overture | *Vlu* |
| overlook | *Vlo* | overturn | *Vln* |
| overmuch | *Vrc* | overweight | *Vra* |
| overpass | *Vp* | overwhelm | *Vl* |
| overpay | *Vpa* | overwise | *Vz* |
| overplus | *Vpx* | overwork | *Vtk* |
| overpower | *VR* | overworked | *Vtk* |
| overprize | *Vpz* | oviferous | *ovfx* |
| overreach | *Vrc* | oviform | *ovf* |
| override | *Vrd* | ovoid | *ovyd* |
| overrule | *Vrl* | ovule | *ovl* |
| overrun | *Vrn* | ovum | *ov* |
| oversea | *Vse* | owe | *o* |
| overseas | *Vsz* | owl | *oul* |
| overseer | *Vse* | owlet | *oull* |
| overshoe | *Vzu* | own | *on* |
| oversight | *Vsu* | owner | *On* |
| overspread | *Vsd* | ownership | *On* |
| overstate | *Vsa* | ox | *x* |
| overstep | *Vsp* | oxen | *xn* |
| overstock | *Vsk* | oxidate | *xda* |
| overstrain | *Vsn* | oxide | *xd* |
| overt | *ovt* | oxidize | *xdz* |
| overtake | *Vtk* | oxygen | *xn* |
| overthrew | *Vtu* | oyster | *yS* |
| overthrow | *Vlo* | ozone | *ozn* |

### P

| | | | |
|---|---|---|---|
| pa | *pa* | pad | *pd* |
| pabulum | *pbl* | paddle | *pdl* |
| pacable | *pkb* | paddock | *pdk* |
| pace | *pas* | padlock | *pdlk* |
| pachyderm | *pkdr* | pagan | *pgn* |
| pachydermatous | *pkdrtx* | paganism | *pgnz* |
| pacific | *psfk* | page | *pg* |
| pacification | *psf* | pageant | *pj* |
| pacifism | *psfz* | pageantry | *Pj* |
| pacifist | *psf* | pagoda | *pgda* |
| pacify | *psf* | paid | *pd* |
| pack | *pk* | pail | *pal* |
| package | *pkj* | pain | *pn* |
| packer | *Pk* | painful | *pnf* |
| packet | *pkt* | painstaking | *pnstk* |
| pact | *pk* | paint | *pa-* |

## PAINTER

| | |
|---|---|
| *painter* | Pa- |
| *pair* (pr) | pa |
| pajama | pjra |
| pajamas | pjras |
| pal | pl |
| palace | pls |
| palanquin | plqn |
| palate | pla |
| palatial | pll |
| palatinate | pllna |
| palatine | plln |
| palaver | Plv |
| pale | pal |
| paleface | plfs |
| palette | pll |
| palfrey | plf |
| palimpsest | plps, |
| palindrome | pl—ro |
| palisade | plsd |
| pall | pal |
| palladium | pld |
| pallbearer | plBa |
| pallet | pl' pll |
| palliasse | pl' |
| palliate | pla |
| palliation | plq |
| palliative | plv |
| palm | p |
| palmist | pr, |
| palmistry | prs, |
| palpable | plpb |
| palpitate | plpta |
| palpitation | plpy |
| palsy | plz, |
| paltry | Pl, |
| pampas | prps |
| pamper | Prp |
| pamphlet | prfll |
| pamphleteer | prflle |
| pan | pn |
| panacea | pnse |
| pancake | pnkk |
| pancreas | pqrs |
| pandemonium | p——m |
| pander | P— |
| pane | pn |

| | |
|---|---|
| panegyric | pnyrk |
| panegyrist | pnyr, |
| panel | pnl |
| pang | pq |
| panic | pnk |
| panicle | pnk |
| pannior | P. |
| panoply | pnp |
| panorama | pnrra |
| pansy | pnz, |
| pant | p- |
| pantaloon | p-ln |
| pantheism | pntez |
| pantheist | pnle, |
| pantheistic | pnle's |
| pantheon | pnlen |
| panther | Pn |
| pantomime | p-rn |
| pantry | p-, |
| pap | pp |
| papa | ppa |
| *paper* | Pp |
| papier-mache | Pp—ja |
| papillary | ppply |
| papoose | ppps |
| papyrus | pppr |
| par | pr |
| parable | Pb |
| parabola | Pbla |
| parabolic | Pblk |
| parabolical | Pblk |
| parachute | Pzu |
| parade | Pds Pd |
| paradise | Pds |
| paradox | Pdx |
| paradoxical | Pdxk |
| paraffin | Pfn |
| paragon | Pqn Pqf |
| paragraph | Pqf |
| parallel | Pll |
| parallelism | Pllz |
| parallelogram | Pllg |
| paralyse | Plz |
| paralysis | Plss |
| paralytic | Plt |
| paramount | P— |

**PARAMOUNT**

| | | | | |
|---|---|---|---|---|
| paramour | | part | | |
| parapet | | partake | | |
| paraphernalia | | partaker | | |
| paraphrase | | partial | | |
| parasite | | partiality | | |
| parasol | | participant | | |
| parboil | | participate | | |
| parcel | | participation | | |
| parch | | participator | | |
| parchment | | participial | | |
| pardon | | participle | | |
| pardonable | | particle | | |
| pare | | particular | | |
| paregoric | | particularity | | |
| parent | | particularize | | |
| parentage | | partisan | | |
| parental | | partition | | |
| parenthesis | | partitive | | |
| parenthetic | | partly | | |
| parenthetical | | partner | | |
| paresis | | partnership | | |
| pariah | | partridge | | |
| parish | | party | | |
| parishioner | | parvenu | | |
| parity | | paschal | | |
| park | | pasha | | |
| parlance | | pass | | |
| parley | | passable | | |
| parliament | | passage | | |
| parliamentary | | passed | | |
| parlor | | passenger | | |
| parochial | | passer | | |
| parody | | passion | | |
| parole | | passionate | | |
| paroxysm | | passive | | |
| parricide | | passiveness | | |
| parrot | | passivity | | |
| parry | | past | | |
| parse | | paste | | |
| parsimonious | | pastel | | |
| parsimony | | pastern | | |
| parsing | | pastil | | |
| parsley | | pastime | | |
| parsnip | | pastor | | |
| parson | | pastoral | | |
| parsonage | | pastorate | | |

PASTORSHIP

| | | | |
|---|---|---|---|
| pastorship....... | | paunch...... | |
| pastry.......... | | pauper....... | |
| pasturage....... | | pauperism.... | |
| pasture......... | | pauperize.... | |
| pat............. | | pause........ | |
| patch.......... | | pave......... | |
| pate........... | | pavement..... | |
| paten.......... | | pavilion...... | |
| patent......... | | paw.......... | |
| paternal........ | | pawn......... | |
| paternity........ | | pawnbroker... | |
| paternoster...... | | pay.......... | |
| path........... | | payable...... | |
| pathetic........ | | payee........ | |
| pathless........ | | payer........ | |
| pathological..... | | paymaster.... | |
| pathologist...... | | payment...... | |
| pathology....... | | pea.......... | |
| pathos.......... | | peace........ | |
| pathway........ | | peaceable.... | |
| patience........ | | peaceful..... | |
| patient......... | | peacemaker... | |
| patois.......... | | peach........ | |
| patriarch........ | | peacock...... | |
| patriarchal...... | | peak......... | |
| patriarchate..... | | peal......... | |
| patriarchic...... | | peanut....... | |
| patrician........ | | pear......... | |
| patricide........ | | pearl........ | |
| patrimonial...... | | peasant...... | |
| patrimony....... | | peasantry.... | |
| patriot.......... | | peat......... | |
| patriotic........ | | pebble....... | |
| patriotism....... | | pecan........ | |
| patristic........ | | peccable..... | |
| patrol.......... | | peccadillo.... | |
| patron.......... | | peccant...... | |
| patronage....... | | peccary...... | |
| patroness....... | | peck......... | |
| patronize........ | | pectoral..... | |
| patronymic...... | | peculate..... | |
| patten.......... | | peculation.... | |
| patter.......... | | peculiar...... | |
| pattern......... | | peculiarity... | |
| patty........... | | pecuniary.... | |
| paucity......... | | pedagog...... | |

PEDAGOG

## PEDAGOGY

| | | | | |
|---|---|---|---|---|
| pedagogy | *pdgs,* | pendulum | *p — l* | |
| pedal | *pdl* | penetrable | *Pnb* | |
| pedant | *pd −* | penetrability | *Pnb)* | |
| pedantic | *pd −k* | penetrate | *Pna* | |
| pedantry | *Pd −,* | penetration | *Pny* | |
| peddler | *Pdl* | penetrative | *Pnv* | |
| pedestal | *pdsl* | penguin | *pngn* | |
| pedestrian | *pdsn* | peninsula | *pnnsla* | |
| pedestrianism | *pdsnz* | penitence | *pnt* | |
| pedigree | *pdge* | penitent | *pnt−* | |
| pediment | *pd −* | penitential | *pntl* | |
| pedlar | *Pdl* | penitentiary | *pntfy* | |
| pedometer | *pdse* | pennant | *pn −* | |
| peek | *pek* | penny | *pn,* | |
| peel | *pel* | pension | *pny* | |
| peep | *pep* | pensionary | *pnyy* | |
| peer | *pe* | pensive | *pv* | |
| peerage | *pej* | pent | *p−* | |
| peeress | *pe'* | pentagon | *p−gn* | |
| peerless | *pel'* | pentameter | *p− se* | |
| peevish | *pvj* | penthouse | *p−hs* | |
| peevishness | *pvj* | penult | *pnll* | |
| peg | *pg* | penultimate | *pnllsa* | |
| pekoe | *pko* | penumbra | *pnsba* | |
| pelage | *ply* | penurious | *pnyx* | |
| pelf | *plf* | penuriousness | *pnyx'* | |
| pelican | *plkn* | penury | *pny* | |
| pelisse | *pls* | peonage | *peny* | |
| pell | *pl* | peony | *pen,* | |
| pellet | *pll* | people | *pp* | |
| pellucid | *plsd* | pepper | *Pp* | |
| pelt | *pll* | peppermint | *Pp−* | |
| pelvis | *plvs* | pepsin | *ppsn* | |
| pen | *pn* | peptic | *ppt* | |
| penal | *pnl* | per | *pr* | |
| penalize | *pnlz* | peradventure | *pav−u* | |
| penalty | *pnll,* | perambulate | *p−bla* | |
| penance | *pn* | perambulation | *p−bly* | |
| pence | *p* | perambulator | *P−bla* | |
| penchant | *pc−* | per annum | *pa* | |
| pencil | *pl* | percale | *pkl* | |
| pendant | *p−−,* | perceivable | *pseb* | |
| pendency | *p−* | perceive | *pse* | |
| pendent | *p−−* | per cent (%) | *pc* | |
| pending | *p−* | percentage | *pcj* | |
| pendulous | *p−lc* | perceptible | *pspt* | |

## PERCEPTION

|  | |  | |
|---|---|---|---|
| perception | *pspy* | periphrase | *Pß Pskp* |
| perceptive | *pspv* | periscope | *Pß* |
| perceptiveness | *pspv* | perish | *Pß Pßb* |
| perch | *pc* | perishable | |
| perchance | *pc* | periwig | *Pq Pql* |
| percolate | *pkla* | periwinkle | |
| percolation | *pkly* | perjure | *pju* |
| percolator | *Pkla* | perjury | *pjy* |
| percussion | *pky* | perk | *pk* |
| perdition | *pdy* | permanency | *pm* |
| peregrinate | *Pgna* | permanent | *pm-* |
| peregrination | *Pgny* | permeable | *prb* |
| peremptory | *prly pnl* | permanganate | *prgna* |
| perennial | | permeate | *pra* |
| *perfect* | *pfk* | permissible | *prsb* |
| *perfection* | *pfky* | permission | *pry* |
| *perfectly* | *pjkl* | permissive | *prsv* |
| perfidious | *pfdx* | permit | *prl* |
| perfidiousness | *pfdx* | permutable | *prub* |
| perfidy | *pfd,* | pernicious | *pnk* |
| perforate | *pfa* | peroration | *poy* |
| perforation | *pfy* | peroxide | *prd* |
| perforator | *Pfa* | perpendicular | *pp— Kl* |
| perforce | *pfs* | perpetrate | *pfa* |
| perform | *pf* | perpetration | *ppy* |
| performance | *pf* | perpetual | *ppil* |
| performer | *pf* | perpetuate | *ppla* |
| perfume | *pfu Pfu* | perpetuation | *ppluy* |
| perfumer | | perplex | *ppx* |
| perfumery | *pfuy* | perplexity | *ppx)* |
| perfunctorily | *pfgy pfgyl* | perquisite | *pqzl* |
| perfunctoriness | *pfgy* | perry | *py* |
| perfunctory | | persecute | *psku* |
| *perhaps* | *pps Pky* | persecution | *psky* |
| pericardium | *Pkrp* | persecutor | *Psku* |
| pericarp | | perseverance | *psve* |
| pericranium | *Pkn* | persevere | *psve* |
| peril | *Pl* | persist | *ps,* |
| perilous | *Plx* | persistence | *pss* |
| perimeter | *Pre Pd* | *person* | *psn* |
| period | | personable | *psnb* |
| periodic | *Pdk* | personage | *psny* |
| periodical | *Pdk* | *personal* | *psnl* |
| periodicity | *Pds)* | personality | *psnl)* |
| peripatetic | *Ppt* | personate | *psna* |
| periphery | *Pfy* | personation | *psny* |

**PERSONATION**

# PERSONIFICATION

| | | | |
|---|---|---|---|
| personification... | *psnf* | petition.......... | *ply* |
| personify....... | *psnf* | petitionary....... | *plyy* |
| perspective...... | *pskv* | petrel............ | *Pel* |
| perspicacious.... | *pskx* | petrification...... | *Pef* |
| perspicacity.... | *psks)* | petrify........... | *Pef* |
| perspicuity...... | *psk)* | petrol............ | *Pel* |
| perspicuous...:.. | *pskx* | petroleum....... | *Pel* |
| perspiration..... | *psy* | petticoat........ | *plko* |
| perspire........ | *psi* | pettifogging..... | *plfg* |
| persuade........ | *psd* | petty............ | *pl,* |
| persuasion...... | *psy* | petulance........ | *pll* |
| persuasive...... | *pssv* | petulant......... | *pll-* |
| persuasiveness.. | *pssv* | pew............. | *pu* |
| pert............ | *pl* | pewter.......... | *Pu* |
| pertly.......... | *pll* | phaeton.......... | *fln* |
| pertain......... | *pln* | phalanx.......... | *flnx* |
| pertinacious..... | *plnx* | phantasm....... | *f-3* |
| pertinacity...... | *plns)* | phantasmagoria... | *f-3rgy* |
| pertinent........ | *pln-* | phantastic....... | *f-5* |
| perturb......... | *plrb* | phantom......... | *f-~* |
| perturbation..... | *plrby* | pharmacist....... | *frs,* |
| peruke......... | *puk* | pharmacy........ | *frs,* |
| perusal......... | *puzl* | phase........... | *fz* |
| peruse......... | *puz* | pheasant........ | *fz-* |
| pervade........ | *pvd* | phenomena...... | *fnma* |
| pervasive....... | *pvsv* | phenomenal..... | *fnml* |
| perverse........ | *pvrs* | phenomenon..... | *fnmn* |
| perversion...... | *pvry* | phial............ | *fl* |
| perversity...... | *pvrs)* | philander........ | *Jl* |
| pervert......... | *pv/* | philanthropical... | *flnlpk* |
| pervious........ | *pvs* | philanthropist.... | *flnlp,* |
| pessimism...... | *psnz* | philanthropy..... | *flnlp,* |
| pessimist....... | *pz,* | philharmonic..... | *flhrmk* |
| pessimistic...... | *ps-5* | philippic........ | *flpk* |
| pest............ | *p,* | philistine........ | *flsn* |
| pester.......... | *ps* | philologist....... | *jlol,* |
| pesthouse....... | *psh-s* | philology........ | *flol* |
| pestiferous...... | *psfx* | philosopher..... | *flsf* |
| pestilence....... | *psl* | philosophic.... | *flsfk* |
| pestilent........ | *psl-* | philosophical ... | *flsfk* |
| pestilential...... | *psl* | philosophize..... | *flsfz* |
| pestle.......... | *psl* | philosophy...... | *flsf* |
| pet............ | *ksle* | phlebotomy..... | *fll,* |
| petal.......... | *pll* | phlegm.. . | *fg-* |
| petard.......... | *pl/* | phlegmatic....... | *fg-* |
| petite.......... | *ple* | phlox............ | *fx* |

**PHLOX**

| | | | | |
|---|---|---|---|---|
| phocine......... | *fsun* | | picker......... | *Pk* |
| phoenix......... | *fnx* | | pickerel........ | *Pkl* |
| phone......... | *fn* | | picket......... | *pkt* |
| phonetic........ | *fnt* | | pickle......... | *pk* |
| phonograph..... | *fngf* | | picnic......... | *pknk* |
| phonographer.... | *fngf* | | pictorial........ | *pkyl* |
| phonographist... | *fngf,* | | picture......... | *pktu* |
| phonography.... | *fngf,* | | picturesque..... | *pktusk* |
| phonologist..... | *fnol,* | | picturesqueness.. | *pktusk'* |
| phonology...... | *fnol* | | pie......... | *pu* |
| phonotype...... | *fntp* | | piebald......... | *publd* |
| phosphate...... | *fsfa* | | *piece*......... | *ps* |
| phosphorescence. | *fsfs* | | piecemeal....... | *psml* |
| phosphorous.... | *fsfx* | | piecework....... | *ps-k* |
| photo......... | *flo* | | pied......... | *pd* |
| *photograph*..... | *flgf* | | pier......... | *pe* |
| photographer.... | *flgf* | | pierce......... | *pes* |
| photogravure.... | *flgvu* | | piety......... | *pu)* |
| photometer..... | *flte* | | pig......... | *pg* |
| photosphere..... | *flsf* | | pigeon......... | *pjn* |
| phrase......... | *fz* | | piggy......... | *pg,* |
| phraseology..... | *fzol* | | pigiron......... | *pgun* |
| phrenologist.... | *fnol,* | | pigment......... | *pg-* |
| phrenology..... | *fnol* | | pike......... | *puk* |
| phthisis......... | *tss* | | pikeman........ | *pks-* |
| phylactery...... | *flky* | | pikestaff........ | *pksf* |
| physic......... | *fzk* | | pilaster......... | *plS* |
| physical........ | *fzk* | | pilchard........ | *plc,* |
| physician....... | *fz1* | | pile......... | *pul* |
| physicist........ | *fzs,* | | piledriver....... | *plDu* |
| physics......... | *fzks* | | pilfer......... | *plf* |
| physiognomy.... | *fzgn,* | | pilferage........ | *plfS* |
| physiography.... | *fzgf,* | | pilgrim......... | *plgu* |
| physiologist..... | *fzol,* | | pilgrimage...... | *plgy* |
| physiology...... | *fzol* | | pill......... | *pl* |
| physique........ | *fzk* | | pillage......... | *plf* |
| phytology....... | *flol* | | pillar......... | *Pl* |
| piacular......... | *pull* | | pillion......... | *pln* |
| pianist......... | *pn,* | | pillory......... | *ply* |
| piano......... | *pno* | | pillow......... | *plo* |
| pianoforte....... | *pnf/a* | | pilot......... | *pll* |
| piaster......... | *pS* | | pimento........ | *p-o* |
| piazza......... | *pza* | | pimp......... | *prp* |
| pibroch......... | *pbk* | | pimpernel....... | *prpnl* |
| *pick*......... | *pk* | | pimple......... | *prp* |
| pickaxe........ | *pkx* | | pin......... | *pn* |

**PINCERS**

| | | | |
|---|---|---|---|
| pincers | | pitiful | |
| pinch | | pitiless | |
| pinchbeck | | pittance | |
| pine | | pity | |
| pineapple | | pivot | |
| pinewood | | placability | |
| pinfold | | placable | |
| pinion | | placard | |
| pink | | placate | |
| pinnace | | place | |
| pinnacle | | placement | |
| pinnate | | placid | |
| pint | | placidity | |
| pioneer | | placidness | |
| pious | | plagiarism | |
| pip | | plagiarist | |
| pipe | | plagiarize | |
| piper | | plagiary | |
| pipkin | | plague | |
| pippin | | plaid | |
| piquancy | | plain | |
| piquant | | plainer | |
| pique | | plainly | |
| piquet | | plainness | |
| piracy | | plainsong | |
| pirate | | plaint | |
| piratical | | plaintiff | |
| pirouette | | plaintive | |
| piscatorial | | plait | |
| pisciculture | | plan | |
| pismire | | planary | |
| pistachio | | plane | |
| pistil | | planer | |
| pistol | | planet | |
| piston | | planetary | |
| pit | | planetoid | |
| pitapat | | plank | |
| pitch | | plant | |
| pitcher | | plantain | |
| pitchfork | | plantation | |
| pitchpipe | | planter | |
| piteous | | plaque | |
| pitfall | | plash | |
| pith | | plaster | |
| pithless | | plastic | |
| pitiable | | plasticity | |

**PLASTICITY**

## PLATE

| | | | |
|---|---|---|---|
| plate | *pa* | pliers | |
| plateau | *plo* | plight | |
| platform | *plf* | plinth | |
| platinum | *pln* | plod | |
| platitude | *pttd* | plot | |
| platoon | *pln* | plough | |
| platter | | ploughman | |
| plaudit | *pdl* | ploughshare | |
| plausibility | *pzb)* | plover | |
| plausible | *pzb* | plow | |
| plausibleness | *pzb'* | plowman | |
| *play* | *pa* | pluck | |
| *player* | *Pa* | pluckiness | |
| playfellow | *paflo* | plucky | |
| *playful* | *paf* | pluff | |
| playground | *pdgr* | plug | |
| playhouse | *pah* | plum | |
| playmate | *pa* | plumage | |
| plaything | *pa* | plumb | |
| plea | *pe* | plumbago | |
| plead | *pd* | plumber | |
| pleasant | *pz* | plume | |
| pleasantness | *pz* | plummet | |
| pleasantry | *pz-,* | plumous | |
| *please* | *po* | plump | |
| *pleasure* | *pz* | plunder | |
| plebeian | *pbn* | plunge | |
| plebiscite | *pbsc* | pluperfect | |
| pledge | *pj* | plural | |
| plenary | *pny* | pluralist | |
| plenipotentiary | *pnptzy* | plurality | |
| plenitude | *pnld* | plus | |
| plenteous | *p-x* | plush | |
| plentiful | *p-f* | plutocracy | |
| plenty | *p-,* | plutocrat | |
| pleonasm | *pnz* | plutocratic | |
| pleonastic | *pns* | pluvial | |
| plethora | *plra* | ply | |
| plethoric | *plrk* | pneumatic | |
| pleura | *pra* | pneumatology | |
| pleurisy | *prs,* | pneumonia | |
| plexus | *plx* | poach | |
| pliability | *pub)* | pock | |
| pliable | *pub* | pocket | |
| pliancy | *pu* | pocketbook | |
| pliant | *pu-* | pod | |

## POEM

| | |
|---|---|
| poem | |
| poesy | |
| poet | |
| poetess | |
| poetic | |
| poetical | |
| poetry | |
| pogrom | |
| poignancy | |
| poignant | |
| poilu | |
| poinsettia | |
| point | |
| pointblank | |
| pointer | |
| poise | |
| poison | |
| poisonous | |
| poke | |
| polar | |
| polarity | |
| polarization | |
| polarize | |
| pole | |
| polemic | |
| police | |
| policeman | |
| policy | |
| polish | |
| polite | |
| politeness | |
| politic | |
| political | |
| politician | |
| politics | |
| polity | |
| polka | |
| poll | |
| pollack | |
| pollard | |
| pollen | |
| pollinate | |
| pollute | |
| pollution | |
| polo | |
| polonaise | |

| | |
|---|---|
| polony | |
| poltroon | |
| polyanthus | |
| polygamist | |
| polygamous | |
| polygamy | |
| polyglot | |
| polygon | |
| polyhedron | |
| polyp | |
| polypetalous | |
| polypode | |
| polysyllable | |
| polytechnic | |
| polytheism | |
| polytheist | |
| pomaceous | |
| pomade | |
| pomegranate | |
| pommel | |
| pomp | |
| pomposity | |
| pompous | |
| pompousness | |
| pond | |
| ponder | |
| ponderable | |
| ponderosity | |
| ponderous | |
| ponderousness | |
| pongee | |
| poniard | |
| pontage | |
| pontiff | |
| pontifical | |
| pontificate | |
| pontoon | |
| pony | |
| poodle | |
| pooh | |
| pool | |
| poop | |
| poor | |
| poorer | |
| poorhouse | |
| poorly | |

**POORLY**

POP

| | | | |
|---|---|---|---|
| pop | | portmanteau | |
| popcorn | | portrait | |
| pope | | portraiture | |
| popery | | portray | |
| popgun | | pose | |
| popinjay | | position | |
| popish | | positiye | |
| poplar | | positively | |
| poplin | | positiveness | |
| poppy | | possess | |
| populace | | possession | |
| popular | | possessive | |
| popularitv | | possessor | |
| popularize | | possibility | |
| popularly | | possible | |
| populate | | post | |
| population | | postage | |
| populous | | postal | |
| populousness | | postcard | |
| porcelain | | postdiluvian | |
| porch | | poster | |
| porcupine | | posterior | |
| pore | | posterity | |
| pork | | postern | |
| porphyraceous | | posthumous | |
| porphyritic | | postil | |
| porphyry | | postillion | |
| porpoise | | postman | |
| porridge | | postmark | |
| porringer | | postmaster(PM) | |
| port | | postmeridian | |
| portable | | postmortem | |
| portage | | postobit | |
| portal | | postoffice | |
| portcullis | | postpone | |
| portend | | postponement | |
| portentous | | postscript (PS) | |
| porter | | postulant | |
| porterage | | postulate | |
| portfolio | | posture | |
| porthole | | posy | |
| portico | | pot | |
| portiere | | potable | |
| portion | | potash | |
| portionist | | potassium | |
| portionless | | potation | |

POTATION

**POTATO**

| | |
|---|---|
| potato......... | preach........... |
| potent.......... | preacher......... |
| potentate....... | preamble........ |
| potential........ | prebend......... |
| potentiality...... | prebendary....... |
| potentiary....... | precarious....... |
| pother.......... | precaution....... |
| pothook........ | precautionary.... |
| potion.........., | precede.......... |
| potsherd........ | precedence....... |
| pottage......... | precedent........ |
| potter.......... | precentor........ |
| pouch.......... | precept.......... |
| poult........... | preceptor........ |
| poulterer........ | preceptress...... |
| poultice......... | precinct......... |
| poultry......... | precious......... |
| pounce.... ... | precipice........ |
| *pound* (lb)...... | precipitance...... |
| poundage....... | precipitant....... |
| pour........... | precipitate....... |
| pout........... | precipitation...... |
| poverty......... | precipitous........ |
| powder ........ | precise.......... |
| *power*.......... | preciseness...... |
| powerful........ | precision.......... |
| *powerless*....... | preclude......... |
| practicable...... | preclusion........ |
| practical........ | preclusive........ |
| *practice*........ | precocious........ |
| practitioner..... | precociousness.... |
| pragmatic....... | precocity......... |
| pragmatism..... | precognition....... |
| pragmatist...... | preconceive....... |
| prairie.......... | preconception.. .. |
| praise.......... | preconcert........ |
| praiseworthy.... | precursor........ |
| prance.......... | predatory........ |
| prank.......... | predecease....... |
| prate........... | predecessor....... |
| prattle......... | predestinate...... |
| prawn.......... | predestination..... |
| pray............ | predestine........ |
| prayer.......... | predeterminate.... |
| prayerful........ | predetermination.. |
| prayerless....... | predetermine...... |

**PREDETERMINE**

PREDICABLE

predicable......
predicament....
predicate......
predication......
predicative.....
predict........
prediction......
predictive......
predilection....
predispose.....
predisposition...
predominance..
predominant....
predominate....
preeminence....
preeminent......
preemption......
preen..........
preengage.......
preexist.........
preexistence.....
preface.........
prefatory..
prefect.........
prefecture.......
prefer.........
preferable.......
preference......
preferment......
prefigurative....
prefigure........
prefigurement...
prefix..........
pregnancy......
pregnant........
prehensible.....
prehensile......
prehension......
prehistoric......
prejudge........
prejudice......
prejudicial......
prelacy.........
prelate.........
prelect..........
prelection.......

preliminary....
prelude........
premature......
premeditate....
premeditation...
premier.........
premiership.....
premise.........
premise........
premium.......
premonish.....
premonition....
premonitory.....
preoccupancy...
preoccupation...
preoccupy......
preordain......
prepaid.........
preparation.....
preparative......
preparatory.....
prepare........
preparedness....
prepay.........
prepayment.....
prepense........
preponderance...
prepopderant....
preponderate....
preposition......
prepositional.....
prepossess......
prepossession....
preposterous.....
prerogative.......
presage..........
presbyter........
presbyterian......
presbytery.......
prescience.......
prescribe........
prescription......
prescriptive....
presence.......
present..........
presentation......

PRESENTATION

## PRESENTED

presented....
presently.. ...
preservation. .
preservative. .
preserve.......
preserver. .
preside......
presidency.
president. . .
presidential.
*press*. .......
*presser* .
pressure. ...
prestige. ...
presumable...
presume. .
presuming.
presumption.
presumptive..
presumptuous..
presuppose......
presupposition...
pretend.........
pretense........
pretension. ....
pretentious......
preternatural...
pretext.......
*prettier*.........
*prettily*.........
*prettiness*.......
*pretty*..........
prevail.........
prevalence......
prevalent.... .
prevaricate......
prevarication..
prevent........
prevention.....
preventive.. ...
previous........
previously......
prey............
*price*....... ...
priceless........
prick.........

prickle. .....
prickly.. .....
pride.. ...
prideful. .
priest....
priestcraft...
priestess.. ...
priesthood. ..
priestly... ....
priestridden..
prig.... ...
priggish. . .
prim........
prima donna..
primal........
primarily. . ..
primary.....
primacy.
primate. .
prime. ..
primer........
primeval.....
primitive. .
primness..
primogenitor.
primogeniture.
primordial..
primrose. .
*prince*... .....
princely.......
princess. ..
principal....
principally....
principality. .
principle. .
prink.. .....
print........
printer.. ......
prior. ....
prioress.. ..
priority.. ...
priory...
prise.. .
prism...
prismatic......
prismatical.....

**PRISMATICAL**

PRISON

| | |
|---|---|
| prison......... | *pzn* |
| prisoner........ | *pzn* |
| pristine......... | *psn* |
| prithee......... | *ple* |
| privacy......... | *pvs,* |
| private......... | *pva* |
| privateer....... | *pvle* |
| privation........ | *pvy* |
| privative....... | *pvv* |
| privet.......... | *pvl* |
| *privilege*....... | *pvly* |
| privily.......... | *pv) pvl* |
| privity.......... | *pv)* |
| privy.......... | *pv;* |
| prize.......... | *pz* |
| probability...... | *pbb)* |
| probable........ | *pbb* |
| probably........ | *pb* |
| probate......... | *pba* |
| probation........ | *pby* |
| probational...... | *pbyl* |
| probationary.... | *pbyy* |
| probative....... | *pbv* |
| probatory....... | *pbly* |
| probe.......... | *pob* |
| probity......... | *pb)* |
| problem........ | *pb* |
| problematic..... | *pbt* |
| problematical.... | *pbtk* |
| proboscis....... | *pbss* |
| procedure....... | *psdu* |
| proceed......... | *psd* |
| process......... | *ps'* |
| procession...... | *psy* |
| proclaim........ | *pkla* |
| proclamation.... | *pkly* |
| proclivity....... | *pklv* |
| proconsul....... | *pksl* |
| proconsular..... | *ptsl* |
| procrastinate.... | *pksna* |
| procrastination.. | *pksny* |
| procreate....... | *pka* |
| procreation...... | *pkey* |
| procreative...... | *pkev* |
| procreator....... | *pka* |
| proctor......... | *pk* |

| | |
|---|---|
| procumbent... | *pkb-* |
| procurable.... | *pkub* |
| procuration.... | *pkuy pkua* |
| procurator..... | *pkua* |
| procure........ | *pku* |
| prodigal....... | *pdgl* |
| prodigality.... | *pdgl)* |
| prodigious..... | *pdjx* |
| prodigy........ | *pdj,* |
| produce........ | *pds* |
| producible..... | *pdsb* |
| product........ | *pdk* |
| production..... | *pdky* |
| productive..... | *pdkv* |
| proem......... | *po* |
| profanation.... | *pfny* |
| profane....... | *pfn* |
| profaneness.... | *pfn'* |
| profanity...... | *pfn'* |
| profess........ | *pf'* |
| profession..... | *pfy* |
| professional.... | *pj' pfyl* |
| professor...... | *pfsyl* |
| professorial.... | *pfsyl* |
| professorship... | *pfs3* |
| proffer........ | *pf* |
| proficiency.... | *pfz* |
| proficient..... | *pfz-* |
| profile........ | *pfl* |
| profit......... | *pfl* |
| profitable..... | *pflb* |
| profiteer....... | *pfle* |
| profitless...... | *pfll* |
| profligacy..... | *pflgs,* |
| profligate...... | *pflga* |
| profound....... | *pf-* |
| profoundness... | *pf;* |
| profundity..... | *pf-)* |
| profuse....... | *pfs* |
| profuseness.... | *pfs'* |
| profusion..... | *pfl pjn* |
| progenitor.... | *pjn,* |
| progeny....... | *pjn,* |
| prognostic...... | *pgns* |
| prognosticate.... | *pgnska* |
| prognostication.. | *pgnsky* |

PROGNOSTICATION

## PROGRAM

program
progress
progression
progressive
prohibit
prohibition
prohibitive
prohibitory
project
projectile
projection
projector
prolate
prolegomenon
proleptic
proletarian
proletariat
prolific
prolificness
prolix
prolixity
prolixness
prolocutor
prologue
prolong
prolongation
promenade
prominence
prominent
promiscuity
promiscuous
promiscuousness
promise
promising
promissory
promontory
promote
promotion
prompt
prompter
promptitude
promptness
promulgate
promulgation
prone
proneness

prong
pronominal
pronoun
pronounce
pronouncement
pronouncing
pronunciation
proof
prop
propaganda
propagandism
propagate
propagation
propel
propeller
propelling
propensity
proper
properly
property
prophecy
prophesy
prophet
prophetess
prophetic
prophetical
propinquity
propitiate
propitiation
propitiatory
propitious
proportion
proportionable
proportional
proportionate
proposal
propose
proposition
propositional
propound
proprietary
proprietor
proprietress
propriety
propulsion
propulsive

**PROPULSIVE**

## PROROGATION

| | |
|---|---|
| prorogation | |
| prorogue | |
| proroguing | |
| prosaic | |
| prosaical | |
| proscenium | |
| proscribe | |
| proscription | |
| proscriptive | |
| prose | |
| prosecute | |
| prosecution | |
| prosecutor | |
| proselyte | |
| proselytism | |
| proselytize | |
| prosody | |
| prospect | |
| prospection | |
| prospective | |
| prospector | |
| prospectus | |
| prosper | |
| prosperity | |
| prosperous | |
| prostitute | |
| prostitution | |
| prostrate | |
| prostration | |
| protect | |
| protection | |
| protective | |
| protector | |
| protectoral | |
| protectorate | |
| protectorial | |
| protectorship | |
| protectory | |
| protectress | |
| protege | |
| protein | |
| protest | |
| protestant | |
| protestation | |
| protocol | |
| protomartyr | |

| | |
|---|---|
| protoplasm | |
| protoplasmic | |
| prototype | |
| protozoa | |
| protract | |
| protraction | |
| protractor | |
| protrude | |
| protrusion | |
| protuberance | |
| protuberant | |
| protuberate | |
| proud | |
| prouder | |
| prove | |
| provender | |
| proverb | |
| proverbial | |
| provide | |
| providence | |
| provident | |
| providential | |
| province | |
| provincial | |
| provincialism | |
| provision | |
| provisional | |
| proviso | |
| provocation | |
| provocative | |
| provoke | |
| provost | |
| provostship | |
| prow | |
| prowess | |
| prowl | |
| proximate | |
| proximity | |
| proximo | |
| proxy | |
| prude | |
| prudence | |
| prudent | |
| prudential | |
| prudery | |
| prudish | |

**PRUDISH**

## PRUDISHNESS

| | |
|---|---|
| prudishness. . | |
| prune...... | |
| prunella.... | |
| prurient.. | |
| pry...... | |
| psalm..... | |
| psalmist...... | |
| psalmody...... | |
| psaltery......... | |
| pseudonym... | |
| pshaw.......... | |
| psittacosis ...... | |
| psychic...... | |
| psychologic..... | |
| psychological | |
| psychologist. | |
| psychology.. ... | |
| ptarmigan. | |
| puberty.. | |
| pubescent...... | |
| public.. .... | |
| publican....... | |
| publication..... | |
| publicity .... | |
| publicly... | |
| publish. | |
| publisher.... | |
| puce..... ... | |
| pucker........ | |
| pudding........ | |
| puddle... | |
| puerile.... | |
| puerility...... | |
| puff.... ... | |
| puffery.. | |
| puffin.. .... | |
| pug.... .. | |
| pugilism.. | |
| pugilist...... | |
| pugnacious...... | |
| pugnacity. .... | |
| puisne......... | |
| puissance....... | |
| puissant....... | |
| puke.......... | |
| pule........... | |

| | |
|---|---|
| pull...... | |
| puller..... | |
| pullet........ | |
| pulley.... | |
| pulmonary.. | |
| pulmonic.... | |
| pulp...... | |
| pulpit........ | |
| pulsate...... | |
| pulsation.... | |
| pulsative..... | |
| pulsatory.... | |
| pulse........ | |
| pulverable.. | |
| pulverizable.. | |
| pulverize..... | |
| pulverous... | |
| puma....... | |
| pumice.. ... | |
| pummel...... | |
| pump........ | |
| pumpkin..... | |
| pun......... | |
| punch...... | |
| puncheon.... | |
| punctilio.... | |
| punctilious. | |
| punctual..... | |
| punctuality.. | |
| punctually... | |
| punctuate.... | |
| punctuation.. | |
| puncture..... | |
| pundit...... | |
| pungency .... | |
| pungent. .. | |
| punish....... | |
| punishable.... | |
| punishment.. | |
| punitive...... | |
| punkah...... | |
| punning...... | |
| punster....... | |
| punt........ | |
| puny........ | |
| pup.......... | |

PUP

**PUPA**

| | | | |
|---|---|---|---|
| pupa | *ppa* | pursuit | *psu* |
| pupil | *pup* | pursuivant | *psv-* |
| pupilage | *pupy* | pursy | *ps,* |
| puppet | *ppl* | purtenance | *p/pul* |
| puppy | *pp,* | purulence | |
| purblind | *plr—* | purulent | *pul-* |
| purchasable | *pcsb* | purvey | *pva* |
| purchase | *pcs* | purveyance | *pva* |
| purchases | *pcss* | purveyor | *Pva* |
| purchaser | *Pcs* | pus | *ps* |
| *pure* | *pu* | push | *psh* |
| *purely* | *pul* | pusillanimity | *psln )* |
| *pureness* | *pu'* | pusillanimous | *psln x* |
| *purer* | *Pu* | pusillanimousness | *psln x'* |
| purgation | *pg/* | puss | *p'* |
| purgative | *pgv* | pussy | *ps,* |
| purgatory | *pgly* | pustular | *Psl* |
| purge | *py* | pustule | *psl* |
| purification | *puf* | pustulous | *psl* |
| purify | *puf* | put | *p* |
| purism | *puz* | putative | *plv* |
| *purity* | *pu)* | putrefaction | *Pufk/* |
| purl | *pl* | putrefy | *Puf* |
| purlieu | *plu* | putrescence | *Pus* |
| purloin | *plyn* | putrid | *Pud* |
| purple | *pp* | putridity | *Pud)* |
| purport | *ppl* | putridness | *Pud'* |
| purpose | *pps* | putt | *pl* |
| purposeful | *ppsf* | putty | *pl,* |
| purposely | *ppsl* | puzzle | *pzl* |
| purr | *pr* | pygmy | *pg',* |
| purse | *ps* | pyramid | *Prd* |
| purseproud | *psprd* | pyramidal | *Prdl* |
| purser | *Ps* | pyrometer | *PrE* |
| purslane | *psln* | pyrotechnic | *Plknk* |
| pursuance | *psu* | pyrotechnical | *Plknl* |
| pursuant | *psu-* | pyrotechnics | *Plknks* |
| pursue | *psu* | pyrotechnist | *Plkn,* |
| pursuer | *Psu* | python | *pln* |

## Q

| | | | |
|---|---|---|---|
| quack | *qk* | quadrant | *q-* |
| quackery | *qky* | quadrate | *qa* |
| quadrangle | *qgl* | quadratic | *qt* |
| quandrangular | *q—glr* | quadrature | *qlu* |

QUADRENNIAL

| | | | |
|---|---|---|---|
| quadrennial | | quaternary | |
| quadrilateral | | quaternion | |
| quadrille | | quatrain | |
| quadrillion | | quaver | |
| quadrinomial | | quay | |
| quadroon | | queen | |
| quadruped | | queenly | |
| quadrupedal | | queer | |
| quadruple | | queerish | |
| quadruplicate | | quell | |
| quaff | | quench | |
| quagga | | quenchable | |
| quaggy | | quenchless | |
| quagmire | | querimonious | |
| quail | | querist | |
| quaint | | quern | |
| quaintness | | querulous | |
| quake | | query | |
| quaker | | quest | |
| qualification | | question | |
| qualify | | questionable | |
| qualitative | | queue | |
| quality | | quibble | |
| qualm | | quick | |
| quandary | | quicken | |
| quantitative | | quickened | |
| quantity | | quicker | |
| quantum | | quickest | |
| quarantine | | quicklime | |
| quarrel | | quickly | |
| quarrelsome | | quickness | |
| quarrier | | quicksand | |
| quarry | | quickset | |
| quarryman | | quicksilver | |
| quart | | quidnunc | |
| quarter | | quiescence | |
| quartering | | quiescent | |
| quarterly | | quiet | |
| quartermaster | | quieter | |
| quartern | | quietly | |
| quarterstaff | | quietness | |
| quartet | | quietude | |
| quarto | | quietus | |
| quartz | | quill | |
| quash | | quillet | |
| quasi | | quilt | |

QUILT

| | |
|---|---|
| quince......... | |
| quinine........ | |
| quinquangular.. | |
| quinquennial... | |
| quinsy......... | |
| quintain....... | |
| quintan........ | |
| quintessence... | |
| quintillion...... | |
| quintuple...... | |
| quip........... | |
| quire.......... | |
| quirk......... | |
| quirky......... | |
| quit.......... | |

| | |
|---|---|
| quitclaim.... | |
| quite........ | |
| quittance.... | |
| quiver....... | |
| quixotic...... | |
| quixotism.... | |
| quiz........ | |
| quoit........ | |
| quondam.... | |
| quorum...... | |
| quota........ | |
| quotation.... | |
| quote........ | |
| quoth........ | |
| quotient..... | |

# R

| | |
|---|---|
| rab............ | |
| rabbet......... | |
| rabbi......... | |
| rabbinic....... | |
| rabbinical...... | |
| rabbit........ | |
| rabble........ | |
| rabid......... | |
| rabies........ | |
| raccoon........ | |
| race.......... | |
| racer.......... | |
| racial......... | |
| raciness....... | |
| rack.......... | |
| racket........ | |
| racoon........ | |
| racy.......... | |
| radiance....... | |
| radiant........ | |
| radiate........ | |
| radiation....... | |
| radiator....... | |
| radical........ | |
| radio......... | |
| radioactive..... | |
| radiograph...... | |
| radish........ | |

| | |
|---|---|
| radius....... | |
| radix........ | |
| raffle....... | |
| raft........ | |
| rafter....... | |
| rag.......... | |
| ragamuffin... | |
| rage........ | |
| ragged....... | |
| ragout....... | |
| raid........ | |
| rail......... | |
| railing...... | |
| raillery...... | |
| railroad...... | |
| railway....... | |
| raiment...... | |
| rain......... | |
| rainbow..... | |
| raindrop..... | |
| rainfall...... | |
| rainy........ | |
| raise....... | |
| raiser....... | |
| raisin....... | |
| rake........ | |
| rakish....... | |
| rally......... | |

### RAM

| | | | |
|---|---|---|---|
| ram | | rareness | |
| ramble | | rarity | |
| rambling | | rascal | |
| ramification | | rascality | |
| ramify | | rascally | |
| ramous | | rash | |
| ramp | | rashness | |
| rampage | | rasp | |
| rampageous | | raspberry | |
| rampant | | rat | |
| rampart | | ratable | |
| ramrod | | ratch | |
| ran | | ratchet | |
| ranch | | rate | |
| rancid | | *rather* | |
| rancidity | | ratify | |
| rancidness | | ratification | |
| rancor | | ratio | |
| rancorous | | ratiocination | |
| random | | ratiocinative | |
| rang | | ration | |
| range | | rational | |
| rank | | rationalism | |
| rankle | | rationalist | |
| rankness | | rationalistic | |
| ransack | | rationality | |
| ransom | | ratline | |
| rant | | rattan | |
| ranunculous | | rattle | |
| rap | | rattlesnake | |
| rapacious | | ravage | |
| rapaciousness | | rave | |
| rapacity | | ravel | |
| rape | | ravelin | |
| *rapid* | | ravelling | |
| rapidity | | raven | |
| *rapidly* | | ravenous | |
| rapidness | | ravine | |
| rapier | | ravish | |
| rapine | | ravishment | |
| rapt | | raw | |
| rapture | | rawness | |
| rare | | ray | |
| *rarefaction* | | raze | |
| rarefy | | razor | |
| rarely | | razure | |

**RAZURE**

**REACH**

| | | | |
|---|---|---|---|
| reach | *rec* | reassure | *razu* |
| react | *rak* | reave | *re* |
| reaction | *raks* | rebate | *rba* |
| reactionary | *rakyy* | rebatement | *rba-* |
| read | *rd* | rebel | *rbl* |
| read | *rd* | rebellion | *rbln* |
| reader | *Rd* | rebellious | *rblx* |
| readier | *Rd,* | rebound | *rbr* |
| readily | *rd,* *rdl* | rebuff | *rbf* |
| readiness | *rd,* | rebuild | *rbld* |
| reading | *rd* | rebuke | *rbk* |
| readjourn | *rajrn* | rebus | *rbx* |
| readjust | *raj,* | rebut | *rbl* |
| readmission | *ra_j* | rebuttable | *rbll-* |
| readmit | *rasl* | rebuttal | *rbll* |
| ready | *rd,* | recalcitrant | *rkls-* |
| reagent | *raj-* | recalcitrate | *rklsa* |
| real | *rl* | recalcitration | *rklsy* |
| reality | *rl)* | recall | *rkl* |
| realization | *rlz* *rlzy* | recant | *rk-* |
| realize | *rlz* | recantation | *rk-1* |
| really | *rl* | recapitulate | *rkp* |
| realm | *rl* | recapitulation | *rkps* |
| ream | *re* | recapitulatory | *rkply* |
| reanimate | *rava* | recapture | *rkpu* |
| reanimation | *ra* | recast | *rk,* |
| reap | *rep* | recede | *rsd* |
| reaper | *Rp* | receipt | *rse* |
| reappear | *rap* | receive | *rse* |
| reappearance | *rap* | receiver | *Rse* |
| rear | *re* | recension | *rsj* |
| rearmouse | *re* | recent | *rs-* |
| rearward | *re/* | recently | *rs-l* |
| reason | *rzn* | receptacle | *rspl* |
| reasonable | *rznb* | reception | *rspj* |
| reasonableness | *rznb* | receptive | *rspv* |
| reasoner | *Rzn* | receptiveness | *rspv* |
| reasoning | *rzn* | receptivity | *rspv)* |
| reassemble | *rasb* | recess | *rs'* |
| reassert | *ras/* | recession | *rsj* |
| reassertion | *ras/* | recessive | *rssv* |
| reassign | *rasın* | recipe | *rspe* |
| reassignment | *rasın-* | recipient | *rsp-* |
| reassume | *rasu* | reciprocal | *rspkl* |
| reassumption | *ras/* | reciprocate | *rspka* |
| reassurance | *razu* | reciprocation | *rspks* |

**RECIPROCATION**

## RECIPROCITY

| | | | |
|---|---|---|---|
| reciprocity | | recourse | |
| recital | | recover | |
| recitation | | recovery | |
| recitative | | recreancy | |
| recite | | recreant | |
| reck | | recreate | |
| reckless | | recreation | |
| recklessness | | recreative | |
| reckon | | recrement | |
| reclaim | | recriminate | |
| reclamation | | recrimination | |
| recline | | recriminative | |
| recluse | | recriminatory | |
| recognition | | recruit | |
| recognizance | | rectangle | |
| recognize | | rectangular | |
| recoil | | rectification | |
| recollect | | rectify | |
| recollection | | rectilineal | |
| recommence | | rectilinear | |
| recommencement | | rectitude | |
| recommend | | rector | |
| recommendation | | rectoral | |
| recommendatory | | rectorate | |
| recommit | | rectorial | |
| recommitment | | rectorship | |
| recommittal | | rectory | |
| recompense | | rectum | |
| reconcilable | | recumbence | |
| reconcile | | recumbency | |
| reconcilement | | recumbent | |
| reconciliation | | recuperate | |
| recondite | | recuperation | |
| reconnaissance | | recuperative | |
| reconnoiter | | recuperatory | |
| reconsider | | recur | |
| reconsideration | | recurred | |
| reconstruct | | recurrence | |
| reconstruction | | recurrency | |
| reconvey | | recurrent | |
| reconveyance | | recurring | |
| record | | recurvate | |
| recorder | | recurvation | |
| recount | | recurvature | |
| recoup | | recurve | |
| recoupment | | recusant | |

**RECUSANT**

## RED

| | |
|---|---|
| red | *rd* |
| redan | *rdn* |
| redbreast | *rdb,* |
| redden | *rdn* |
| redder | *Rd* |
| reddest | *rd,* |
| reddish | *rdz* |
| reddition | *rdy* |
| redeem | *rde* |
| redeemer | *Rde* |
| redemption | *rdy* |
| redemptive | *rd-w* |
| redemptory | *rd-dy* |
| redintegrate | *rd-ga* |
| redintegration | *rd-gj* |
| redirect | *rdrk* |
| redness | *rd'* |
| redolence | *rdl* |
| redolency | *rdl/* |
| redolent | *rdl-* |
| redouble | *rdb* |
| redoubt | *rd ̃* |
| redoubtable | *rd ̃tb* |
| redoubted | *rd ̃* |
| redound | *rd—* |
| redress | *rd'* |
| reduce | *rds* |
| reduction | *rdkj* |
| redundance | *rd—/* |
| redundancy | *rd—/* |
| redundant | *rd——* |
| reduplicate | *rdpka* |
| reduplication | *rdpkj* |
| re-echo | *reko* |
| reed | *rd* |
| reedy | *rd,* |
| reef | *ref* |
| reefy | *rf,* |
| reek | *rek* |
| reeky | *rk,* |
| reel | *rl* |
| reelect | *relk* |
| reelection | *relkj* |
| reembark | *rbrk* |
| reembarkation | *rbrkj* |
| reenact | *rnak* |
| reenactment | *rnak-* |
| reenforce | *rnfs* |
| reenforcement | *rnfs-* |
| reenter | *rN* |
| reentry | *rN,* |
| reestablish | *resl* |
| reestablishment | *resl-* |
| reeve | *re* |
| reexamination | *re-mj* |
| reexamine | *re-m* |
| refection | *rfkj* |
| refectory | *rfky* |
| refer | *rf* |
| referable | *rfb* |
| referee | *rfe* |
| reference | *rf* |
| referendum | *rf—* |
| refill | *rfl* |
| refine | *rfe* |
| refinement | *rfe-* |
| refinery | *rfy* |
| refit | *rfl* |
| reflect | *rflk* |
| reflection | *rflkj* |
| reflective | *rflkw* |
| reflector | *rflk* |
| reflex | *rfl* |
| reflexive | *rflw* |
| refluent | *rflu-* |
| reflux | *rflx* |
| reform | *rf* |
| reformation | *rf y* |
| reformative | *rf w* |
| reformatory | *rf dy* |
| refract | *rfk* |
| refraction | *rfkj* |
| refractive | *rfkw* |
| refractory | *rfky* |
| refrain | *rfn* |
| refrangible | *rfjb* |
| refresh | *rff* |
| refreshment | *rff-* |
| refrigerant | *r jj-* |
| refrigerate | *r jja* |
| refrigerative | *r jjw* |
| refrigerator | *r jjar* |

**REFRIGERATOR**

refrigeratory....

refuge.........

refugee.........

refulgence......

refulgent........

refund..........

refusal.........

refuse..........

refuses.........

refutation.......

refute..........

regain..........

regal...........

regale..........

regalia.........

regard..........

regarding.......

regardless......

regatta.........

regency.........

regenerate......

regeneration.....

regenerative.....

regent..........

regentship......

regicide........

regime..........

regimen........

regiment........

regimental......

region..........

register.........

registrar........

registration.....

registry.........

regnancy........

regnant.........

regress.........

regression......

regressive.......

regret..........

regretful........

regular.........

regularity.......

regulate........

regulation ......

regulative........

regulator.........

rehabilitate......

rehabilitation.....

rehearsal........

rehearse.........

reign.............

reimburse........

reimbursement...

rein.............

reindeer.........

reinforce.........

reinforcement....

reinstate.........

reinstatement....

reintroduce......

reintroduction....

reinvest.........

reinvestment.....

reinvigorate......

reinvigoration....

reissue..........

reissuance.......

reiterate.........

reiteration.......

reject............

rejection.........

rejoice...........

rejoicing.........

rejoin...........

rejoinder........

rejuvenescence...

rejuvenescent....

rekindle.........

relapse..........

relate...........

relation..........

relationship......

relative..........

relax............

relaxation........

relay............

release..........

relegate.........

relegation........

relent...........

| | | | |
|---|---|---|---|
| relentless | *rl-l'* | remonstrant | |
| relevance | | remonstrate | |
| relevancy | | remorse | |
| relevant | | remorseful | |
| reliability | | remorsefulness | |
| reliable | | remorseless | |
| reliance | | remorselessness | |
| reliant | | remote | |
| relic | | remoteness | |
| relict | | remount | |
| relief | | removable | |
| relieve | | removal | |
| religion | | remove | |
| religious | | remover | |
| religiousness | | remunerate | |
| relinquish | | remuneration | |
| reliquary | | remunerative | |
| relish | | renascent | |
| reluctance | | renal | |
| reluctancy | | rencounter | |
| reluctant | | rend | |
| reluctantly | | render | |
| rely | | rendition | |
| remain | | rendezvous | |
| remainder | | renegade | |
| remand | | renew | |
| remanent | | renewable | |
| remark | | renewal | |
| remarkable | | reniform | |
| remediable | | rennet | |
| remedial | | renitent | |
| remedy | | renounce | |
| remember | | renouncement | |
| remembrance | | renovate | |
| remind | | renovation | |
| reminder | | renown | |
| reminiscence | | rent | |
| remiss | | rentable | |
| remission | | rental | |
| remissness | | renter | |
| remit | | renunciation | |
| remittance | | reopen | |
| remittent | | reorganization | |
| remnant | | reorganize | |
| remodel | | repaid | |
| remonstrance | | repair | |

## REPAIRER

| | |
|---|---|
| repairer......... | |
| reparable....... | |
| reparation....... | |
| repartee........ | |
| repast.......... | |
| repatriate....... | |
| repatriation..... | |
| repay.......... | |
| repayment...... | |
| repeal.......... | |
| repeat.......... | |
| repeatedly...... | |
| repel........... | |
| repellent....... | |
| repent.......... | |
| repentance...... | |
| repentant....... | |
| repercussion.... | |
| repercussive.... | |
| repertoire...... | |
| repertory....... | |
| repetition....... | |
| repine.......... | |
| replace......... | |
| replacement..... | |
| replenish....... | |
| replenishment... | |
| replete......... | |
| repleteness...... | |
| repletion........ | |
| replica.......... | |
| replication...... | |
| reply........... | |
| *report*.......... | |
| *reporter*........ | |
| repose.......... | |
| repository....... | |
| repossess....... | |
| repossession.... | |
| reprehend....... | |
| reprehensible.... | |
| reprehension.... | |
| reprehensive.... | |
| reprehensory.... | |
| represent....... | |
| representation... | |

| | |
|---|---|
| representative... | |
| repress......... | |
| repression...... | |
| repressive....... | |
| reprieve........ | |
| reprimand...... | |
| reprint.......... | |
| reprisal........ | |
| reproach........ | |
| reproachable.... | |
| reproachful...... | |
| reprobate....... | |
| reprobation..... | |
| reproduce....... | |
| reproduction.... | |
| reproductive.... | |
| reproductory.... | |
| reproof........ | |
| reprovable.... | |
| reprove......... | |
| reptile......... | |
| republic........ | |
| republican...... | |
| republicanism... | |
| republication.... | |
| republish....... | |
| repudiate....... | |
| repudiation...... | |
| repugnance..... | |
| repugnancy.... | |
| repugnant....... | |
| repulse......... | |
| repulsion....... | |
| repulsive........ | |
| repurchase...... | |
| reputable....... | |
| reputation....... | |
| repute.......... | |
| request........ | |
| requiem........ | |
| *require*......... | |
| requirement.... | |
| requisite........ | |
| *requisition*...... | |
| requisitionist.... | |
| requital........ | |

**REQUITAL**

| | | | | |
|---|---|---|---|---|
| requite | *rqu* | resourceful | *rsrsf* |
| reredos | *rrds* | resources | *rsrss* |
| rescind | *rs—* | respect | *rsk* |
| rescript | *rskp* | respectability | *rsb)* |
| rescue | *rsku* | respectable | *rskt* |
| research | *rsc* | respectful | *rskf* |
| resemblance | *rz t* | respective | *rskv.* |
| resemble | *rz t* | respiration | *rsy* |
| resent | *rz-* | respirator | *Rsa* |
| resentful | *rz-f* | respiratory | *rsly* |
| resentment | *rz--* | respire | *rsc* |
| reservation | *rsvy* | respite | *rsc* |
| reserve | *rsv* | resplendence | *rs—* |
| reservoir | *rsv a* | resplendent | *rs——* |
| reset | *rsl* | respond | *rs—* |
| reside | *rzd* | response | *rs* |
| residence | *rzd* | responsibility | *rs b)* |
| residency | *rzd* | responsible | *rs t* |
| resident | *rzd-* | responsibleness | *rs t'* |
| residential | *rzdc* | responsive | *rsv* |
| residentiary | *rzd-y* | rest | *r,* |
| residual | *rzdl* | restaurant | *rs—* |
| residuary | *rzdy* | restaurateur | *rslu* |
| residue | *rzdu* | restful | *rsf* |
| residuous | *rzdc* | restfulness | *rsf'* |
| residuum | *rzd* | restitution | *rsly* |
| resign | *rzn* | restive | *rsv* |
| resignation | *rzgnf* | restless | *rsl'* |
| resile | *rzl* | restlessness | *rs "* |
| resiliency | *rzl* | restoration | *rsy* |
| resilient | *rzl-* | restorative | *rsv* |
| resin | *rzn* | restore | *rs* |
| resinous | *rznx* | restorer | *rsr* |
| resiny | *rzn,* | restrain | *rsn* |
| resist | *rz'* | restraint | *rs—* |
| resistance | *rzs* | restrict | *rsk* |
| resistible | *rzsl* | restrictive | *rskv* |
| resistless | *rzsl'* | result | *rsl* |
| resolute | *rzlu* | resultant | *rsl-* |
| resolution | *rzly* | resume | *rzu* |
| resolve | *rzlv* | resumption | *rz y* |
| resonance | *rzf* | resurgence | *rsf* |
| resonant | *rzn-* | resurgent | *rsf-* |
| resort | *rz/* | resurrection | *rskf* |
| resound | *rzu—* | resuscitate | *rssta* |
| resource | *rsrs* | resuscitation | *rssly* |

**RETAIL**

| | | | |
|---|---|---|---|
| retail | | reunion | |
| retain | | reunite | |
| retainer | | reveal | |
| retaliate | | revel | |
| retaliation | | revelation | |
| retaliative | | revelry | |
| retaliatory | | revenge | |
| retard | | revengeful | |
| retardation | | revenue | |
| retch | | reverberate | |
| retention | | reverberation | |
| retentive | | revere | |
| retentiveness | | reverence | |
| reticence | | reverend | |
| reticent | | reverent | |
| reticulate | | reverential | |
| reticule | | reverie | |
| reticle | | reversal | |
| retiform | | reverse | |
| retina | | reversible | |
| retinue | | reversion | |
| retire | | reversionary | |
| retirement | | revert | |
| retort | | review | |
| retouch | | revile | |
| retrace | | revisal | |
| retract | | revise | |
| retractible | | revision | |
| retractile | | revisit | |
| retraction | | revival | |
| retreat | | revivalism | |
| retrench | | revivalist | |
| retrenchment | | revive | |
| retribution | | revivify | |
| retributive | | revocable | |
| retributory | | revocation | |
| retrieve | | revoke | |
| retrocede | | revolt | |
| retrocession | | revolting | |
| retrograde | | revolute | |
| retrogression | | revolution | |
| retrogressive | | revolutionary | |
| retrospect | | revolutionist | |
| retrospection | | revolutionize | |
| retrospective | | revolve | |
| return | | revolver | |

**REVOLVER**

| | | | |
|---|---|---|---|
| revulsion | *rvl/* | rider | *Rd* |
| reward | *r/* | ridge | *ry* |
| reynard | *rn/* | ridicule | *rdkl* |
| rhapsodist | *rpsd,* | ridiculous | *rdkle* |
| rhapsody | *rpsd,* | riding | *rd_* |
| rheostat | *rost* | rife | *ruf* |
| rhetoric | *Rk* | riff-raff | *rfrf* |
| rhetorical | *Rg RK* | rifle | *rfl* |
| rhetorician | *Rg* | rifleman | *rfl-* |
| rheum | *r* | rift | *rf* |
| rheumatic | *rt* | rig | *rg* |
| rheumatism | *rtz* | rigger | *Rg* |
| rhinoceros | *rnsrs* | right | *ru* |
| rhododendron | *rdd—n* | righteous | *rut* |
| rhomb | *r* | righteousness | *rut'* |
| rhomboid | *rbyd* | rightful | *ruf* |
| rhombus | *rbt* | rightly | *ru' rul* |
| rhubarb | *rbrb* | rightness | *ru'* |
| rhumb | *r* | rigid | *ryd* |
| rhyme | *ru* | rigidity | *ryd)* |
| rhymer | *Ru* | rigidness | *ryd'* |
| rhymster | *ruS* | rigmarole | *rgrrl* |
| rhythm | *rt* | rigor | *Rg* |
| rhythmic | *rtsk* | rigorous | *Rgx* |
| rhythmical | *rtrk* | rile | *rul* |
| rib | *rb* | rill | *rl* |
| ribald | *rbld* | rim | *r* |
| ribaldry | *rbldr,* | rime | *ru* |
| ribband | *rt—* | rimple | *rp* |
| ribbon | *rbn* | rind | *ru—* |
| rice | *rus* | rinderpest | *R—p,* |
| rich | *rc* | ring | *rg* |
| richer | *Rc* | ringer | *Rg* |
| riches | *rcs* | ringlet | *rgll* |
| richly | *rcl* | ringworm | *rgr* |
| richness | *rc'* | rinse | *r* |
| rick | *rk* | riot | *rut* |
| rickets | *rkls* | riotous | *rulx* |
| rickety | *rkl,* | rip | *rp* |
| rickshaw | *rkza* | riparian | *rpyn* |
| ricochet | *rkza* | ripe | *rup* |
| rid | *rd* | ripen | *rpn* |
| riddance | *rd* | ripeness | *rp'* |
| ridden | *rdn* | ripple | *rp* |
| riddle | *rdl* | rippler | *Rp* |
| ride | *rd* | rise | *rz* |

## RISEN

risen.......... *rzn*

risibility........ *rzb)*

risible......... *rzb*

risk............ *rsk*

rite............ *ru*

ritual.......... *rtl*

ritualistic....... *rtls*

rival........... *rul*

rivalled........ *rul*

rivalling........ *rul*

rivalry......... *rulr,*

rive............ *ru*

riven........... *run*

*river* .......... *Rv*

riverside........ *Rvsd*

rivet.......... *rul*

rivulet.......... *rull*

roach.......... *roc*

*road* .......... *rd*

roadside........ *rdsd*

roadstead...... *rdsd*

roadster....... *rds*

roadsters....... *rdss*

roadway....... *rd-a*

roam.......... *ro*

roan........... *rn*

roar........... *ro*

roast........... *ro,*

roaster......... *Ro,*

rob............ *rb*

robber......... *Rb*

robbery........ *rby*

robe........... *rob*

robin.......... *rbn*

robust......... *rb,*

roc............ *rk*

rochet......... *rcl*

*rock* .......... *rk*

rocker......... *Rk*

rockery........ *rky*

rocket......... *rkl*

rocky.......... *rk,*

rod............ *rd*

rode........... *rd*

rodent......... *rd-*

rodomontade.... *rd-d*

roe............ *ro*

roebuck....... *rbk*

rogation....... *rgf*

rogue.......... *rog*

roguery........ *rgy*

roguish........ *rgs*

roister......... *rys*

role........... *rol*

roll............ *rol*

*roller* .......... *Rl*

rollick......... *rlk*

romance........ *rn*

romantic....... *rnt*

romanticism.... *rn-sz*

romp........... *rnp*

romper........ *Rnp*

rompish........ *rnps*

rondeau........ *r-o*

rood........... *rd*

*roof* ........... *ruf*

roofing......... *ruf-*

roofless......... *rfl*

rook........... *rk*

rookery........ *rky*

room........... *rn*

*roomer* ........ *Rn,*

roominess...... *rn;*

roomy.......... *rn;*

roost........... *ru,*

rooster......... *Ru,*

root............ *ru*

rootlet......... *rull*

rope........... *rop*

ropery......... *rpy*

ropiness........ *rp'*

rosaceous...... *rzx*

rosary......... *rzy*

*rose* .......... *rz*

roseate........ *rza*

rosebud........ *rzbd*

rosemary...... *rznr*

rosette......... *rzl*

rosewood...... *rz-d*

rosin.......... *rzn*

rostral......... *rSl*

rostrate........ *rSa*

## ROSTRATE

**ROSTRUM**

| | | | |
|---|---|---|---|
| rostrum......... | *rs* | rubbish....... | *rbz* |
| rosy............ | *rz,* | rubble........ | *rb* |
| rot............. | *rt* | rubicund...... | *rbk —* |
| rotary.......... | *roy* | rubric........ | *rbk* |
| rotate.......... | *roa* | ruby.......... | *rb,* |
| rotation........ | *roj* | rudder........ | *rd' Rd* |
| rotatory........ | *roty* | ruddiness..... | *rd'* |
| rote............ | *ro* | ruddy......... | *rd,* |
| rotten.......... | *rtn* | rude.......... | *rd* |
| rottenness...... | *rtn'* | rudeness...... | *rd'* |
| rotund......... | *rt —* | rudiment...... | *rd -* |
| rotunda........ | *rt — a* | *rudimental*..... | *rd - l* |
| rotundity....... | *rt —)* | rudimentary... | *rd - y* |
| rotundness..... | *rt —'* | rue........... | *ru* |
| rouble......... | *rb* | rueful........ | *ruf* |
| rouge.......... | *rzh* | ruefulness..... | *ruf'* |
| rough.......... | *rf* | rueing........ | *ru* |
| roughen........ | *rfn* | ruff.......... | *rf* |
| roulette........ | *rlt* | ruffian....... | *rfn* |
| *round*......... | *r —* | ruffianism...... | *rfnz* |
| roundel........ | *r — l* | ruffianly...... | *rfnl* |
| roundelay...... | *r — la* | ruffle........ | *rf* |
| *rounder*....... | *R —* | rufous....... | *rfx* |
| roundly........ | *r — l* | rug........... | *rg* |
| roundness..... | *r —'* | rugged....... | *rgd' rg* |
| rouse.......... | *r z rl* | ruggedness..... | *rgd'* |
| rout........... | *rl* | ruin.......... | *run* |
| route.......... | *ru* | ruinous....... | *runx* |
| routine........ | *run* | *rule*.......... | *rul* |
| rove........... | *ro* | ruler......... | *Rl* |
| rover.......... | *Ro* | rum.......... | *r* |
| row........... | *ro* | rumble....... | *rb* |
| row........... | *r* | ruminant...... | *rm -* |
| rowan......... | *rn* | ruminate...... | *rma* |
| rowboat....... | *robo* | rumination..... | *rmy* |
| rowdy......... | *rd,* | rummage...... | *rR* |
| rowdyism...... | *rdz* | rumor........ | |
| rowel......... | *rl* | rump......... | *rp* |
| rower......... | *Ro* | rumple....... | *rp* |
| rowlock........ | *rolk* | *run*.......... | *rn* |
| royal.......... | *ryl* | runabout...... | *rnab* |
| royalism....... | *rylz* | runagate...... | *rnga* |
| royalist........ | *ryl* | runaway...... | *rna a* |
| royalty........ | *ryll,* | rune......... | *rn* |
| rub........... | *rb* | rung......... | *rg* |
| rubber........ | *Rl* | runlet........ | *rnll* |

| | | | |
|---|---|---|---|
| runner | *Ro* | russet | *rsl* |
| runt | *r-* | rust | *r,* |
| rupee | *rpe* | rustic | *rS* |
| rupture | *rpu* | rusticate | *rska* |
| rural | *rrl* | rustle | *rsl* |
| ruralize | *rrlz* | rusty | *rs,* |
| ruse | *rz* | rut | *rl* |
| rush | *rZ* | ruth | *rul* |
| rushing | *rZ-* | ruthless | *rll'* |
| rushlight | *rZli* | rye | *ru* |
| rusk | *rsk* | ryot | *rul* |

## S

| | | | |
|---|---|---|---|
| Sabbath | *sbl* | saddlery | *sdly* |
| saber | *Sb* | sadness | *sd'* |
| sable | *sb* | safe | *saf* |
| sabot | *sbl* | safeguard | *sfg/* |
| sabotage | *sbly* | safely | *sfl* |
| sac | *sk* | safer | *Sf* |
| saccharine | *Skn* | safety | *sf,* |
| sacerdotal | *ssdll* | safety-valve | *sf, vlv* |
| sacerdotalism | *ssdllz* | saffron | *sfn* |
| sachet | *sza* | sag | *sq* |
| sack | *sk* | saga | *sga* |
| sackbut | *skbl* | sagacious | *sgx* |
| sackcloth | *skkll* | sagacity | *sgs)* |
| sacrament | *sk-* | sage | *saj* |
| sacramental | *sk-l* | sagely | *sjl* |
| sacramentally | *sk-l* | sageness | *sj'* |
| sacred | *sked* | sago | *sgo* |
| sacredness | *skd'* | sahib | *shb* |
| sacrifice | *skfs* | said | *sd* |
| sacrificial | *skfx* | sail | *sal* |
| sacrificially | *skfx* | sailboat | *slbo* |
| sacrilege | *skly* | sailor | *Sl* |
| sacrilegious | *sklyx* | saint (st) | *sa-* |
| sacrilegiously | *sklyxl* | saintlike | *s-lk* |
| sacrist | *sk,* | saintly | *s-l* |
| sacristan | *sksn* | saith | *sal* |
| sacristy | *sks,* | sake | *sk* |
| sad | *sd* | salaam | *sl* |
| sadden | *sdn* | salacious | *slx* |
| sadder | *Sd* | salad | *sld* |
| saddle | *sdl* | salamander | *Sl-* |
| saddler | *Sdl* | salary | *sly* |

SALE

| | | | |
|---|---|---|---|
| sale | *sal* | sanctimoniousness | *sqmi'* |
| saleable | *slb* | sanctimony | *sqm,* |
| salesman | *slsz-* | sanction | *sqi* |
| salient | *sl-slf* | sanctity | *sq)* |
| salify | *slf* | sanctuary | *sqy* |
| saline | *sli* | sanctum | *sq'* |
| saliva | *slva* | *sand* | *s—* |
| salival | *slvl* | sandal | *s—l* |
| salivary | *slvy* | sandalwood | *s—lwd* |
| salivate | *slva* | sandman | *s—n-* |
| salivation | *slvy* | sandpiper | *s—Pp* |
| sallow | *slo* | sandwich | *s—wc* |
| sallowness | *slo'* | sandy | *s—,* |
| sally | *sl,* | sane | *sn* |
| salmon | *sm* | saneness | *sn'* |
| saloon | *sln* | sang | *sq* |
| *salt* | *sll* | sang-froid | *sqfyd* |
| saltant | *sll-* | sanguinary | *sqny* |
| saltatory | *slltty* | sanguine | *sqn* |
| *salter* | *Sll* | sanguineous | *sqnx* |
| saltiness | *sli'* | sanitary | *snly* |
| salubrious | *slbx* | sanitation | *snly* |
| salubriousness | *slbx'* | sanity | *sn)* |
| salubrity | *slb)* | sank | *sq* |
| salutary | *slly* | sansculotte | *snskll* |
| salutation | *sly* | sap | *sp* |
| salutatory | *sluly* | sapid | *spd* |
| salute | *slu* | sapidity | *spd)* |
| salvage | *slvy* | sapience | *sp* |
| salvation | *slvy* | sapient | *sp-* |
| salve | *sv* | sapless | *spl'* |
| salver | *Sv* | sapling | *spg* |
| salvo | *svo* | saponaceous | *spnx* |
| *same* | *sa* | sapphire | *sfr* |
| sameness | *sa'* | sappy | *sp,* |
| samite | *sn* | sarcasm | *srkz* |
| samphire | *sfr* | sarcastic | *srk5* |
| sample | *sp* | sarcastical | *srkst* |
| sampler | *Srp* | sarcastically | *srkst* |
| sanable | *snb* | sarcenet | *srsnl* |
| sanative | *snv* | sarcophagus | *srkfgx* |
| sanatorium | *snly* | sardine | *s/n* |
| sanatory | *snly* | sardonic | *s/nk* |
| sanctification | *sqf* | sardonyx | *s/nx* |
| sanctify | *sqf* | sarsaparilla | *srspla* |
| sanctimonious | *sqmi* | sartorial | *s/yl* |

**SARTORIAL**

## SASH

| | | | |
|---|---|---|---|
| sash | | savior | |
| sat | | savor | |
| satchel | | savory | |
| sate | | savoy | |
| sateen | | saw | |
| satellite | | sawdust | |
| satiable | | sawmill | |
| satiate | | sawpit | |
| satiety | | sawyer | |
| satin | | saxifrage | |
| satinet | | saxophone | |
| satinwood | | say | |
| satiny | | scab | |
| satire | | scabbard | |
| satiric | | scabbedness | |
| satirical | | scabbiness | |
| satirically | | scaffold | |
| satirist | | scaffolding | |
| satirize | | scald | |
| satisfaction | | scale | |
| satisfactory | | scalene | |
| satisfy | | scallop | |
| satrap | | scallywag | |
| saturate | | scalp | |
| saturation | | scalpel | |
| Saturday | | scaly | |
| saturnalia | | scammony | |
| saturnalian | | scamp | |
| saturnine | | scamper | |
| satyr | | scampish | |
| sauce | | scan | |
| saucepan | | scandal | |
| saucer | | scandalize | |
| sauciness | | scandalous | |
| saucy | | scant | |
| saunter | | scantiness | |
| saurian | | scantle | |
| sausage | | scantling | |
| savage | | scantness | |
| savageness | | scanty | |
| savagery | | scape | |
| savanna | | scapegoat | |
| save | | scapegrace | |
| saveloy | | scapular | |
| saver | | scapulary | |
| saving | | scar | |

**SCAR**

### SCARAB

| | | | |
|---|---|---|---|
| scarab......... | *skab* | schoolboy...... | *sklby* |
| scarce......... | *skrs* | schoolhouse.... | *sklh* |
| scarcely........ | *skrsl* | schoolmaster... | *skl S* |
| scarceness...... | *skrs'* | schoolroom..... | *sklr* |
| scarcity........ | *skrs)* | schooner....... | *Skn* |
| scare.......... | *ska* | sciagraph...... | *sigf* |
| scarecrow....... | *skako* | sciatic........ | *si* |
| scarf.......... | *skrf* | sciatica........ | *silka* |
| scarification..... | *skyf* | science........ | *si* |
| scarify......... | *skyf* | scientific...... | *si-fk* |
| scarlatina....... | *skrltna* | scientist....... | *si-,* |
| scarlet......... | *skrll* | scimitar....... | *Srl* |
| scathe......... | *skai* | scintilla........ | *s-la* |
| scatheless...... | *skil'* | scintillate...... | *s-la* |
| scathing........ | *skal* | scintillation.... | *s-ly* |
| scatter......... | *Ska* | sciolism....... | *silz* |
| scavenger....... | *Skvy* | sciolist........ | *sil,* |
| scavengering.... | *Skvy_* | scion.......... | *sin* |
| scavengery..... | *skvyy* | scirrhus....... | *skrx* |
| scene.......... | *sn* | scissors........ | *szs* |
| scenery........ | *sny* | scoff.......... | *skf* |
| scenic......... | *snk* | scoffer........ | *Skf* |
| scenical........ | *snl* | scoffingly...... | *skfl* |
| scenographic.... | *sngfk* | scold.......... | *skol* |
| scenographical... | *sngfl* | sconce......... | *sk* |
| scent.......... | *s-* | scoop......... | *skup* |
| scepter........ | *Sp skpt* | scope......... | *skop* |
| sceptic........ | *skpt* | scorbutic...... | *sklt* |
| sceptical...... | *skpt* | scorch........ | *skc* |
| scepticism..... | *skpsz* | score......... | *sko* |
| sceptred........ | *Sp* | scoria........ | *skya* |
| schedule....... | *skdl* | scorn......... | *skn* |
| scheme........ | *ske* | scorner....... | *Skn* |
| scheming....... | *ske* | scornful....... | *sknf* |
| schism......... | *sz* | scorpion....... | *skpn* |
| schismatic...... | *sz* | scotch........ | *skc* |
| schismatical..... | *szll* | scoundrel...... | *sk—l* |
| schist.......... | *?* | scoundrelism... | *sk—lz* |
| scholar......... | *Skl* | scour......... | *sk-r* |
| scholarly........ | *Skll* | scourge........ | *skry* |
| scholarship..... | *Skl* | scout......... | *sk l* |
| scholastic....... | *skl S* | scowl........ | *sk l* |
| scholiast........ | *skl,* | scrag......... | *skrg* |
| scholiastic...... | *skl S* | scraggy........ | *skg* |
| scholium........ | *skl* | scramble....... | *sk-b* |
| *school*.......... | *skl* | scrap. ... ... | *skrp* |

## SCRAPE

scrape..........
scraper.........
scratch.........
scrawl..........
scream.........
screech.........
screen..........
screenings......
screw..........
scribble.........
scribe..........
scrim..........
scrimmage......
scrimp..........
scrip..........
script..........
scriptural......
scripture........
scrivener......
scrofula.........
scrofulous.......
scroll..........
scrub..........
scruple........
scrupulosity....
scrupulous......
scrupulousness..
scrutineer......
scrutinize.......
scrutiny........
scud..........
scuffle..........
scull..........
sculler..........
scullery.........
scullion.........
sculptor.........
sculpture.......
scum..........
scupper.........
scurf..........
scurfiness.......
scurrile.........
scurrility........
scurrilous.......
scurrilousness...

scurry..........
scurvily.........
scurviness......
scurvy..........
scutage.........
scutiform.......
scuttle..........
scythe..........
sea.............
seacoast........
seafarer.........
seafaring.......
seal............
seam...........
seamen........
seance.........
seaport.........
sear....
search. .......
seashore........
seasick ........
seaside.........
season..........
seasonable......
seasoning........
seat...........
seaward.........
sebaceous........
secant..........
secede..........
secession........
seclude.........
seclusion........
seclusive.......
second (sec).....
secondary.......
secrecy.........
secret..........
secretarial......
secretariate......
secretary (secy)..
sect.............
section..........
sector..........
secure..........
security.........

## SECURITY

SEDAN

| | |
|---|---|
| sedan | *sdn* |
| sedate | *sda* |
| sedateness | *sda'* |
| sedative | *sdv* |
| sedentary | *sd-y* |
| sedge | *sj* |
| sedgy | *sj,* |
| sediment | *sd-* |
| sedimentary | *sd-y* |
| sedition | *sdy* |
| seditious | *sdx* |
| seduce | *sds* |
| seducement | *sds-* |
| seduction | *sdkj* |
| seductive | *sdkv* |
| sedulous | *sdle* |
| see | *se* |
| seed | *sd* |
| seedling | *sdlg* |
| seedsman | *sds-* |
| seedtime | *sdle* |
| seeing | *se* |
| seek | *sek* |
| seeker | *sk* |
| seem | *se* |
| seemingly | *sel* |
| seemliness | *sel'* |
| seemly | *sel* |
| seen | *sn* |
| seer | *se* |
| seesaw | *sesa* |
| seethe | *sel* |
| segment | *sg-* |
| segregate | *sgga* |
| segregation | *sggj* |
| seignior | *snr* |
| seigniory | *sny* |
| seismic | *ssrk* |
| seismograph | *ssrgf* |
| seismometer | *ssre* |
| seize | *sz* |
| seizure | *szj* |
| selah | *sla* |
| seldom | *sld* |
| select | *slk* |
| selection | *slkj* |

| | |
|---|---|
| self | *s* |
| selfish | *sj* |
| selfishness | *sj'* |
| selfless | *sl'* |
| selfsame | *ssa* |
| sell | *sl* |
| seller | *sl* |
| selvedge | *slvj* |
| selves | *sl* |
| semaphore | *sfo* |
| semblance | *sbl* |
| semester | *ss* |
| semibreve | *sbe* |
| semicircle | *scl* |
| semicircular | *sclr* |
| semicolon | *skln* |
| semiconscious | *skx* |
| semidiameter | *sd e* |
| seminal | *sml* |
| seminary | *smy* |
| semiquaver | *sqa* |
| semitone | *stn* |
| semitransparent | *s Ip-* |
| semivocal | *svkl* |
| semivowel | *svl* |
| semolina | *slna* |
| sempiternal | *splnl* |
| sempstress | *ss'* |
| senate | *sna* |
| senator | *sna* |
| senatorial | *snlyl* |
| send | *s—* |
| sender | *s—* |
| seneschal | *snx* |
| senile | *snl* |
| senility | *snl)* |
| senior | *sr* |
| seniority | *sr)* |
| senna | *sna* |
| sensation | *sj* |
| sensational | *sjl* |
| sense | *sl'* |
| senseless | *sl'* |
| sensibility | *sb)* |
| sensible | *sb* |
| sensibly | *sb* |

SENSIBLY

| | | | |
|---|---|---|---|
| sensitive | *sv* | seraphic | *sfk* |
| sensorial | *syl* | seraphical | *sfk* |
| sensory | *sy* | seraphim | *sf* |
| sensual | *sl* | serenade | *synd* |
| sensualism | *slz* | serene | *srn* |
| sensualist | *sl,* | sereneness | *srn'* |
| sensuality | *sl)* | serenity | *srn)* |
| sensuous | *sx* | serf | *sf* |
| sent | *s-* | serfdom | *sfd* |
| sentence | *s-l* | serge | *sj* |
| sentential | *s-x* | sergeant | *sj-* |
| sententious | *s-nx* | serial | *syl* |
| sentient | *snj* | series | *sys* |
| sentiment | *s--* | serious | *syx* |
| sentimental | *s--l* | seriously | *syxl* |
| sentimentalism | *s--lz* | seriousness | *syx'* |
| sentimentalist | *s--l,* | sermon | *s-m* |
| sentimentality | *s--l)* | sermonize | *s-mz* |
| sentinel | *s-nl* | serous | *sx* |
| sentry | *s-,* | serpent | *sp-* |
| separable | *spb* | serpentine | *sp-n* |
| separate | *spa* | serrate | *sra* |
| separately | *spal* | serried | *sy* |
| separation | *spj* | serum | *sr* |
| separatist | *spa,* | servant | *sv-* |
| separator | *spa* | serve | *sv* |
| sepia | *spa* | server | *sv* |
| sepoy | *spy* | service | *svs* |
| September | *sp* | serviceable | *svsb* |
| septenary | *spny* | servile | *svl* |
| septennial | *spnl* | servility | *svl)* |
| septic | *spt* | servitor | *sv* |
| septuagenarian | *spjnyn* | servitude | *svld* |
| septum | *sp* | sesame | *sse* |
| sepulcher | *splck* | sesquipedalian | *ssqpdln* |
| sepulchral | *splkl* | session | *sj* |
| sepulture | *spltu* | set | *sl* |
| sequel | *sql* | seton | *sln* |
| sequence | *sq* | settee | *sle* |
| sequester | *sqs* | setter | *sl* |
| sequestrate | *sqsa* | settle | *sll* |
| sequestration | *sqsj* | settlement | *sll-* |
| sequestrator | *sqsar* | settler | *sll* |
| sequin | *sqn* | seven | 7 |
| seraglio | *srlo* | sevenfold | 7 *fol* |
| seraph | *sf* | seventeen | 17 |

## SEVENTEEN

## SEVENTEENTH

seventeen ... *17L*
seventh ....... *7L*
seventy ........ *70*
sever........... *Sv*
*several*......... *sv*
*severally*........ *Sv svl*
severance....... *Sv sve*
severe.......... *sve*
severities....... *svr))*
severity......... *svr)*
severeness...... *sve'*
sew ............ *so*
sewage......... *suy*
sewer........... *Su*
sewerage....... *Suy*
sex............. *sx*
sexagenarian.... *sxgnyn*
sexennial....... *sxnl*
sextant......... *sx-*
sexton.......... *sxn*
sextuple........ *sxp*
sexual.......... *sxl*
shabbily........
shabbiness......
shabby.........
shackle.........
shackless.......
shad...........
*shade*..........
shadow.........
shadowy........
shady..........
shaft...........
shagginess......
shaggy.........
shagreen.......
shah...........
shake..........
shaker.........
shako..........
*shall*..........
shalloon........
shallop.........
shallot.........
shallow.........
shallowness .....

shalt...........
sham...........
shamble........
shame..........
shameful.......
shamefulness....
shameless......
shamelessness...
shamming......
shammy........
shampoo........
shamrock.......
shank..........
shan't..........
shanty.........
*shape*..........
shapeless.......
shapely........
share..........
shareholder.....
shark..........
sharp..........
sharpen........
sharpener.......
sharper........
sharpness......
sharpshooter....
shatter.........
shave..........
shaveling......
shaven.........
shaver.........
shaving........
shaw..........
shawl..........
she............
sheaf..........
shear..........
shearling.....
sheathe.......
sheathing......
sheaves.......
shebeen........
*shed*...........
sheen..........
*sheep*...........

**SHEEP**

## SHEEPISHNESS

| | |
|---|---|
| sheepishness.... | shoal........ |
| sheepshearing... | shock........ |
| sheer.......... | shod........ |
| sheet.......... | shoddy...... |
| sheik.......... | shoe........ |
| shekel......... | shoemaker... |
| shelf.......... | *shoes*........ |
| shell.......... | shone........ |
| shellac........ | shook........ |
| sheller........ | shoot........ |
| shelter........ | shooter...... |
| shelve......... | *shop*........ |
| shelvy......... | shopkeeper... |
| shepherd....... | shoplifter.... |
| shepherdess..... | shopman..... |
| sherbet........ | *shopper*...... |
| sheriff........ | shopwalker... |
| sheriffdom...... | *shore*........ |
| sheriffship...... | shoreless.... |
| sherry......... | shorn........ |
| she's.......... | *short*........ |
| shew.......... | shortage..... |
| shibboleth...... | shorten...... |
| shield......... | *shorter*...... |
| shift.......... | shorthand.... |
| shifting........ | *shortly*...... |
| shiftless........ | shot......... |
| shiftlessness.... | shotgun...... |
| shillelah........ | *should*...... |
| shilling........ | *shoulder*..... |
| shilly-shally..... | shouldst..... |
| shimmer........ | *shout*....... |
| shin.......... | shove........ |
| *shine*......... | shovel....... |
| shingle........ | show........ |
| shining........ | *shower*...... |
| *ship*.......... | showery..... |
| shipment....... | shrank...... |
| *shipper*........ | shrapnel..... |
| shipwreck...... | shred....... |
| shipyard....... | shrewd...... |
| shire.......... | shrewish..... |
| shirk.......... | shrewishness. |
| shirt.......... | shriek....... |
| shirting........ | shrievalty.... |
| shiver......... | shrift....... |

**SHRIFT**

## SHRILL

| | |
|---|---|
| shrill | |
| shrillness | |
| shrimp | |
| shrine | |
| shrink | |
| shrive | |
| shrivel | |
| shrivelling | |
| shriven | |
| shroud | |
| shrub | |
| shrubbery | |
| shrubby | |
| shrug | |
| shrunk | |
| shudder | |
| shuffle | |
| shun | |
| shunt | |
| *shut* | |
| *shutter* | |
| shuttle | |
| shy | |
| sibilant | |
| sibyl | |
| sibylline | |
| *sick* | |
| sicken | |
| sickle | |
| *sickly* | |
| sickness | |
| *side* | |
| sideboard | |
| sidelong | |
| sidereal | |
| sidewalk | |
| sidewise | |
| siege | |
| sienna | |
| sierra | |
| siesta | |
| sieve | |
| sift | |
| sigh | |
| *sight* | |
| sightless | |

| | |
|---|---|
| sightly | |
| sign | |
| signal | |
| signalize | |
| signalling | |
| signatory | |
| signature | |
| signet | |
| significance | |
| significant | |
| signification | |
| signify | |
| silence | |
| silent | |
| silhouette | |
| silica | |
| siliceous | |
| *silk* | |
| silken | |
| silkworm | |
| sill | |
| sillabub | |
| silliness | |
| silly | |
| silo | |
| silt | |
| *silver* | |
| silverware | |
| silvery | |
| similar | |
| similarity | |
| simile | |
| similitude | |
| simmer | |
| simony | |
| simoom | |
| simoon | |
| simper | |
| *simple* | |
| simpleness | |
| simpleton | |
| simplicity | |
| simplification | |
| simplify | |
| simply | |
| simulate | |

## SIMULATION

| | |
|---|---|
| simulation...... | *srlg* |
| simulator....... | *srla* |
| simultaneity..... | *srlln)* |
| simultaneous.... | *srllnx* |
| simultaneousness | *srllnx'* |
| sin............. | *sn* |
| *since*........... | *s/* |
| sincere......... | *sse* |
| sincerity........ | *s/r)* |
| sinciput......... | *spl* |
| sine............ | *sin* |
| sinecure........ | *snku* |
| sinecurist....... | *snku,* |
| sinew.......... | *snu* |
| sinewy......... | *snu,* |
| sinful.......... | *snf* |
| sinfulness....... | *snf'* |
| *sing*........... | *sq* |
| singe.......... | *sy* |
| *singer*......... | *Sq* |
| *single*......... | *sgl* |
| *singly*......... | *Sgl* *sgl* |
| *singular*....... | *Sgl* |
| singularity...... | *Sgl)* |
| sinister........ | *sns* |
| sink........... | *snl'* *sq* |
| sinless......... | *snl'* |
| sinner......... | *Sn* |
| sinning........ | *sn* |
| sinuate........ | *sna* |
| sinuosity....... | *snus)* |
| sinuous........ | *snux* |
| sinus.......... | *snx* |
| sip............ | *sp* |
| siphon......... | *sfn* |
| siphonal....... | *sfnl* |
| siphonate...... | *sfna* |
| siphonic....... | *sfnk* |
| *sir*........... | *sr* |
| sire........... | *su* |
| siren.......... | *srn* |
| sirloin........ | *slyn* |
| sirocco........ | *srko* |
| sirup.......... | *srp* |
| sis........... | *ss* |
| *sister*......... | *ss* |
| sisterhood....... | *sshd* |
| sisterlike........ | *sslk* |
| *sisterly*......... | *ssl* |
| *sit*............. | *sl* |
| site............ | *su* |
| situate.......... | *sla* |
| situation........ | *sul* |
| six .......... | *6* |
| sixfold ..... | *6p* *6fol* |
| sixpence .. | *6p* *16* |
| sixteen ...... | *16l* |
| sixteenth .... | |
| sixth ........ | *6l* |
| sixthly ..... | *6l* |
| sixty ........ | *60* |
| sizar........... | *Sz* |
| size........... | *sz* |
| skate.......... | *ska* |
| skein.......... | *skn* |
| skeleton....... | *sklln* |
| skeptic........ | *skp* |
| sketch......... | *skc* |
| skew.......... | *sku* |
| skewer........ | *Sku* |
| ski........... | *ske* |
| skid.......... | *skd* |
| skies......... | *skz* |
| skiff......... | *skf* |
| skilful........ | *sklf* |
| skill......... | *skl* |
| skillet........ | *skll* |
| skim......... | *sk* |
| skin......... | *skn* |
| skinny........ | *skn,* |
| *skins*......... | *skns* |
| skip......... | *skp* |
| skipper....... | *Skp* |
| skirmish....... | *skr* |
| skirt......... | *sk/* |
| skit......... | *skl* |
| skittish....... | *skl?* |
| skittles....... | *skils* |
| skulk......... | *sklk* |
| skull......... | *skl* |
| skunk........ | *skq* |
| *sky*......... | *ski* |

## SKYBLUE

| | | | |
|---|---|---|---|
| skyblue | *skibu* | slice | *sis* |
| skylark | *skilok* | slid | *sd* |
| skylight | *skil* | slide | *sd* |
| skyscraper | *skiskp* | slieve | *sv* |
| skyward | *ski/* | slight | *si* |
| slab | *sb* | slim | *s* |
| slack | *sk* | slime | *si* |
| slacken | *skn* | slimy | *si* |
| slackness | *sk* | sling | *sq* |
| slag | *sq* | slink | *sq* |
| slain | *sn* | slip | *sp* |
| slake | *sk* | slipper | *sp* |
| slam | *s* | slippery | *sp* |
| slander | *s* | slipshod | *spzd* |
| slanderous | *s—x* | slit | *sl* |
| slang | *sq* | slobber | *sb* |
| slant | *s-* | sloe | *so* |
| slap | *sp* | slog | *sq* |
| slash | *sf* | slogan | *sgn* |
| slat | *sl* | sloop | *sup* |
| slate | *sa* | slop | *sp* |
| slattern | *sn* | slope | *sop* |
| slatternly | *snl* | slopping | *sp-sl* |
| slaughter | *sa* | slot | *sl* |
| slave | *sa* | sloth | *sl* |
| slavery | *say* | slothful | *slf* |
| slavish | *saf* | slothfulness | *slf* |
| slay | *sa* | slouch | *src* |
| slayer | *sa* | slouching | *src* |
| sled | *sd* | slough | *s* |
| sledge | *sf* | sloughy | *sf* |
| sleek | *sek* | sloven | *svn* |
| *sleep* | *sep* | slovenliness | *svnl* |
| sleeper | *sp sf* | *slow* | *so* |
| *sleepiness* | *sp sf* | *slower* | *so* |
| sleepless | *spl* | slowness | *so* |
| sleepy | *sp* | slue | *su* |
| sleet | *se* | slug | *sq* |
| sleeve | *se* | sluggard | *sqf* |
| sleeveless | *sel* | sluggish | *sqf* |
| sleigh | *sa* | sluggishly | *sqfl* |
| sleight | *sa* | sluggishness | *sqf* |
| slender | *s* | sluice | *sus* |
| slenderness | *s* | slum | *s* |
| slept | *sp* | slumber | *snb* |
| slew | *su* | slumberous | *snbs* |

**SLUMBEROUS**

## SLUMP

| | | | |
|---|---|---|---|
| slump | _srp_ | snack | _snk_ |
| slung | _sg_ | snaffle | _snfl_ |
| slunk | _sg_ | snag | _sng_ |
| slur | _sr_ | snaggy | _sng,_ |
| slush | _slʒ_ | snail | _snal_ |
| slut | _sl_ | snake | _snk_ |
| sluttish | _slʒ_ | snap | _snp_ |
| sluttishness | _slʒ'_ | snapdragon | _snpdgn_ |
| sly | _si_ | snare | _sna_ |
| slyly | _sil_ | snarl | _snrl_ |
| slyness | _si'_ | snatch | _snc_ |
| smack | _s rk_ | sneak | _snek_ |
| *small* | _sra_ | sneakiness | _snk'_ |
| *smaller* | _Sra_ | sneer | _sne_ |
| smart | _sr/_ | sneeze | _snʒ_ |
| smartness | _sr'_/ | sniff | _snf_ |
| smash | _s rʒ_ | snip | _snp_ |
| smatter | _Sra_ | snipe | _snp_ |
| smatterer | _Srar_ | snipping | _snp_ |
| smattering | _Sra_ | snivel | _snvl_ |
| smear | _sre_ | snivelling | _snvl_ |
| smell | _srl_ | snob | _snb_ |
| smelt | _srll_ | snobbery | _snby_ |
| *smile* | _s rl_ | snobbish | _snbʒ_ |
| smilingly | _isrll_ | snobbishness | _snbʒ'_ |
| smilingness | _srlg_ | snood | _snd_ |
| smirch | _srrc_ | snooze | _snʒ_ |
| smirk | _srrk_ | snore | _sno_ |
| smite | _sr_ | snort | _sn/_ |
| smith | _srl_ | snout | _snl_ |
| smithery | _s rly_ | *snow* | _sno_ |
| smithy | _srl,_ | snowball | _snobl_ |
| smitten | _srln_ | snowdrop | _snodp_ |
| smock | _srk_ | snowflake | _snoflk_ |
| *smoke* | _s rok_ | snowy | _sno,_ |
| *smoker* | _Srk_ | snub | _snb_ |
| smooth | _srl_ | snubbing | _snb_ |
| smoothness | _srl'_ | snuff | _snf_ |
| smote | _sro_ | snuffle | _snfl_ |
| smother | _Sro_ | snug | _sng_ |
| smothery | _Sro,_ | so | _so_ |
| smoulder | _Srl_ | soak | _sok_ |
| smug | _srg_ | soap | _sop_ |
| smuggle | _srgl_ | soapsuds | _spsds_ |
| smut | _srl_ | soar | _so_ |
| smutting | _srl_ | sob | _sb_ |

## SOBBING

| | |
|---|---|
| sobbing......... | *sb* |
| sober........... | *sb* |
| soberness....... | *sb'* |
| sobriety........ | *sb)* |
| sobriquet...... | *sbka* |
| sociability...... | *szb)* |
| sociable........ | *szb* |
| sociableness..... | *szb'* |
| social.......... | *sx* |
| socialist........ | *sx,* |
| socialistic....... | *sx5* |
| socialize........ | *sxz* |
| society......... | *ss)* |
| sock........... | *sk* |
| socket......... | *skl* |
| sod........... | *sd* |
| soda.......... | *sda* |
| sodality........ | *sdl)* |
| sodden........ | *sdn* |
| soever......... | *sov* |
| sofa.......... | *sfa* |
| soft........... | *sf* |
| soften......... | *sfn* |
| softer......... | *sf* |
| softly......... | *sfl* |
| softness....... | *sf'* |
| soil.......... | *syl* |
| soiree......... | *sra* |
| sojourn........ | *syrn* |
| sojourner...... | *syrn* |
| solace......... | *sls* |
| solar.......... | *sl* |
| sold.......... | *sol* |
| solder......... | *sd* |
| soldier......... | *slj* |
| soldierlike...... | *sljlk* |
| soldiership..... | *sljp* |
| soldiery........ | *slj,* |
| sole.......... | *sol* |
| solecism....... | *slsz* |
| solemn........ | *sl* |
| solemnity...... | *sl m)* |
| solemnize...... | *sl mz* |
| sol-fa......... | *slfa* |
| solicit......... | *slsl* |
| solicitation..... | *slsy* |

| | |
|---|---|
| solicitor........ | *sls* |
| solicitous...... | *slslx* |
| solicitude...... | *slsld* |
| solid.......... | *sld* |
| solidarity..... | *sld)* |
| solidification.... | *sldf* |
| solidify........ | *sldf* |
| solidity........ | *sld)* |
| solidness...... | *sld'* |
| soliloquize..... | *sllqz* |
| soliloquy...... | *sllq,* |
| soliped........ | *slpd* |
| solitaire....... | *slla* |
| solitary........ | *slly* |
| solitude....... | *slld* |
| solo.......... | *slo* |
| soloist......... | *slo,* |
| solstice........ | *slss* |
| solstitial....... | *slsx* |
| solubility...... | *slb)* |
| soluble........ | *slb* |
| solution........ | *sly* |
| solve.......... | *slv* |
| solvability...... | *slvb)* |
| solvable....... | *slvb* |
| solvency....... | *slv* |
| solvent........ | *slv-* |
| somber........ | *srb* |
| somberly...... | *srbl* |
| somberness..... | *srb'* |
| some.......... | *s* |
| somebody...... | *srbd,* |
| somehow...... | *sh* |
| someone....... | *si* |
| somersault..... | *srsll* |
| something..... | *sr* |
| sometime...... | *stu* |
| somewhat...... | *sra* |
| somewhere..... | *srr* |
| somnambulate... | *s m rbla* |
| somnambulism.. | *s m rblz* |
| somnambulist... | *s m rbll* |
| somniferous..... | *smfx* |
| somnolence..... | *srhl,* |
| somnolency..... | *s ml* |
| somnolent...... | *s ml-* |

**SOMNOLENT**

## SON

| | | | |
|---|---|---|---|
| son | *sn* | soubriquet | *sbka* |
| sonata | *snta* | souchong | *sfq* |
| song | *sq* | sough | *sf* |
| songster | *sgs* | sought | *st* |
| songstress | *sgs'* | soul | *sol* |
| sonnet | *snt* | soulless | *sol'* |
| sonneteer | *snte* | *sound* | *sr—* |
| sonometer | *snre* | sounder | *sr—* |
| sonorous | *snr* | *soundness* | *sr—'* |
| sonorousness | *snr'* | soup | *sup* |
| *soon* | *sn* | sour | *sr* |
| soot | *su* | source | *srs* |
| sooth | *sut* | sourness | *sr'* |
| soothe | *sut* | souse | *ss* |
| soothsayer | *stsa* | *south* | *S* |
| sooty | *st,* | southeast | *St* |
| sop | *sp* | *southeastern* | *Strn* |
| sophism | *sfz* | *southerly* | *Srl* |
| sophist | *sf,* | southern | *Srn* |
| sophistic | *sfs* | southernmost | *Srnro,* |
| sophistical | *sfst* | *southward* | *Sf* |
| sophisticate | *sfska* | southwest | *SU* |
| sophistry | *sfs,* | southwestern | *SUrn* |
| sophomore | *sfro* | souvenir | *sune* |
| soporiferous | *spfr* | sovereign | *Srn* |
| soporific | *spfk* | sovereignty | *Sr—,* |
| soprani | *spn,* | sow | *so* |
| sopranist | *spn,* | sow | *sr* |
| soprano | *spnd* | *space* | *sas* |
| sorcerer | *Srs* | spacious | *sx* |
| sorceress | *sro'* | spade | *sd* |
| sorcery | *srsy* | spaghetti | *sgt,* |
| sordid | *sjd* | spake | *sk* |
| sordidness | *sjd'* | span | *sn* |
| sore | *so* | spandrel | *s—l* |
| soreness | *so'* | spangle | *sgl* |
| sorority | *srr)* | spaniel | *snl* |
| sorrel | *srl* | spank | *sq* |
| sorrow | *sro* | spar | *sa* |
| sorrowful | *srof* | spare | *sa* |
| sorry | *sy* | spareness | *sa'* |
| sort | *sf* | sparingness | *sag'* |
| *sorter* | *sf* | spark | *srk* |
| sortie | *sf,* | sparkle | *srkl* |
| sot | *st* | sparrow | *sro* |
| sottish | *stj* | sparse | *srs* |

SPARSE

## SPARSELY

| | | | |
|---|---|---|---|
| sparsely | *srsl* | speculum | *skl* |
| sparseness | *srs'* | sped | *sd* |
| sparsity | *srs)* | speech | *sec* |
| spasm | *sz* | speechless | *scl'* |
| spasmodic | *sz-rdk* | speechlessness | *scl'* |
| spasmodical | *sz-rdl* | speed | *sd* |
| spat | *st* | speedometer | *sd ze* |
| spate | *sa* | Speedtyping | *sdtp* |
| spatter | *Sa* | Speedwriter (S/r) | *sdlr* |
| spavin | *svn* | Speedwriting (S/) | *sdrz* |
| spawn | *san* | speedy | *sd,* |
| spawner | *San* | spell | *sl* |
| *speak* | *sek* | spellbound | *slbz* |
| *speaker* | *Sk* | spelt | *sll* |
| spear | *se* | spencer | *S/* |
| spearman | *se ,-* | *spend* | *s—* |
| spearmint | *se - .* | *spender* | *s—* |
| *special* | *sx* | spendthrift | *s—y* |
| specialist | *sx,* | spent | *s-* |
| *specialization* | *sxzj* | sperm | *sz* |
| specialty | *sxl,* | spermaceti | *szsl,-* |
| species | *sz,,* | spermatic | *szr* |
| specific | *ssfk* | spermatical | *szrk* |
| specification | *ssf* | spew | *su* |
| specify | *ssf* | sphere | *sfe* |
| specimen | *ss-m* | spherical | *sfk* |
| specious | *sx* | sphericity | *sfs)* |
| speciousness | *sx'* | spheroid | *sfyd* |
| speck | *sk* | spheroidal | *sfydl* |
| speckle | *sk* | sphincter | *sfg.* |
| spectacle | *skt* | sphinx | *sfx* |
| spectacular | *sktl* | spice | *sts* |
| spectator | *Ska* | spicery | *ssy* |
| specter | *Sk* | spick | *sk* |
| spectra | *Sk* | spicy | *ss,* |
| spectral | *Skl* | spider | *Se* |
| spectroscope | *Skskp* | spigot | *sgl* |
| spectrum | *Sk,* | spike | *stk* |
| specula | *skla* | spikelet | *skel* |
| specular | *Skl* | spikenard | *skn/* |
| speculate | *skla* | spiky | *sk,* |
| speculation | *skly* | spile | *sil* |
| speculatist | *skll,* | spill | *sl* |
| speculative | *sklv* | spilt | *sll* |
| speculator | *Skla* | spin | *sn* |
| speculatory | *skly* | spinach | *snc* |

**SPINACH**

## SPINAL

|  | |  | |
|------|------|------|------|
| spinal......... | _snl_ | spondee......... | _s—e_ |
| spindle........ | _s—l_ | sponge.......... | |
| spine.......... | _sn_ | spongy......... | |
| spinet......... | _snt_ | sponsal......... | |
| spinneret...... | _snt_ | sponsor......... | |
| spinnery....... | _sny_ | spontaneity..... | _s—n)_ |
| spinose........ | _sns_ | spontaneous..... | _s—ns_ |
| spinous........ | _sns_ | spontaneousness.. | _s—nt'_ |
| spinster....... | _sns_ | spool.......... | _sul_ |
| spiny.......... | _sn,_ | spoon......... | _sn_ |
| spiracle....... | _srk_ | spoonful....... | _snf_ |
| spiral......... | _srl_ | spoor......... | _sr_ |
| spire.......... | _sr_ | sporadic....... | _srdk_ |
| _spirit_........ | _srt_ | spore......... | _so_ |
| spiritless...... | _srtl'_ | sporran....... | _srn_ |
| spiritual....... | _srtl_ | sport......... | _s/_ |
| spiritualism.... | _srtlz_ | sportful....... | _s/b_ |
| spiritualist..... | _srtl,_ | sportive....... | _s/v_ |
| spirituality..... | _srtl)_ | sportsman..... | _s//_ |
| spiritualize..... | _srtlz_ | _spot_......... | _st_ |
| spirituous..... | _srts_ | spotless....... | _stl'_ |
| spit........... | _st_ | spousal....... | _szl_ |
| spite.......... | _st_ | spouse....... | _sz_ |
| spiteful........ | _stf_ | spout........ | _st_ |
| spitefulness.... | _stf'_ | spouter...... | _st_ |
| spittoon........ | _stn_ | sprain........ | _sn_ |
| splash......... | _s?_ | sprang....... | _sq_ |
| splay......... | _sa_ | sprat........ | _st_ |
| spleen........ | _sn_ | sprawl....... | _sal_ |
| splendent...... | _s——_ | spray....... | _sa_ |
| splendid...... | _s—d_ | _spread_...... | _sd_ |
| splendor...... | _s—_ | spreader..... | _sd_ |
| splenetic...... | _snt_ | spree....... | _se_ |
| splice......... | _sus_ | sprig....... | _sl_ |
| splint......... | _s—_ | sprightly..... | _srl_ |
| splinter....... | _s—_ | _spring_...... | _sq_ |
| split.......... | _st_ | springtide.... | _sqtd_ |
| splitting.... | _st_ | springtime..... | _sqt_ |
| splutter........ | _st_ | sprinkle...... | _sql_ |
| spoil........ | _syl_ | sprint....... | _s—_ |
| spoiler........ | _syl_ | sprite....... | _st_ |
| _spoke_........ | _sok_ | sprout...... | _st_ |
| _spoken_....... | _skn_ | spruce..... | _sus_ |
| spokesman..... | _sks_ | sprung...... | _sq_ |
| spoliation...... | _sly_ | spry........ | _se_ |
| spondaic...... | _s—ak_ | spume...... | _su_ |

**SPUME**

## SPUMOUS

|  | |  | |
|---|---|---|---|
| spumous | | stack | |
| spumy | | stadium | |
| spun | | staff | |
| spunk | | stag | |
| spur | | stage | |
| spurge | | stagger | |
| spurious | | stagnant | |
| spurn | | stagnate | |
| spurring | | stagnation | |
| spurt | | staid | |
| sputter | | stain | |
| spy | | stainless | |
| squab | | stair | |
| squabble | | staircase | |
| squad | | stairway | |
| squadron | | stake | |
| squalid | | stalactite | |
| squalidness | | stalagmite | |
| squall | | stale | |
| squally | | staleness | |
| squalor | | stalk | |
| squander | | stall | |
| *square* | | stallage | |
| *squarely* | | stallion | |
| squash | | stalwart | |
| squat | | stamen | |
| squaw | | stamina | |
| squeak | | staminal | |
| squeal | | staminate | |
| squeamish | | stammer | |
| squeamishness | | stamp | |
| squeeze | | stampede | |
| squeezer | | stance | |
| squib | | stanch | |
| squill | | stanchion | |
| squint | | *stand* | |
| squire | | standard | |
| squirrel | | standing | |
| squirt | | stank | |
| stab | | stannary | |
| stability | | stanza | |
| stable | | staple | |
| stableness | | stapler | |
| stabling | | *star* | |
| stablish | | starboard | |
| staccato | | starch | |

STARCH

STARE

| | | | |
|---|---|---|---|
| stare | *ra* | steady | *rd,* |
| stark | *sk* | steak | *rk* |
| starlight | *sli* | steal | *rel* |
| starling | *s, slq* | stealth | *rll* |
| starry | *s,* | stealthy | *rli,* |
| start | *sl* | steam | *re* |
| starter | *str* | steamboat | *rebo* |
| startle | *sll* | steamer | *rer* |
| startling | *sllg* | steamship (SS) | *rez* |
| starvation | *svy* | steed | *rd* |
| starve | *sv* | steel | *rel* |
| starveling | *svlq* | steelyard | *rly/* |
| state | *ra* | steep | *rep* |
| State | *ra,* | steeple | *rp* |
| stateliness | *ral'* | steepness | *rp'* |
| stately | *ral* | steer | *re* |
| statement | *ra-* | steerage | *rey* |
| stateroom | *rar* | steersman | *res,-* |
| statesman | *ras,-* | stellar | *slr* |
| statesmanlike | *ras,-lk* | stellate | *rla* |
| statesmanship | *ras,-z* | stellular | *rllr* |
| static | *r* | stellulate | *rlla* |
| statical | *rs rk* | stem | *r* |
| statics | *rs* | stench | *rc* |
| station | *ry* | stencil | *rl.* |
| stationary | *ryy* | stencilling | *rll* |
| stationer | *ryr* | stenographer | *rngf* |
| stationery | *ryy* | stenographic | *mgfk* |
| statist | *ra,* | stenographical | *mgfk* |
| statistical | *rsk* | stenography | *mgf,* |
| statistician | *rsy* | stenotype | *mlp* |
| statistics | *rss* | stentorian | *r yn* |
| statuary | *rly* | step | *rp* |
| statue | *rlu* | stepmother | *rp ro rp* |
| statuesque | *rlusk* | steppe | *rp* |
| stature | *rlu* | stepping | *rp* |
| status | *ral* | stereoscope | *sskp* |
| statute | *rlu* | stereotype | *slp sl* |
| statutory | *rtty* | sterile | *sl* |
| staunch | *rac* | sterility | *sl,* |
| stave | *ra* | sterling | *slq* |
| stay | *ra* | stern | *sn* |
| stead | *rd* | sternum | *sn* |
| steadfast | *rdf,* | sternutation | *snly* |
| steadfastness | *rdfs'* | sternutative | *snlv* |
| steadily | *rdl* | sternutatory | *sntty* |

| | |
|---|---|
| stertorous....... | stitch........ |
| stertorousness... | stithy........ |
| stethoscope..... | stiver........ |
| stethoscopic..... | stoat........ |
| stethoscopical.... | stock........ |
| stevedore....... | stockade..... |
| stew | stocking...... |
| steward........ | stoic........ |
| stewardess...... | stoical........ |
| stewardship..... | stoke........ |
| stick.......... | stokehole..... |
| stickleback..... | stoker........ |
| stickler........ | stole........ |
| stiff.......... | stolen........ |
| stiffen........ | stolid........ |
| stiffness........ | stolidity...... |
| stifle.......... | stolidness.... |
| stigma......... | stomach...... |
| stigmata....... | stomacher.... |
| stigmatize...... | stomachical... |
| stile........... | stone......... |
| stiletto........ | stony........ |
| still.......... | stood......... |
| stillness........ | stool......... |
| stilly.......... | stoop........ |
| stilt.......... | stop......... |
| stimulant....... | stopgap...... |
| stimulate....... | stoppage...... |
| stimulation...... | stopper....... |
| stimulative...... | stopping...... |
| stimuli......... | stopple...... |
| stimulus........ | storage....... |
| sting........... | store......... |
| stinginess....... | storehouse.... |
| stingy.......... | storekeeper... |
| stink.......... | stork........ |
| stint........... | storm........ |
| stipe.......... | stormy....... |
| stipend........ | story......... |
| stipendiary...... | stout........ |
| stipulate........ | stoutness..... |
| stipulation...... | stove........ |
| stipulator....... | stow......... |
| stipule......... | stowage...... |
| stir............ | stowaway..... |
| stirrup......... | straddle..... |

## STRAGGLE

| Word | Shorthand |
|---|---|
| straggle | *Sgl* |
| straggler | *Sglr* |
| straight | *Sa* |
| straighten | *San* |
| straighter | *Sar* |
| straightforward | *Saf* |
| straightness | *Sa'* |
| straightway | *Sa-a* |
| strain | *Sn* |
| strainer | *Snr* |
| strait | *Sa* |
| straiten | *San* |
| straitness | *Sa'* |
| strand | *S—* |
| strange | *Sy* |
| strangely | *Syl* |
| strangeness | *Sy'* |
| stranger | *Syr* |
| strangle | *Sgl* |
| strangulation | *Sgly* |
| strap | *Sp* |
| strata | *Sla* |
| stratagem | *Sly* |
| strategic | *Slyk* |
| strategical | *Slyl* |
| strategist | *Sly,* |
| strategy | *Sly,* |
| strath | *Sl* |
| strathspey | *Slspa* |
| stratification | *Slf* |
| stratiform | *Slf* |
| stratify | *Slf* |
| stratum | *Sl* |
| stratus | *Sls* |
| straw | *Sa* |
| strawberry | *Saby* |
| stray | *Sa* |
| streak | *Sek* |
| stream | *Se* |
| streamer | *Ser* |
| streamlet | *Sell* |
| street | *sl* |
| strength | *S* |
| strengthen | *Sn* |
| strenuous | *Snu* |
| stress | *S'* |
| stretch | *Sc* |
| stretcher | *Scr* |
| strew | *Su* |
| strewn | *Sn* |
| stricken | *Skn* |
| strict | *Sk* |
| strictness | *Sk'* |
| stricture | *Sku* |
| stride | *Sd* |
| strident | *Sd-* |
| stridently | *Sd-l* |
| stridulous | *Sdlu* |
| strife | *Sf* |
| strike | *Sek* |
| striker | *Skr* |
| string | *Sg* |
| stringency | *Sy'* |
| stringent | *Sy-Sg,* |
| stringy | *Sg,* |
| strip | *Sp* |
| stripe | *Sip* |
| stripling | *Spg* |
| strive | *Se* |
| striving | *Se* |
| strode | *Sd* |
| stroke | *Sok* |
| stroll | *Sol* |
| strong | *Sg* |
| stronger | *Sgr* |
| stronghold | *Sghl* |
| strop | *Sp* |
| strove | *So* |
| struck | *Sk* |
| structural | *Skul* |
| structurally | *Skul* |
| structure | *Sku* |
| struggle | *Sgl* |
| strum | *S* |
| strung | *Sg* |
| strut | *Sl* |
| strychnia | *Skna* |
| strychnine | *Sknn* |
| stub | *sb* |
| stubble | *sb* |
| stubborn | *sbrn* |
| stubbornness | *sbrn'* |

**STUBBORNNESS**

## STUCCO

| | | | |
|---|---|---|---|
| stucco......... | *rko* *rk* | subject......... | *sl* |
| stuck.......... | | subjection...... | *sll* |
| stud........... | *rd* | subjective....... | *sjv* *sll* |
| student........ | *rd-* | subjoin......... | *sjyn* |
| studied........ | *rd,* | subjugate....... | *sjga* |
| studio......... | *rdo* | subjugation..... | *sjgl* |
| studious....... | *rdx* | subjunctive..... | *sjgv* |
| *study*.......... | *rd,* | sublease........ | *slo* |
| stuff.......... | *rf* | sublimate....... | *slra* |
| stultify........ | *rlf* | sublime......... | *slr* |
| stumble....... | *rb* | sublimity....... | *sl,)* |
| stumblingblock.. | *rbgbk* | sublunar........ | *sln* |
| stump......... | *rp* | sublunary....... | *slny* |
| stun........... | *rn* | submarine...... | *srn* |
| stung......... | *rg* | submerge....... | *srf* |
| stunk......... | *rg* | submergence.... | *srf* |
| stunt......... | *rl* | submersion..... | *srf* |
| stuntedness.... | *rd'* | submission..... | *srf* |
| stupefaction.... | *rpfkf* | submissive..... | *srsv* |
| stupefy........ | *rpf* | submit......... | *srl* |
| stupendous..... | *rp—x* | submitted...... | *srl* |
| stupendousness.. | *rp—x'* | subordinate..... | *s/na* |
| stupid......... | *rpd* | subordination... | *s/nf* |
| stupidity....... | *rpd)* | suborn......... | *srn* |
| stupor......... | *rpr* | subornation.... | *srnf* |
| sturdiness..... | *Sd'* | subpoena....... | *spna* |
| sturdy......... | *Sd,* | subscribe....... | *sskb* |
| sturgeon....... | *Sjn* | subscriber..... | *sskb* |
| stutter......... | *rlr* | subscription.... | *sskpf* |
| sty............ | *ru* | subsequence.... | *ssf* |
| style.......... | *rl* | subsequent..... | *ssg-* |
| stylish......... | *rl,* *rlf* | subsequently.... | *ssg-l* |
| stylist......... | *rl,* | subserve....... | *ssv* |
| stylograph..... | *rlgf* | subservience.... | *ssv* |
| stylus......... | *rlu* | subserviency... | *ssv* |
| styptic........ | *rpl* | subservient.... | *ssv-* |
| suasion........ | *sf* | subside........ | *ssd* |
| suasive........ | *srsv* | subsidence..... | *ssd* |
| suave.......... | *srv* | subsidency..... | *ssd* |
| suavity........ | *srv)* | subsidiarily.... | *ssdyl* |
| subaltern...... | *saltn* | subsidiary..... | *ssdy* |
| subaqueous.... | *sagx* | subsidize....... | *ssdz* |
| subdivide...... | *sdvd* | subsidy........ | *ssd,* |
| subdivision..... | *sdvj* | subsist........ | *ss,* |
| subdue........ | *sdu* | subsistence..... | *sss* |
| subjacent...... | *sjs-* | subsoil......... | *ssyl* |

### SUBSTANCE

substance....... *ss*

substantial...... *sse*

substantiality.... *sse)*

substantialize... *ssez*

substantially.... *sse*

substantiate..... *ssnza*

substantive..... *ss-v*

substitute....... *sstu*

substitution..... *ssly*

substitutional.... *sslyl*

substitutionary.. *sslyy*

substrata....... *ssla*

substratum...... *ssl*

substructure.... *ssku*

subtenant...... *stn-*

subtend........ *st-*

subterfuge...... *sfy*

subterranean.... *snn*

subterraneous... *snr*

subtile.......... *sll*

subtility........ *sll)*

subtle.......... *sll*

subtlety........ *slll,*

subtract........ *slk*

subtraction...... *slk*

subtrahend...... *slh-*

suburb......... *sub*

suburban....... *subn*

subvention...... *svy*

subversion...... *svry*

subvert........ *svf*

subway........ *sra*

succeed........ *suc*

*success*........ *suc*

successful...... *suc*

succession...... *sucy*

successive...... *sucv*

successor....... *suc*

succinct........ *sksg*

succor......... *skl-*

succulent...... *skl-*

succumb........ *sk*

*such*.......... *sc*

suck.......... *sk*

suckle.......... *sk*

suckling........ *sk*

suction....... *skf*

sudatory...... *sdly*

sudden....... *sdn*

suddenly..... *sdnl*

suddenness... *sdn'*

sudorific...... *sdfk*

suds......... *sds*

sue.......... *su*

suede........ *sd*

suet.......... *sul*

suety........ *sul,*

*suffer*........ *sf*

sufferable..... *sfl*

sufferance.... *sf*

sufferer.... *Sf*

suffering...... *sf*

suffice........ *sfs*

sufficiency.... *sfy*

*sufficient*...... *sfy-*

*sufficiently*.... *sfy-l*

suffix......... *sfx*

suffocate...... *sfka*

suffocation.... *sfky*

suffragan..... *sfgn*

suffrage....... *sfy*

suffragette.... *sfyl*

suffragist..... *sfy,*

suffuse....... *sfs*

suffusion...... *sfy*

*sugar*......... *zgr*

sugary........ *zgy*

suggest........ *sy,*

suggestion..... *syy*

suggestive.... *syv*

suicidal....... *susdl*

suicide........ *susd*

*suit*.......... *su*

suitability..... *sub)*

suitable....... *sub*

suitableness... *sub'*

suite......... *se*

*suitor*........ *Su*

sulk.......... *slk*

sulkiness...... *slk'*

sulks......... *slks*

sulky......... *slk,*

**SULKY**

## SULLEN

|  | |  | |
|---|---|---|---|
| sullen | | superannuate | |
| sullenness | | superannuation | |
| sully | | superb | |
| sulphate | | supercargo | |
| sulphur | | superciliary | |
| sulphuretted | | supercilious | |
| sulphuric | | supereminent | |
| sulphurous | | supererogation | |
| sultan | | supererogatory | |
| sultana | | superexcellent | |
| sultriness | | superficial | |
| sultry | | superficiality | |
| sum | | superficialness | |
| summarily | | superfine | |
| summarize | | superfluity | |
| summary | | superfluous | |
| summation | | superhuman | |
| *summer* | | superimpose | |
| summit | | superimposed | |
| summon | | superincumbent | |
| sumpter | | superinduce | |
| sumptuary | | superintend | |
| sumptuous | | superintendence | |
| sun | | superintendent (supt) | |
| sunbeam | | superior | |
| sunburn | | superiority | |
| *Sunday* | | superlative | |
| sunder | | superman | |
| sundown | | supernal | |
| sundry | | supernatural | |
| sunflower | | supernumerary | |
| sung | | superpose | |
| sunk | | superposition | |
| sunken | | superscribe | |
| sunless | | superscription | |
| sunlight | | supersede | |
| sunny | | superstition | |
| sunrise | | superstitious | |
| sunset | | superstructure | |
| sunshine | | supervene | |
| sup | | supervisal | |
| superabound | | supervise | |
| superabundance | | supervision | |
| superabundant | | supervisor | |
| superadd | | supine | |

**SUPINE**

## SUPINENESS

| Word | Shorthand |
|---|---|
| supineness | |
| supper | |
| supplant | |
| supple | |
| supplement | |
| supplemental | |
| supplementary | |
| suppliant | |
| supplicate | |
| supplication | |
| supplicatory | |
| *supply* | |
| support | |
| supportable | |
| supporter | |
| *suppose* | |
| supposed | |
| *supposition* | |
| suppress | |
| suppressible | |
| suppression | |
| suppressive | |
| suppurate | |
| supramundane | |
| supremacy | |
| supreme | |
| surcharge | |
| surd | |
| *sure* | |
| surely | |
| *sureness* | |
| *surer* | |
| surety | |
| surf | |
| surface | |
| surfaceman | |
| surfeit | |
| surge | |
| surgeon | |
| surgery | |
| surgical | |
| surliness | |
| surly | |
| surmise | |
| surmount | |

| Word | Shorthand |
|---|---|
| surmountable | |
| surname | |
| surpass | |
| surpassable | |
| surplice | |
| surplus | |
| surplusage | |
| *surprise* | |
| surrender | |
| surreptitious | |
| surrey | |
| surrogate | |
| *surround* | |
| surtax | |
| surtout | |
| surveillance | |
| survey | |
| surveyor | |
| surveyorship | |
| survival | |
| survive | |
| survivor | |
| susceptibility | |
| susceptible | |
| susceptive | |
| suspect | |
| suspend | |
| suspender | |
| suspense | |
| suspension | |
| suspensory | |
| suspicion | |
| suspicious | |
| sustain | |
| sustentation | |
| sutler | |
| suttee | |
| sutural | |
| suture | |
| suzerain | |
| suzerainty | |
| swab | |
| swabbing | |
| swaddle | |
| swag | |

SWAG

## SWAIN

| | | | |
|---|---|---|---|
| swain | *sm* | swinish | *srns* |
| swallow | *solo* | swirl | *srl* |
| swam | *sm* | switch | *src* |
| swamp | *srp* | switchboard | *srcb* |
| swan | *sn* | swivel | *srvl* |
| swanlike | *snlk* | swollen | *sln* |
| swap | *sp* | swoon | *sn* |
| sward | *sr* | swoop | *srp* |
| sware | *sra* | sword | *sl* |
| swarm | *srn* | swordsman | *sll-* |
| swarthy | *srl* | swordsmanship | *sll-z* |
| swastika | *srska* | swore | *so* |
| swath | *sl* | sworn | *srn* |
| swathe | *sal* | swum | *sn* |
| sway | *sra* | swung | *sg* |
| swear | *sra* | sycamore | *shr* |
| sweat | *sl* | sycophancy | *skf* |
| sweater | *sl* | sycophant | *skf-* |
| sweep | *srep* | sycophantic | *skf-k* |
| sweeper | *srp* | sycophantical | *skf-k* |
| sweeping | *srep* | sycophantism | *skf-z* |
| sweepstake | *spsk* | syllabic | *slbk* |
| *sweet* | *sre* | syllabical | *slbk* |
| sweetbread | *srebd* | syllable | *slb* |
| sweetbrier | *sreBr* | syllogism | *slz* |
| sweeten | *sren* | syllogistic | *sljs* |
| *sweeter* | *sre* | syllogistical | *slysl* |
| sweetheart | *sreh* | syllogize | *slz* |
| *sweetness* | *sre* | sylph | *slf* |
| swell | *srl* | sylvan | *slvn* |
| swelter | *sl* | symbol | *srb* |
| swept | *sp* | symbolic | *srbk* |
| swerve | *srv* | symbolical | *srbl* |
| swift | *sf* | symbolism | *srbz* |
| swiftness | *sf* | symbolize | *srbz* |
| swill | *sl* | symmetrical | *srek* |
| swim | *sn* | symmetry | *sre* |
| swimmer | *sr* | sympathetic | *srpl* |
| swimming | *sn* | sympathize | *srplz* |
| swimmingly | *srl* | sympathy | *srpl* |
| swindle | *sr-l* | symphonious | *srfn* |
| swindler | *sr-l* | symphony | *srfn* |
| swindling | *sr-l* | symposium | *srpz* |
| swine | *srn* | symptom | *srnt* |
| swing | *sg* | symptomatic | *srnt* |
| swinge | *sg* | symptomatical | *srdk* |

## SYNAGOGUE

| | |
|---|---|
| synagogue..... | syntax......... |
| synchronal..... | synthesis....... |
| synchronous.... | synthetical...... |
| syncopate...... | syphon......... |
| syncope........ | syringe......... |
| syndicalism.... | syrup.......... |
| syndicate...... | system......... |
| synod......... | systematic...... |
| synonym....... | systematical..... |
| synonymous.... | systematically... |
| synopsis....... | systematize..... |
| synoptical..... | systole......... |
| syntactic....... | systolic......... |
| syntactical..... | |

## T

| | |
|---|---|
| tab........... | tactile.......... |
| tabard........ | tactual......... |
| tabaret........ | tadpole......... |
| tabby......... | taffeta......... |
| tabernacle...... | taffrail......... |
| tablature....... | tag............ |
| *table*......... | tail............ |
| tableaux....... | tailor.......... |
| tablecloth...... | tailoress........ |
| tablespoon..... | taint.......... |
| tablespoonful... | *take*.......... |
| tablet......... | taking......... |
| tableware...... | talcum......... |
| taboo......... | tale........... |
| tabor......... | talent......... |
| taboret........ | talisman........ |
| tabular........ | talismanic....... |
| tabulate....... | *talk*.......... |
| tabulation...... | talkative........ |
| tabulator....... | *talker*........ |
| tacit.......... | *tall*.......... |
| taciturn........ | *taller*........ |
| taciturnity...... | *tallness*........ |
| tack.......... | tallow......... |
| tackle......... | tally.......... |
| tact.......... | talon.......... |
| tactical........ | tamable........ |
| tactician....... | tamarind........ |
| tactics........ | tamarisk........ |

TAMARISK

## TAMBOUR

| | | | |
|---|---|---|---|
| tambour | | tart | |
| tambourine | | tartan | |
| tame | | tartar | |
| tameness | | tartaric | |
| tam-o'-shanter | | tartarous | |
| tamper | | task | |
| tan | | taskmaster | |
| tanager | | tassel | |
| tandem | | *taste* | |
| tang | | *tastefully* | |
| tangent | | tasteless | |
| tangential | | *taster* | |
| tangibility | | tasty | |
| tangible | | tatter | |
| tangibleness | | tatterdemalion | |
| tangle | | tattle | |
| tank | | tattoo | |
| tankard | | taught | |
| tanner | | taunt | |
| tannery | | tautologic | |
| tannic | | tautological | |
| tannin | | tautology | |
| tansy | | tavern | |
| tantalize | | tawdriness | |
| tantamount | | tawdry | |
| tap | | tawny | |
| tape | | tax | |
| taper | | taxation | |
| tapestry | | taxicab | |
| tapeworm | | taximeter | |
| tapioca | | tea | |
| tapir | | *teach* | |
| tapping | | *teachable* | |
| tapster | | teachableness | |
| tar | | *teacher* | |
| tarantula | | teak | |
| tardiness | | teakettle | |
| tardy | | teal | |
| tare | | team | |
| target | | teamster | |
| targeteer | | teapot | |
| tariff | | *tear* | |
| tarn | | *tearful* | |
| tarnish | | tearless | |
| tarpaulin | | tease | |
| tarry | | teasel | |

**TEASEL**

## TEASPOON

| | | | |
|---|---|---|---|
| teaspoon | *lsn* | tempt | |
| teat | *le* | temptation | |
| technic | *lknk* | tempter | |
| technical | *lknl* | tempting | |
| technicality | *lknkl)* | ten (10) | *10* |
| technique | *lknk,* | tenable | *lnb* |
| technological | *lknolk* | tenacious | *lnx* |
| technologist | *lknol,* | tenacity | *lns)* |
| technology | *lknol* | tenancy | *ln,* |
| ted | *ld* | tenant | *ln-* |
| tedious | *ldx* | tenantless | *ln-l²* |
| tedium | *lds* | tenantry | *ln-r,* |
| tee | *le* | tench | *lc* |
| teem | *le* | tend | *l——* |
| teeth | *lel* | tendency | *l——* |
| teetotal | *ttl* | tender | *J—²* |
| teetotaler | *Jttl* | *tenderness* | *J—²* |
| tegument | *lg-* | tendon | *l——m* |
| tegumentary | *lg-y* | tendril | *J—l* |
| telegram | *llg,* | tenebrous | *lnbx* |
| *telegraph* | *llgf* | tenement | *ln-* |
| telegrapher | *llgf* | tenet | *lnl* |
| telegraphic | *llgk* | tenfold | *10fol* |
| telegraphist | *llgf,* | tennis | *lns* |
| telegraphy | *llgf,* | tenon | *lnn* |
| teleology | *llol* | tenor | *Jn* |
| telepathy | *llpl,* | tenpence | *10p* |
| telephone | *llfn* | tense | *Vl* |
| telephonic | *llfnk* | tensible | *Vb* |
| telescope | *llskp* | tensile | *Vl* |
| telescopic | *llskpl* | tension | *lny* |
| *tell* | *ll* | tent | *l-* |
| *teller* | *Jl* | tentacle | *l-K* |
| temerity | *Jr)* | tentation | *l-1* |
| temper | *Jrp* | tentative | *l-v* |
| temperament | *lrp-* | tenter | *J-* |
| temperance | *lrp,* | tenth (10t) | *10l* |
| temperate | *lrpa* | tenuity | *lnu)* |
| temperature | *lrplu* | tenuous | *lnx* |
| tempest | *lrp,* | tenure | *lnu* |
| tempestuous | *lrpsx* | tepefaction | *lpfkj* |
| temple | *lrp* | tepefy | *lpf* |
| temporal | *lrpl* | tepid | *lpd* |
| temporality | *lrpl)* | tepidity | *lpd)* |
| temporary | *lrpj* | tepidness | *lpd²* |
| temporize | *lrpz* | teraphim | *lrf* |

## TERAPHIM

# TERCENTENARY

| | | | |
|---|---|---|---|
| tercentenary | *vrs—my* | tetanus | *ttnx* |
| teredo | *vrdo* | tether | *Je* |
| tergiversation | *Jrvsj* | tetragon | *Jlgn* |
| term | *vr* | tetrahedron | *JlHn* |
| termagant | *vrg—* | tetralogy | *Jlol* |
| terminable | *vrmb* | tetrarch | *Jlak* |
| terminal | *vrml* | tetrasyllable | *Jsll* |
| terminate | *vrma* | tetter | *Jl* |
| termination | *vrmj* | text | *lx* |
| terminational | *vrmjl* | textile | *lxl* |
| terminative | *vrmb* | texture | *lxu* |
| terminology | *vrmol* | than | *ln* |
| tern | *ln* | thane | *ln* |
| ternary | *lny* | thank | *lg* *lgf* *lgf'* |
| ternate | *lna* | thankful | *lgf* |
| terrace | *vrs* | thankfulness | *lgl'* |
| terracotta | *vrkla* | thankless | *lgl* |
| terraqueous | *vrgx* | thanksgiving | *lgsgt* |
| terrene | *lyn* | that | *la* |
| terrestrial | *vrsl* | thatch | *lc* |
| terrible | *lyb* | thaumaturgical | *ldryk* |
| terrier | *Jy* | thaumaturgy | *ldy, la* |
| terrific | *lyfk* | thaw | |
| terrify | *lyf* | the | |
| territorial | *lylyl* | theater | *Je Jek* |
| territory | *lyly* | theatrical | |
| terror | *Jr* | thee | *le* |
| terse | *vrs* | theft | *4 z* |
| tersely | *vrsl* | their | |
| terseness | *vrs'* | theism | *lez le,* |
| tertian | *vy* | theist | |
| tertiary | *vrjy* | theistic | *leS lest* |
| tesselate | *lsla* | theistical | |
| tesselation | *lslj* | them | *l* |
| test | *l,* | theme | *le* |
| testaceous | *lsx* | themselves | *lrs ln* |
| testament | *ls—* | then | *y ln* |
| testamentary | *ls-y* | thence | *V* |
| testate | *lsa* | thenceforth | *Vfl* |
| testator | *Jsa* | thenceforward | *Vfl* |
| testatrix | *Jsax* | theocracy | *leks, lekJ* |
| tester | *l8* | theocratic | |
| testify | *lsf* | theocratical | *lekll ledli* |
| testimonial | *lsml* | theodolite | |
| testimony | *lsm,* | theogony | *legn,* |
| testy | *ls,* | theologian | *leoln* |

THEOLOGICAL

| theological | *leolk leol* |
| theology | |
| theorem | *ler* |
| theoretic | *lert* |
| theoretical | *lerlt ler,* |
| theorist | |
| theorize | *lerz ley* |
| theory | |
| theosophist | *lesf, lesf,* |
| theosophy | |
| therapeutic | *lrpT* |
| *there* | *l* |
| thereabout | *lab laf* |
| thereafter | |
| thereat | *ll* |
| thereby | *lb lf* |
| therefor | |
| therefore | *lf lm* |
| therein | |
| thereinto | *lnl* |
| thereof | *lo lv* |
| thereon | *lo* |
| thereto | *llo* |
| thereupon | *lpn* |
| therewith | *lwl lw* |
| therewithal | |
| thermal | *brl, brrl* |
| thermodynamical | *brdmk* |
| thermodynamics | *brdmks* |
| thermometer | *brmle* |
| thermometric | *brmlek* |
| thermometrical | *brmlekl* |
| thesaurus | *lzrr lz* |
| *these* | |
| thesis | *lss* |
| theurgy | *lrj,* |
| thew | *lu ly* |
| *they* | |
| they'll | *lyl* |
| they're | *lyr lyr* |
| they've | *lyv lk* |
| *thick* | |
| thicken | *lkn lk* |
| *thicker* | |
| thicket | *lkl lk'* |
| thickness | |

| thief | *lef* |
| thieve | *le* |
| thievery | *ley lez* |
| thievish | |
| thigh | *li* |
| thimble | *lrb.* |
| thin | *ln* |
| thine | *ln* |
| thing | *lg lg* |
| think | *lg 2g* |
| thinker | |
| thinner | *ln ln* |
| thinness | *ln'* |
| third | *3d lr,* |
| thirst | |
| thirsty | *lrs, 13* |
| thirteen | |
| thirteenth | *13l 30l* |
| thirtieth | |
| thirty | *30* |
| *this* | *lh lsl* |
| thistle | *lsl* |
| thistly | *lsl* |
| thither | *2l l* |
| thitherward | *lol* |
| thole | |
| thong | *lg* |
| thorax | *lrx* |
| thorn | *lrn lrnbk* |
| thornback | |
| thorny | *lrn, lro* |
| thorough | |
| thoroughbred | *lrobd lrofa* |
| thoroughfare | |
| thoroughgoing | *lrog lro'* |
| thoroughness | |
| thorp | *lrp los* |
| those | |
| *thou* | *lu lo* |
| *though* | |
| thought | *tt* |
| those | *los* |
| *thou* | *lu lo* |
| *though* | |
| thought | *tt ttf* |
| thoughtful | |

THOUGHTFUL

## THOUGHTLESS

| | | | |
|---|---|---|---|
| thoughtless | | thumb | |
| *thousand* | | thumbkin | |
| thousandfold | | thumbscrew | |
| thousandth | | thump | |
| thraldom | | thumper | |
| thrall | | thumping | |
| thrash | | thunder | |
| thread | | thunderbolt | |
| threadbare | | thunderous | |
| threat | | thunderstorm | |
| threaten | | thunderstruck | |
| threatening | | thundery | |
| three | | *Thursday* | |
| threefold | | *thus* | |
| threepence | | *thusly* | |
| threeply | | thwack | |
| threescore | | thwart | |
| threnody | | thy | |
| thresh | | thyme | |
| threshold | | thyself | |
| threw | | tiara | |
| thrice | | tick | |
| thrift | | ticket | |
| thriftless | | tickle | |
| thrifty | | tidal | |
| thrill | | tide | |
| thrive | | tideway | |
| throat | | tidings | |
| throb | | tidy | |
| throe | | *tie* | |
| throne | | tier | |
| throng | | tierce | |
| throstle | | tiffin | |
| throttle | | tiger | |
| *through* | | tight | |
| throughout | | tighten | |
| *throw* | | tightness | |
| thrown | | tigress | |
| thrum | | tile | |
| thrumming | | *till* | |
| thrush | | *tiller* | |
| thrust | | tilt | |
| thud | | timber | |
| thug | | timbre | |
| thuggery | | timbrel | |
| thuggism | | *time* | |

**TIME**

187

| | | | |
|---|---|---|---|
| timeliness | | toadstool | |
| timely | | toady | |
| timeworn | | toadyism | |
| timid | | toast | |
| timidity | | tobacco | |
| timidness | | tobacconist | |
| timorous | | toboggan | |
| timothy | | tock | |
| tin | | tocsin | |
| tinctorial | | today | |
| tincture | | toddle | |
| tinder | | toddy | |
| tine | | toe | |
| tinfoil | | toga | |
| tinge | | together | |
| tingle | | toil | |
| tinker | | toilet | |
| tinkle | | toilsome | |
| tinsel | | token | |
| tint | | told | |
| tinfinnabulation | | tolerable | |
| tiny | | tolerant | |
| tip | | tolerate | |
| tippet | | toleration | |
| tipple | | toll | |
| tipstaff | | tomahawk | |
| tiptoe | | tomato | |
| tirade | | tomb | |
| tire | | tombstone | |
| tiresome | | tome | |
| tissue | | tomfoolery | |
| tit | | tomorrow | |
| titanic | | tomtit | |
| titbit | | ton | |
| tithe | | tone | |
| tither | | tongs | |
| tithing | | tongue | |
| titillate | | tonic | |
| titillation | | tonight | |
| title | | tonnage | |
| titmouse | | tonsil | |
| titter | | tonsilitis | |
| tittle | | tonsure | |
| titular | | tontine | |
| to | | too | |
| toad | | took | |

TOOK

## TOOL

| | | | |
|---|---|---|---|
| tool........... | *lul* | tournament.... | *brn—* |
| toot........... | *lu* | tourney........ | *brn,* |
| tooth........... | *lul* | tourniquet..... | *brnkl* |
| toothache....... | *ttak* | tout........... | *lul* |
| toothpick....... | *ttpk* | tow........... | *lo* |
| toothsome...... | *tts* | towage........ | *loy* |
| *top*............. | *lp* | *toward*........ | *ly* |
| topaz.......... | *lpos* | towel.......... | *lul* |
| toper.......... | *Jp* | towelling....... | *lul* |
| topic.......... | *lpk* | tower.......... | *lun* |
| topical......... | *lpl* | *town*.......... | *lun* |
| topmost........ | *lpro,* | township..... | *luns* |
| topographic..... | *lpgfk* | townsman...... | *luns* |
| topographical.... | *lpgfl* | toxic ......... | *lcik* |
| topography...... | *lpgf,* | toxicology..... | *lckol* |
| topple.......... | *lp lpslro;* | toy........... | *ly* |
| topsy-turvy..... | | toyish......... | *lyz* |
| torch.......... | *brc* | trace.......... | *las Zsb* |
| tore........... | *lo* | traceable...... | *Zsy* |
| torment........ | *br—* | tracery........ | *Zho* |
| tormentor....... | *Jr—* | trachea........ | *Zkl,* |
| torn........... | *brn* | tracheotomy.... | *las Zk* |
| tornado........ | *brndo* | tracing........ | *Zk'* |
| torpedo........ | *lrpdo* | track.......... | *Zkl' Zk"* |
| torpid......... | *lrpd* | trackless....... | *Zk lkb)* |
| torpidity....... | *lrpd)* | tracklessness... | *Zk* |
| torpor......... | *Jrp* | tract.......... | *Zkb lkl'* |
| torque......... | *brk* | tractability..... | |
| torrefy......... | *lyf* | tractable....... | *Zkl' Zk* |
| torrent........ | *br—* | tractableness... | *Zkl Zky* |
| torrid.......... | *brd* | tractile........ | *Zko Jk* |
| torsion........ | *brj* | traction........ | *ld* |
| tortoise........ | *l/s* | tractive........ | *Jd'* |
| torture......... | *l/u l'* | tractor......... | *Zds Jd'* |
| toss........... | *tt* | trade.......... | *Zdy* |
| tot............. | *ttl* | trader......... | |
| total.......... | *ttl)* | tradesman..... | *ldyl Zdyy* |
| totality......... | *til* | tradition....... | *lds lfk* |
| totally......... | *tts* | traditional..... | *Zydn Zyd,* |
| totem.......... | *Jl* | traditionary.... | *Zyk Zyl* |
| totter......... | *lc* | traduce........ | |
| *touch*........... | *lc'* | traffic......... | |
| *touchiness*...... | *lf lu* | tragedian...... | |
| tough.......... | *lu,* | tragedy........ | |
| tour........... | | tragic......... | |
| tourist......... | | tragical........ | |

## TRAGICAL

# TRAIL

trail...........

train..........

trainer.........

trait...........

traitor.........

traitorous.......

traitress........

trajection.......

trajectory.......

tram...........

trammel........

trammelling....

tramp..........

trample.........

trance..........

tranquil........

tranquilize......

tranquillity......

transact........

transaction......

transalpine......

transatlantic.....

transcend.......

transcendent....

transcendental...

transcribe.......

transcript.......

transcription....

transept........

transfer.........

transferable.....

transference.....

transferring.....

transfiguration...

transfigure......

transfigurement..

transfix.........

transform.......

transformation...

transformer.....

transfuse........

transfusible.....

transfusion......

transgress.......

transgression....

transgressor....

transient..........

transit.............

transition..........

transitive..........

transitory..........

translate...........

translation.........

translucency.......

translucent.........

transmigrate.......

transmigration......

transmissible.......

transmission.......

transmit...........

transmittal.........

transmutable.......

transmutation......

transmute..........

transom...........

transparence......

transparency.......

transparent........

transpire..........

transplant..........

transport...........

transportation......

transposal..........

transpose..........

transposition......

transubstantiation...

transversal.........

transverse..........

trap...............

trapeze.............

trapezoid...........

trapping...........

trash..............

trashy.............

travail.............

travel..............

traveler............

traverse............

travesty............

trawl..............

trawler............

tray...............

**TRAY**

| | | | |
|---|---|---|---|
| treacherous | | tribune | |
| treachery | | tributary | |
| treacle | | tribute | |
| tread | | trice | |
| treadle | | tricentenary | |
| treadmill | | trichinosis | |
| treason | | trick | |
| treasonable | | trickery | |
| treasure | | trickish | |
| treasurer | | trickle | |
| treasury | | trickster | |
| treat | | tricky | |
| treatise | | tricolor | |
| treatment | | tricycle | |
| treaty | | trident | |
| treble | | tried | |
| tree | | triennial | |
| trefoil | | tries | |
| trellis | | trifle | |
| tremble | | trifling | |
| tremendous | | trifoliate | |
| tremor | | trig | |
| tremulous | | trigger | |
| trench | | triglyph | |
| trenchant | | trigonometric | |
| trencher | | trigonometrical | |
| trend | | trigonometry | |
| trental | | trihedral | |
| trepan | | trilateral | |
| trephine | | trilingual | |
| trepidation | | triliteral | |
| trespass | | trill | |
| tress | | trillion | |
| trestle | | trilogy | |
| tret | | trim | |
| triad | | trimeter | |
| trial | | trinity | |
| triangle | | trinket | |
| triangular | | trinomial | |
| triangulate | | *trio | |
| triangulation | | triolet | |
| tribal | | trip | |
| tribe | | tripartite | |
| tribrach | | tripe | |
| tribulation | | tripedal | |
| tribunal | | triphthongal | |

TRIPLE

| | | | |
|---|---|---|---|
| triple | | trousers | |
| triplet | | trousseau | |
| triplicate | | trout | |
| tripod | | trow | |
| tripos | | trowel | |
| triptych | | troy | |
| trireme | | truancy | |
| trisect | | truant | |
| trisection | | truantship | |
| trisyllabic | | truce | |
| trisyllable | | truck | |
| trite | | truckage | |
| triturable | | truckle | |
| triturate | | truculence | |
| trituration | | truculency | |
| triumph | | truculent | |
| triumphal | | trudge | |
| triumphant | | *true* | |
| triumvir | | *truer* | |
| triumvirate | | truffle | |
| triune | | truism | |
| trivet | | trull | |
| trivial | | truly | |
| triviality | | trump | |
| trivialness | | trumpery | |
| trochee | | trumpet | |
| trod | | trumpeter | |
| trodden | | truncate | |
| troglodyte | | truncheon | |
| troll | | trundle | |
| trolley | | trunk | |
| trombone | | trunnion | |
| troop | | truss | |
| *troops* | | trust | |
| trope | | trustee | |
| trophy | | trustful | |
| tropic | | trustworthiness | |
| tropical | | trustworthy | |
| trot | | trusty | |
| troth | | *truth* | |
| troubadour | | truthful | |
| *trouble* | | truthfulness | |
| troublesome | | truthless | |
| troublous | | try | |
| trough | | tryst | |
| trounce | | tsetse | |

TSETSE

## TUB

| | | | |
|---|---|---|---|
| tub............ | | turbulent...... | |
| tube........... | | tureen......... | |
| tuber.......... | | turf.......... | |
| tubercle....... | | turfy......... | |
| tuberculosis..... | | turgent....... | |
| tuberculous..... | | turgescent..... | |
| tubular......... | | turgid........ | |
| tubule......... | | turkey........ | |
| tubulous........ | | turmoil....... | |
| tuck........... | | *turn*.......... | |
| *Tuesday*........ | | turnery....... | |
| tuft........... | | turning........ | |
| tufty.......... | | turnip........ | |
| tug............ | | turnover...... | |
| tuition......... | | turnpike...... | |
| tulip.......... | | turnstile...... | |
| tulle.......... | | turpentine.... | |
| tumble......... | | turpitude.. .. | |
| tumbler........ | | turquoise..... | |
| tumbrel....... | | turret........ | |
| tumefaction..... | | turtle........ | |
| tumefy......... | | tush.......... | |
| tumid......... | | tusk.......... | |
| tumor......... | | tussle........ | |
| tumult......... | | tut........... | |
| tumultuary....... | | tutelage....... | |
| tumultuous...... | | tutelar........ | |
| tumulus........ | | tutelary....... | |
| tun............ | | tutor.......... | |
| tune........... | | tutorage....... | |
| tuneful......... | | tutoress....... | |
| tunefulness..... | | tutorial........ | |
| tuneless........ | | tutorship...... | |
| tunic.......... | | twaddle........ | |
| tunnage........ | | twain......... | |
| tunnel......... | | twang........ | |
| tunny......... | | tweak......... | |
| tup............ | | tweed........ | |
| turban.......... | | tweezers...... | |
| turbary........ | | twelfth........ | |
| turbid........ | | twelve........ | |
| turbinate...... | | twelvemonth... | |
| turbine........ | | twentieth...... | |
| turbot........ | | twenty........ | |
| turbulence...... | | twice.......... | |
| turbulency...... | | twig.......... | |

twilight........
twill..........
twin..........
twine..........
twinge........
twinkle........
twirl..........
twist..........
twit..........
twitch........
twitter........
two ........
twofold ...
tympanum....
type..........
typewriter......

typewriting........
typhoid..........
typhoon..........
typhus..........
typical..........
typify..........
typographic......
typographical......
typography........
tyrannic ..........
tyrannical ........
tyrannize........
tyrannous.........
tyranny..........
tyrant..........
tyro..............

# U

ubiquitous.....
ubiquity........
udder..........
ugliness........
ugly............
ukase..........
ukulele........
ulcer..........
ulcerate........
ulceration......
ulcerous........
ulster..........
*ulterior* ........
ultimate........
ultimatum.....
ultimo........
ultramarine.....
ultramontane...
umbel........
umber..........
umbilic........
umbilical........
umbrage........
umbrella........
umpire........
unabashed.....
unabated......

unable............
unabridged........
unaccented........
unacceptable......
unaccommodating..
unaccompanied....
*unaccountable* .....
unaccustomed.....
unacknowledged...
unacquainted......
unadorned........
unadulterated....
unadvisable.......
unadvised........
unaffected........
*unafraid* ..........
unaided..........
unalloyed........
unalterable........
unambitious.......
unamiable........
unanimity........
unanimous........
unanswerable.....
unappalled........
unappreciated....
unapproachable....

**UNAPT**

| | |
|---|---|
| unapt.......... *uap* | unchain........... *ucn* |
| unarm.......... *uas* | unchanged........ *ucj* |
| unasked........ *usk* | uncharitable...... *ucylb* |
| unassailable.... *uaslb* | uncharitableness... *ucylb'* |
| unassuming.... *uasy* | unchaste.......... *uc,* |
| unattached...... *uate* | unchecked........ *uck* |
| unattainable..... *uatnb* | unchurch..... *ucrc* |
| unattended...... *uat* | uncial............ *ux* |
| unattractive..... *uakv* | unciform.......... *usf* |
| unauthorized.... *udj* | uncircumcision.... *uCsy* |
| unavailable..... *uavlb* | uncircumcised..... *uCsj* |
| unavailing...... *uavl* | uncivil........... *usvl* |
| unavoidable..... *uavyb* | uncivilized....... *usvlj* |
| unaware........ *uara* | unclasp........... *uklsp* |
| unbalanced..... *ubal* | uncle............ *ugl* |
| unbar.......... *uba* | unclean.......... *ukln* |
| unbearable...... *ubab* | uncleanness....... *ukln'* |
| unbecoming..... *ubk* | unclose........... *uklz* |
| unbegot........ *ubgt* | unclothed......... *uklt* |
| unbegotten ..... *ubgtn* | unclouded........ *ukld* |
| unbelief........ *ublf* | uncoil............ *ukyl* |
| unbend......... *ub* | uncomely....... *ukl* |
| unbending...... *ub* | uncomfortable..... *ukflb* |
| unbiased........ *ube,* | uncommon........ *ukn* |
| unbidden....... *ubdn* | uncomplaining.... *ukpn* |
| unbind......... *ube* | uncompromising... *ukpz* |
| unbelieving..... *uble* | unconcern........ *ukkn* |
| unbleached..... *ube* | unconditional...... *ukdgl* |
| unblemished.... *ubz* | uncongenial....... *ukjnl* |
| unblessed....... *ub,* | unconnected...... *uknk* |
| unblushing...... *ubz* | unconquerable..... *ukgl* |
| unbolt.......... *ublt* | unconscionable..... *ukjb* |
| unborn......... *ubrn* | unconscious....... *ukx* |
| unbosom........ *ubz* | unconsidered...... *ukto* |
| unbound........ *ubd* | unconstitutional... *ukslyl* |
| unbrace........ *ubo* | unconstrained...... *ukf* |
| unbreakable..... *ubkb* | uncontested........ *ukto* |
| unbridled....... *ubdl* | uncontrollable...... *uktlb* |
| unbroken........ *ubkn* | unconverted........ *ukvj* |
| unbuckle....... *ubk* | uncork........... *ukrk* |
| unburden........ *ub/n* | uncounted........ *ukt* |
| unbutton........ *ubtn* | uncouple........ *ukp* |
| uncalled........ *ukt* | uncourteous....... *uk/x* |
| unceasing....... *uss* | uncouth........... *ukt* |
| uncertain........ *us/n* | uncover........... *ukv* |
| uncertainty...... *us/-,* | uncrowned......... *uk* |

**UNCROWNED**

## UNCTION

unction.........
unctuous........
uncultivated.....
uncurl..........
uncut...........
undaunted......
undeceive.......
undecided......
undefended.....
undefiled.......
undefined.......
undelivered.....
undeniable......
under..........
underbid........
underbrush.....
undercurrent....
undercut........
underdone......
underestimate...
underfoot.......
undergo........
underground....
undergrowth....
underhand......
underlay........
underline.......
underling.......
undermine......
undermost......
underneath.....
underpaid.......
underpin........
underrate.......
underscore......
undersell........
undershirt......
undersign.......
undersized......
understand......
understanding...
understood......
understudy......
undertake.......
undertaker......
undertaking.....

undertone......
undertook......
undervalue.....
underwaist.....
underwear.....
underwent......
Underwood.....
underwrite......
undeserved.....
undesigned.....
undesirable.....
undetected......
undetermined...
undeviating.....
undigested......
undignified......
undiminished...
undiscernible....
undiscerning....
undisciplined....
undisguised.....
undismayed.....
undisputed.....
undisturbed.....
undivided.......
undo...........
undoing........
undone.........
undoubted......
undress.........
undulate........
undulation......
undulatory......
unduly.........
undutiful.......
undying........
unearned.......
unearth........
unearthly.......
uneasy.........
uneducated.....
unembarrassed..
unembodied.....
unemployed.....
unending.......
unengaged......

UNENGAGED

| | | | | |
|---|---|---|---|---|
| unenlightened... | | unfulfilled....... | |
| unenviable...... | | unfurl.......... | |
| unenvied....... | | unfurnished..... | |
| unequal......... | | ungainly ....... | |
| unequivocal..... | | ungentle........ | |
| unerring........ | | ungird.......... | |
| unessential.... | | ungodly......... | |
| uneven......... | | ungracious...... | |
| uneventful...... | | ungrateful...... | |
| unexampled..... | | ungrounded..... | |
| unexceptionable. | | ungrudging...... | |
| unexhausted.... | | unguarded....... | |
| unexpected...... | | unguent........ | |
| unexplained..... | | unhallowed..... | |
| unexplored..... | | unhand.......... | |
| unexpressed ..... | | unhandy........ | |
| unfaded........ | | unhappy........ | |
| unfailing....... | | unharmed...... | |
| unfair......... | | unharnessed.... | |
| unfaithfulness... | | unhealthful..... | |
| unfamiliar...... | | unhealthy...... | |
| unfashionable... | | unheard........ | |
| unfasten........ | | unheeding...... | |
| unfathomable... | | unhesitating..... | |
| unfavorable..... | | unhinge........ | |
| unfeeling....... | | unholy......... | |
| unfeigned...... | | unhonored...... | |
| unfelt.......... | | unhook......... | |
| unfettered...... | | unhorse........ | |
| unfilial......... | | unhoused...... | |
| unfinished...... | | unhurt.......... | |
| unfit........... | | unicorn......... | |
| unflagging...... | | unification...... | |
| unflattering... | | uniform......... | |
| unfledged....... | | uniformity...... | |
| unflinching..... | | uniformly...... | |
| unfold.......... | | unify.......... | |
| unforeseen..... | | unilateral...... | |
| unforetold..... | | unimpaired..... | |
| unforgiving..... | | unimpeachable... | |
| unformed....... | | unimportant..... | |
| unfortunate..... | | unimproved.... | |
| unfounded...... | | uninjured....... | |
| unfrequented.... | | unintelligible.... | |
| unfriendly...... | | uninterrupted.... | |
| unfruitful....... | | union........... | |

# UNIQUE

| Word | Shorthand |
|---|---|
| unique.......... | *uk* |
| unison.......... | *usn* |
| unit............ | *ul* |
| *unite*........... | *unu* |
| unity........... | *u)* |
| univalve....... | *uvlv* |
| universal...... | *uvrsl* |
| universality..... | *uvrsl)* |
| universe........ | *uvrs* |
| university....... | *uvrs)* |
| *unjust*......... | *uj,* |
| unkempt........ | *uk* |
| *unkept*........ | *ukp* |
| *unkind*........ | *uki* |
| unkindness...... | *uki'* |
| *unknown*....... | *uno* |
| unlawful........ | *ulaf* |
| *unlearn*........ | *uln* |
| unlearned....... | *ulñ* |
| *unless*......... | *ul'* |
| unlettered...... | *ul̄* |
| unlike.......... | *ulk* |
| *unload*......... | *uld* |
| unlock.......... | *ulk* |
| unlocked....... | *ulk* |
| unloose......... | *ulus* |
| *unloving*........ | *ulv* |
| unlucky......... | *ulk,* |
| unmake........ | *umk* |
| unman......... | *um-* |
| unmeaning...... | *umn* |
| unmoor........ | *umr* |
| *unmount*....... | *um-* |
| *unmove*........ | *umv* |
| unmoved....... | *umṽ* |
| unmuffle........ | *umfl* |
| unmuzzle....... | *umzl* |
| unnatural....... | *uNal* |
| unnecessary..... | *unec* |
| unnerve........ | *unrv* |
| *unnoticed*....... | *unt,* |
| unoccupied...... | *uokpī* |
| *unopen*......... | *uop* |
| unpack......... | *upk* |
| unpaid.......... | *upd* |
| unparalleled..... | *ull* |
| unpeople......... | *upp* |
| unpitied.......... | *up)* |
| unpleasant....... | *upz* |
| unprecedented.... | *upsd=* |
| unpretending..... | *upt—* |
| unprincipled....... | *uppī* |
| unprofitable....... | *upfll* |
| unpunished....... | *upnz* |
| unqualified...... | *uglf* |
| unquestionable.... | *ugb* |
| unquestioned...... | *uḡ* |
| unquiet.......... | *ugl* |
| unravel.......... | *urvl* |
| unreal.......... | *url* |
| unreason........ | *urzn* |
| unreasonable...... | *urznl* |
| unrest.......... | *ur,* |
| unrestrained..... | *urs—* |
| unrighteous....... | *urx* |
| unrighteousness... | *urx'* |
| unruly.......... | *url,* |
| unsafe.......... | *usf* |
| unsaid.......... | *usd* |
| unsay.......... | *usa* |
| unscathed........ | *uskt* |
| unscrew........ | *usku* |
| unscrupulous..... | *uskplt* |
| unsearchable...... | *uscb* |
| unseat......... | *use* |
| *unseemly*........ | *usel* |
| unseen.......... | *usn* |
| unselfish........ | *usf* |
| unsettled........ | *ustl* |
| unshaken........ | *uzkn* |
| unsheathe....... | *uzt* |
| unship.......... | *uz* |
| unsightly........ | *usl* |
| unskilful.......... | *usklf* |
| unsought........ | *usl* |
| unsound......... | *us—* |
| unspeakable....... | *uskb* |
| unspotted........ | *ust* |
| unstable......... | *usb* |
| unstained........ | *usn̄* |
| unsteady......... | *usd,* |
| unstop.......... | *usp* |

| | | | | |
|---|---|---|---|---|
| unstring........ | *usg* | upheld......... | *phl* | |
| unsuccessful..... | *usuc* | uphill.......... | *phl* | |
| *unsuitable*...... | *usub* | uphold......... | *phol* | |
| unsuspected..... | *ussk* | upholster....... | *phls* | |
| untaught........ | *utt* | upholstery..... | *phls,* | |
| *unteachable*.... | *ulcb* | upland......... | *pl—* | |
| unthinking ..... | *ulg* | uplift.......... | *plf* | |
| unthread........ | *uld* | *upon*.......... | *pn* | *p* |
| untidy.......... | *uld,* | upper.......... | | |
| *untie*.......... | *uli* | uppermost...... | *P–o,* | |
| *until*.......... | *ul* | upright......... | | *pru* |
| untimely........ | *uhl* | uprightness..... | *pri'* | |
| untiring......... | *uli* | uprise......... | *prz* | |
| unto........... | *ulo* | uproar........ | *pro* | |
| *untold*......... | *ulol* | uproarious..... | | *prox* |
| *untouched*...... | *uli* | uproot........ | *pru* | |
| untoward....... | *ul/* | upset.......... | *psl* | |
| untried........ | *uli* | upshoot........ | *pzu* | |
| untrod......... | *uld* | upside........ | *psd* | |
| *untrue*......... | *ulu* | upstairs........ | *psas* | |
| untruth........ | *utt* | upstart........ | *psl* | |
| unturn......... | *uln* | upward........ | *p/* | |
| untwine....... | *ulwn* | urban.......... | *ubn* | |
| *unusual*........ | *ul* | urbane......... | *ubn* | |
| unveil.......... | *uvl* | urbanity....... | *ubn)* | |
| unwarp........ | *uwrp* | urchin........ | *ucn* | |
| *unwearable*..... | *uwab* | urge.......... | *uj* | *uy* |
| unweary........ | *uwry* | urgency........ | | |
| unweave........ | *uwe* | urgent......... | *uy-* | |
| unwed.......... | *uwd* | urn........... | *un* | |
| unwelcome...... | *uwlk* | *us*........... | | *us* |
| unwept........ | *uwp* | U. S. ........ | *US* | |
| unwieldy....... | *uwld,* | usable......... | *uzb* | |
| *unwilling*....... | *ul* | usage......... | *usy* | |
| *unwind*........ | *uw—* | *use*.......... | *us'* | *uz* |
| unwise........ | *uwz* | *useful*........ | *usf* | |
| unwittingly..... | *uwll* | useless........ | *usl'* | |
| *unworthy*...... | *uwrl,* | usher......... | *Uz* | |
| unwoven........ | *uwon* | using.......... | *uz* | |
| unwrap........ | *uwrp* | *usual*......... | *x* | |
| unyoke........ | *uyk* | usurp......... | *usp* | |
| *up*............ | *p* | usurpation...... | *uspy* | |
| upbraid......... | *pbd* | usurious........ | *usx* | |
| upbraiding...... | *pbd* | usury......... | *usy* | |
| upheaval........ | *phel* | utensil......... | *utl* | |
| upheave....... | *phe* | utilitarian....... | *ullyn* | |

## UTILITARIANISM

utilitarianism...
utility........
utilize........
utmost........
utter..........

utterable......
utterance.....
utterly........
uttermost.....
uvula.........

## V

vacancy........
vacant.........
vacate.........
vacation.......
vaccinate......
vaccination.....
vaccine.........
vacillant.......
vacillate.......
vacillation......
vacillatory......
vacuity........
vacuous........
vacuum........
vagabond......
vagabondage....
vagabondism....
vagary.........
vagrancy.......
vagrant........
vague..........
vagueness......
vail...........
vain...........
vainglorious....
valance........
vale...........
valediction.....
valedictory......
valentine.......
valerian........
valet..........
valetudinarian..
valiant.........
valiantly.......
valid..........
validity........
validness......

valise........
valley........
valor.........
valorous......
valuable......
valuation......
valuator......
value.........
valued........
valve.........
valvular......
vamp.........
vampire......
van..........
vandalism.....
vane.........
vanguard......
vanilla........
vanish........
vanity........
vanquish......
vantage.......
vapid.........
vapidity.......
vapidness.....
vapor.........
vaporization...
vaporize.......
vaporous......
vapory........
variable.......
variance.......
variation......
varicose......
variegated....
variety.......
various.......
varlet........

## VARNISH

| | |
|---|---|
| varnish | *vrnʒ* |
| vary | *vry* |
| vase | *vas* |
| vassal | *vsl* |
| vassalage | *vslʒ* |
| vast | *vs,* |
| vastness | *vs`* |
| vat | *vt* |
| vaticinate | *vtsna* |
| vaticination | *vtsnʒ* |
| vaudeville | *vdvl* |
| vault | *vll* |
| vaunt | *va-* |
| veal | *vel* |
| vedette | *vdt* |
| veer | *ve* |
| vegetable | *vgtb* |
| vegetarian | *vgtyn* |
| vegetarianism | *vgtynz* |
| vegetate | *vgta* |
| vegetation | *vgly* |
| vegetative | *vgtv* |
| vehemence | *vr* |
| vehemency | *vr* |
| vehement | *v-* |
| vehicle | *vk* |
| vehicular | *vkl* |
| veil | *val* |
| vein | *vn* |
| vellum | *vl* |
| velocipede | *vlspd* |
| velocity | *vls)* |
| velvet | *vlvt* |
| velveteen | *vlvtn* |
| velvety | *vlvt,* |
| venal | *vnl* |
| venality | *vnl)* |
| vend | *v—* |
| vendetta | *v—la* |
| vendible | *v—b* |
| vendor | *V—* |
| veneer | *vne* |
| veneering | *vne* |
| venerable | *Vnb* |
| venerate | *Vna* |
| veneration | *Vny* |

| | |
|---|---|
| venery | *vny* |
| Venetian | *vny* |
| vengeance | *vʒ* |
| vengeful | *vʒl* |
| venial | *vnl* |
| venison | *vnsn* |
| venom | *vn* |
| venomous | *vn-v* |
| vent | *v-* |
| ventilate | *v-la* |
| ventilation | *v-lʒ* |
| ventilator | *V-la* |
| ventral | *V-l* |
| ventricle | *V-K* |
| ventriloquism | *V-lgz* |
| ventriloquist | *V-lg,* |
| ventriloquy | *V-lg,* |
| venture | *v-u* |
| venturesome | *v-us* |
| venturous | *v-ux* |
| venue | *vnu* |
| veracious | *vrx* |
| veracity | *vrs)* |
| veranda | *vr—a* |
| verb | *vrb* |
| verbal | *vrbl* |
| verbatim | *vrbt* |
| verbena | *vrbna* |
| verbiage | *vrby* |
| verdant | *v-/* |
| verdict | *v/k* |
| verdigris | *v/gs* |
| verdure | *v/u* |
| verge | *vry* |
| verger | *Vry* |
| verifiable | *vfb* |
| verification | *vf* |
| verify | *vf* |
| verily | *vl* |
| verisimilar | *vsrl* |
| verisimilitude | *vsrlld* |
| veritable | *vtb* |
| verity | *vr)* |
| verjuice | *vrjs* |
| vermicelli | *vrssl* |
| vermicular | *Vrkl* |

**VERMICULAR**

# VERMICULATE

| | |
|---|---|
| vermiculate | *vr kla* |
| vermiculation | *vr kly* |
| vermiform | *vrf* |
| vermillion | *vr* |
| vermin | *vr m* |
| vernacular | *vrnll* |
| vernal | *vrnl* |
| vernation | *vrny* |
| vernier | *vrne* |
| versatile | *vrsll* |
| versatility | *vrsll)* |
| verse | *vrs* |
| versification | *vrsf* |
| versify | *vrsf* |
| version | *vry* |
| verst | *vr,* |
| versus | *vs* |
| vertebra | *v/ba* |
| vertebrae | *v/bl* *v/be* |
| vertebral | *v/bl* |
| vertebrate | *v/ba* |
| vertex | *v/x* *v/K* |
| vertical | *v/K* |
| vertigo | *v/9* |
| vervain | *vrm* |
| verve | *vrv* |
| *very* | *v* |
| vesicle | *vsK* |
| vesicular | *Vskl* |
| vesiculous | *vsklx* |
| vesper | *Vs -* |
| vessel | *vsl* |
| vest | *v,* |
| vestal | *vsl* |
| vestibule | *vsbl* |
| vestige | *vsy* |
| vestment | *vs-* |
| vestry | *vs,* |
| vestryman | *vs -* |
| vesture | *vsu* |
| vetch | *vc* |
| veteran | *Vln* |
| veterinary | *Vlny* |
| veto | *vlo* |
| vetoist | *vlo,* |
| vex | *vx* |

| | |
|---|---|
| vexation | *vy* |
| vexatious | *vx* |
| via | *v* |
| viaduct | *vdk* |
| vial | *vl* |
| viameter | *v se* |
| viand | *v ___* |
| viaticum | *vlk* |
| vibrate | *vba* |
| vibration | *vby* *vbly* |
| vibratory | *vbly* |
| vicar | *Vk* *vk* |
| vicarage | *vhy* |
| vicarial | *Vkl* |
| vicariate | *vkr* *Vka* |
| vicarious | *vkx* |
| vicarship | *vk3* |
| vice | *vs* |
| vicegerent | *vsyr-* |
| viceregal | *vsrgl* |
| viceroy | *vsry* |
| viceroyalty | *vsryll,* |
| vicinage | *vsny* |
| vicinity | *vsn)* |
| vicious | *vc* |
| vicissitude | *vssld* |
| victim | *vk* |
| victimize | *vk3* *vk* |
| victor | *Vkx* |
| victorious | *Vkx* |
| victory | *Vk,* |
| victual | *vll* |
| *view* | *vu* |
| viewless | *vul'* |
| vigil | *vyl* *vyl* |
| vigilance | *vyl* |
| vigilant | *vyl-* |
| vignette | *vnl* *Vg* |
| vigor | *Vgx* |
| vigorous | *Vgx* |
| vile | *vl'* *vl* |
| vileness | *vl'* |
| vilify | *vlf* |
| vilipend | *vlp —* |
| villa | *vla* |
| *village* | *vly* |

### VILLAGER

| | |
|---|---|
| villager......... | |
| villain.......... | |
| villainous....... | |
| villainy......... | |
| vincible......... | |
| vinculum........ | |
| vindicate........ | |
| vindication...... | |
| vindicator....... | |
| vindictive....... | |
| vine............ | |
| vinegar......... | |
| vinery.......... | |
| vineyard........ | |
| vintage......... | |
| viol............ | |
| viola........... | |
| violable........ | |
| violate......... | |
| violation........ | |
| violator......... | |
| violence........ | |
| violent.......... | |
| violet........... | |
| violin.......... | |
| violinist........ | |
| violoncello...... | |
| viper........... | |
| viperous........ | |
| virago.......... | |
| virgin.......... | |
| virginal......... | |
| virginity........ | |
| viridity......... | |
| virile........... | |
| virility.......... | |
| virtual.......... | |
| virtually........ | |
| virtue.......... | |
| virtuoso........ | |
| virtuous........ | |
| virulence........ | |
| virulent......... | |
| virus........... | |
| visage.......... | |
| viscera......... | |

| | |
|---|---|
| viscid......... | |
| viscidity...... | |
| viscosity...... | |
| viscount...... | |
| vise.......... | |
| vise.......... | |
| visibility...... | |
| visible........ | |
| visibleness.... | |
| vision........ | |
| visionary...... | |
| visit ......... | |
| visitation..... | |
| visitor........ | |
| visor......... | |
| vista......... | |
| visual........ | |
| vital......... | |
| vitality....... | |
| vitalize....... | |
| vitamines..... | |
| vitiate........ | |
| vitreous...... | |
| vitrify........ | |
| vitriol........ | |
| vituperate..... | |
| vituperation.. | |
| vituperative... | |
| vivacious...... | |
| vivacity...... | |
| vivid... ...... | |
| vividness..... | |
| vivification.... | |
| vivify........ | |
| viviparous..... | |
| vivisection.... | |
| vixen.. ...... | |
| vizier......... | |
| vocable....... | |
| vocabulary.... | |
| vocal......... | |
| vocalist....... | |
| vocalize....... | |
| vocation...... | |
| vocative...... | |
| vociferate..... | |

### VOCIFERATE

## VOCIFERATION

| | | | | |
|---|---|---|---|---|
| vociferation | *vsff* | voluptuary | *vlpy* |
| vociferous | *vsfx* | voluptuous | *vlpx* |
| vogue | *voq* | volute | *vlu* |
| voice | *vy vyl* | vomit | *vol* |
| voiceless | | vomitory | *voly* |
| void | *vyd* | voracious | *vrx* |
| voidable | *vydb* | voracity | *vrs)* |
| voil | *vyl* | vortex | *v/x* |
| volant | *vl-* | vortices | *v/ss* |
| volatile | *vlll* | votaress | *vo'* |
| volatileness | *vell'* | votary | *Vo,* |
| volatility | *vlil)* | vote | *vo* |
| volatilize | *vlllz* | voter | *Vo* |
| volcanic | *vlkk* | vouch | *vvc* |
| volcano | *vlko* | voucher | *vvc* |
| vole | *vol* | vow | *v* |
| volition | *vly* | vowel | *vvl* |
| volley | *vl,* | voyage | *vyf* |
| volt | *vll* | vulcanize | *vlkz* |
| voltaic | *vllak* | vulgar | *Vlg* |
| voltaism | *vllz* | vulgarism | *Vlgz* |
| voluble | *vlb* | vulgarity | *Vlg)* |
| volubility | *vlb)* | vulgarize | *Vlgz* |
| volume | *vol* | vulnerability | *Vlnb)* |
| voluminous | *vl-x* | vulnerable | *Vlnb* |
| voluntary | *vl-y* | vulture | *vllu* |
| voluntaryism | *vl-yz* | vulturine | *vllun* |
| volunteer | *vl-e* | vulturish | *vlluz* |

## W

| | | | | |
|---|---|---|---|---|
| wabble | *b* | waggle | *gl* |
| wad | *d* | wagon | *gn gn* |
| waddle | *dl* | wagoner | *gn* |
| wade | *d* | waif | *af* |
| wady | *d,* | wail | *al* |
| wafer | *f* | wailing | *al* |
| wafery | *fy* | wain | *n* |
| waffle | *fl* | wainscot | *nskt* |
| waft | *f* | waist | *a,* |
| wag | *g* | waistband | *sb-* |
| wage | *aj* | waistcoat | *sko* |
| wager | *j* | wait | *a a* |
| waggery | *gy* | waiter | *a'* |
| wagging | *g-* | waitress | *a'* |
| waggishness | *gz'* | waive | *a* |

WAIVE

## WAKE

| | | | |
|---|---|---|---|
| wake........... | | warrant....... | |
| wakeful......... | | warrantable.... | |
| wakefulness..... | | warranter..... | |
| waken.......... | | warranty...... | |
| *walk*........... | | warrantise.... | |
| *walker*.......... | | warren........ | |
| *wall*............ | | warrior....... | |
| wallet.......... | | warship....... | |
| walloon........ | | wart.......... | |
| wallop......... | | wary......... | |
| wallow........ | | *was*.......... | |
| walnut......... | | *wash*......... | |
| walrus........ | | *washable*..... | |
| waltz.......... | | washboard..... | |
| wampum........ | | washer........ | |
| wan........... | | wasn't........ | |
| wand.......... | | wasp......... | |
| wander........ | | waspish....... | |
| wanderer...... | | wassail....... | |
| wane.......... | | wassailer..... | |
| *want*.......... | | *wast*......... | |
| wantage........ | | *waste*......... | |
| wanted........ | | wasteful...... | |
| wanting........ | | waster........ | |
| wanton........ | | wastrel....... | |
| wantonness..... | | *watch*........ | |
| *war*........... | | *watcher*....... | |
| warble........ | | watchful...... | |
| warbler........ | | watchman..... | |
| ward ........ | | watchword..... | |
| warden........ | | water......... | |
| warder........ | | watercourse.... | |
| wardrobe....... | | watercress..... | |
| ware.......... | | waterfall...... | |
| warehouse...... | | waterfowl..... | |
| warfare. ....... | | waterman..... | |
| wariness........ | | watermelon.... | |
| warlike........ | | waterproof..... | |
| warlock........ | | waterspout..... | |
| *warm*.......... | | watery........ | |
| *warmer*........ | | watt.......... | |
| warmness...... | | wattle......... | |
| warmth........ | | waul.......... | |
| warn.......... | | *wave*......... | |
| warning........ | | waveless...... | |
| warp.......... | | wavelet....... | |

**WAVELET**

| | | | |
|---|---|---|---|
| waveless | | weedy | |
| wavelet | | *week* | |
| *waver* | | weekday | |
| wax | | *weekly* | |
| waxen | | ween | |
| waxy | | weep | |
| *way* | | weevil | |
| wayfarer | | weft | |
| waylay | | weigh | |
| wayless | | *weight* | |
| wayside | | weighty | |
| *wayward* | | weir | |
| *we* | | weird | |
| weak | | welaway | |
| weaken | | welcome | |
| *weaker* | | weld | |
| weakling | | welfare | |
| *weakness* | | welkin | |
| weal | | *well* | |
| weald | | well (adjective) | |
| wealth | | we'll | |
| wealthy | | welladay | |
| wean | | well-known | |
| weapon | | welsh | |
| *wear* | | welt | |
| *wearable* | | welter | |
| *wearer* | | wen | |
| weariness | | wench | |
| wearisome | | wend | |
| weary | | *went* | |
| weasand | | wept | |
| weasel | | *were* | |
| *weather* | | we're | |
| weatherbeaten | | wergild | |
| weathercock | | wert | |
| weave | | *west* | |
| weaver | | westerly | |
| web | | western | |
| wed | | *westward* | |
| we'd | | wet | |
| wedding | | wetness | |
| wedge | | wettish | |
| wedlock | | we've | |
| *Wednesday* | | wey | |
| wee | | whack | |
| weed | | whale | |

WHALEBONE

| | | | |
|---|---|---|---|
| whalebone | | whet | |
| whaler | | whether | |
| whaling | | whetstone | |
| wharf | | whew | |
| wharfage | | whey | |
| wharfinger | | which | |
| wharves | | whichever | |
| *what* | | whichsoever | |
| whate'er | | whiff | |
| whatever | | whiffle | |
| whatnot | | *while* | |
| whatsoever | | whilst | |
| wheal | | whim | |
| *wheat* | | whimper | |
| wheaten | | whimsey | |
| wheedle | | whimsical | |
| *wheel* | | whine | |
| wheelbarrow | | whinny | |
| wheeler | | whinstone | |
| wheelwright | | whip | |
| wheeze | | whippet | |
| whelk | | whir | |
| whelm | | whirl | |
| whelp | | whirligig | |
| *when* | | whirlpool | |
| whence | | whirlwind | |
| whencesoever | | whisk | |
| whene'er | | whisker | |
| whenever | | whisky | |
| whensoever | | whisper | |
| *where* | | whist | |
| whereas | | whistle | |
| whereat | | whit | |
| whereby | | *white* | |
| wherefore | | whiten | |
| wherein | | *whiteness* | |
| whereof | | *whiter* | |
| whereon | | whitewash | |
| wheresoever | | whither | |
| whereto | | whithersoever | |
| whereunto | | whitish | |
| whereupon | | whitlow | |
| wherever | | whittle | |
| wherewith | | whiz | |
| wherewithal | | *who* | |
| wherry | | whoever | |

WHOEVER

WHOLE

| | | | |
|---|---|---|---|
| whole | | wily | |
| wholeness | | wimble | |
| wholesale | | wimple | |
| wholesome | | win | |
| wholly | | wince | |
| whom | | winch | |
| whoop | | wind | |
| whore | | windage | |
| whorl | | windbound | |
| whortleberry | | windfall | |
| whose | | winding | |
| whosoever | | windlass | |
| whoso | | windmill | |
| why | | window | |
| wick | | windpipe | |
| wicked | | windward | |
| wickedness | | windy | |
| wicker | | wine | |
| wicket | | wine-bibber | |
| wide | | wing | |
| widely | | wink | |
| widen | | winkle | |
| wider | | winner | |
| widow | | winning | |
| widower | | winnow | |
| widowhood | | winsome | |
| width | | winter | |
| wield | | wintry | |
| wieldy | | wipe | |
| wife | | wire | |
| wifely | | wiredraw | |
| wig | | wireless | |
| wight | | wis | |
| wigwam | | wisdom | |
| wild | | wise | |
| wilder | | wiseacre | |
| wilderness | | wisely | |
| wildfire | | wiser | |
| wildly | | wish | |
| wile | | wisher | |
| wilful | | wishful | |
| will (noun) | | wishfulness | |
| will (verb) | | wisp | |
| willing | | wist | |
| willow | | wistful | |
| wilt | | wit | |

WIT

## WITCH

witch . . . . . . . . . . .
witchcraft . . . . . . .
witching . . . . . .
*with* . . . . . . . . . . .
withal . . . . . . . . .
withdraw . . . . . . .
withdrawal . . . . .
withdrew . . . . . . .
withe . . . . . . . . . .
wither . . . . . . . . . .
withers . . . . . . . . .
withheld . . . . . . . .
withhold . . . . . . . .
*within* . . . . . . . . . .
without . . . . . . . . .
withstand . . . . . . .
withstood . . . . . . .
witless . . . . . . . . .
witness . . . . . . . . .
witty . . . . . . . . . . .
wives . . . . . . . . . . .
wizard . . . . . . . . :
wizen . . . . . . . . . .
woe . . . . . . . . . . . .
woebegone . . . . . .
woeful . . . . . . . . . .
woke . . . . . . . . . . .
wold . . . . . . . . . . .
wolf . . . . . . . . . . . .
wolfish . . . . . . . . .
wolverene . . . . . . .
wolves . . . . . . . . . .
*woman* . . . . . . . . .
womanhood . . . . .
womanish . . . . . . .
womankind . . . . . .
*womanly* . . . . . . . .
womb . . . . . . . . . .
*women* . . . . . . . . .
won . . . . . . . . . . . .
*wonder* . . . . . . . . .
wonderful . . . . . . .
wonderfully . . . . .
wonderland . . . . .
wonderment . . . . .
wondrous . . . . . . .

wont . . . . . . . . . .
won't . . . . . . . . . .
woo . . . . . . . . . . .
*wood* . . . . . . . . . .
woodbine . . . . . .
woodchuck . . . . . .
woodcock . . . . . .
woodcutter . . . . .
wooden . . . . . . . .
woodland . . . . . .
woodman . . . . . .
woodpecker . . . .
woodruff . . . . . . .
woodward . . . . . .
woodwork . . . . . .
woody . . . . . . . . .
woof . . . . . . . . . .
wool . . . . . . . . . .
woolen . . . . . . . .
woolly . . . . . . . .
*word* . . . . . . . . . .
wordiness . . . . . .
wore . . . . . . . . . .
*work* . . . . . . . . . .
*workable* . . . . . .
worker . . . . . . . .
workman . . . . . .
workmanship . . .
workshop . . . . . .
*world* . . . . . . . . .
worldliness . . . . .
worldling . . . . . .
*worldly* . . . . . . . .
worm . . . . . . . . .
wormy . . . . . . . .
worn . . . . . . . . . .
worry . . . . . . . . .
worse . . . . . . . . .
worship . . . . . . . .
worshipper . . . . .
worshipping . . . .
worst . . . . . . . . . .
worsted . . . . . . . .
wort . . . . . . . . . .
*worth* . . . . . . . . .
*worthily* . . . . . . .

## WORTHLESS

| | |
|---|---|
| worthless...... | wrest......... |
| worthy....... | wrestle........ |
| wot........... | wretch......... |
| *would*........ | wretched....... |
| wouldn't....... | wretchedness... |
| wouldst........ | wriggle....... |
| wound........ | wright......... |
| wound........ | wring......... |
| wove......... | wringer........ |
| woven........ | wrinkle........ |
| wrack........ | wrist......... |
| wraith........ | writ........... |
| wrangle....... | *write*......... |
| wrangler...... | writer......... |
| wrap......... | writhe........ |
| wrapper....... | *written*...... |
| wrapping...... | *wrong*....... |
| wrath........ | wrongful....... |
| wrathful...... | wrongheaded.. |
| wreak........ | wrote......... |
| wreath....... | wroth......... |
| wreathe...... | wrought....... |
| wreck........ | wrung........ |
| wren......... | wry........... |
| wrench........ | wryly......... |

## X

| | |
|---|---|
| xebec......... | xylography..... |
| X-ray......... | xylonite........ |
| xylograph...... | xylophone...... |
| xylographer.... | xyst........... |
| xylographic.... | xystus........ |

## Y

| | |
|---|---|
| yacht......... | yawn......... |
| yak.......... | ye........... |
| yam.......... | yea.......... |
| Yankee....... | yean......... |
| *yard*......... | yeanling...... |
| yărdstick...... | *year*......... |
| yarn......... | yearling....... |
| yarrow........ | yearly........ |
| yaw.......... | yearn........ |
| yawl......... | yearning...... |

**YEARNING**

YEAST

| | | | |
|---|---|---|---|
| yeast | *ye,* | yonder | |
| yeasty | | yore | |
| yell | | you | |
| yellow | | you'd | |
| yelp | | you'll | |
| yeoman | | young | |
| yeomanry | | younger | |
| yes | | youngish | |
| yesterday | | youngster | |
| yesternight | | your | |
| yet | | you're | |
| yew | | yours | |
| yield | | yourself | |
| yielding | | yourselves | |
| yodel | | youth | |
| yoke | | youthful | |
| yokel | | you've | |
| yolk | | Yule | |
| yon | | Yule-tide | |

## Z

| | | | |
|---|---|---|---|
| zany | | zincography | |
| zeal | | zither | |
| zealot | | zodiac | |
| zealous | | zollverein | |
| zebra | | zone | |
| zebu | | zoo | |
| zed | | zoological | |
| zemindar | | zoologist | |
| zenana | | zoology | |
| zenith | | zoophyte | |
| zephyr | | zoophytic | |
| zeppelin | | zoophytical | |
| zero | | zounds | |
| zest | | zymometer | |
| zigzag | | zymosis | |
| zinc | | zymotic | |

SUMMARY

of

BRIEF FORMS

## BRIEF FORMS

| | | | |
|---|---|---|---|
| about | *al* | at, it | *l* |
| above | *bv* | avoid | *avy* |
| absolute | *abs* | because | *ks* |
| acknowledge | *ak* | been | *b* |
| advantage | *avj* | being | *b* |
| advertise | *avz* | begin | *bg* |
| advice | *vrs* | benefit | *bnf* |
| again, against | *ag* | beneficial | *bfl* |
| allow | *l* | between | *bl* |
| almost | *lso* | black | *⌐* |
| already | *lr* | both | *bo* |
| also | *lso* | business | *bs* |
| always | *l* | busy | *bz* |
| America,-n | *a* | but | *b* |
| am | *⌐* | buy | *b* |
| an | *a* | by | *b* |
| and | *&* | call | *kl* |
| appear | *ap* | came | *k* |
| approximate,-ly | *apx* | can | *k* |
| arrive | *rv* | charge | *cg* |
| around | *r* | child | *cc* |
| as | *as* | children | *cl* |
| ask | *sk* | circumstance | *C,* |

| collect | | fine | |
| come | | fire | |
| coming | | first | |
| communicate | | for | |
| country | | full, -y | |
| day | | girl | |
| deal | | give | |
| definite, -ly | | given | |
| deliver, -ery | | go, -ing | |
| describe | | good | |
| description | | great | |
| difficult, -y | | had | |
| during | | happen | |
| east | | has | |
| easy | | have, -ing | |
| else | | he | |
| equal, -ly | | held | |
| establish | | help | |
| even | | her | |
| fail | | him | |
| farm | | his, is | |
| feel | | hole, whole | |
| field | | hour | |
| find | | hundred | |

| | | | |
|---|---|---|---|
| idea | *id* | market | *mkt* |
| importance | *ip* | million | *ml* |
| important | *ip* | mine | *mn* |
| in | *n* | minimum | *mn* |
| initial | *il* | move | *mv* |
| intelligent, -ence | *Nj* | necessary | *nec* |
| is, his | *s* | necessarily | *nec* |
| it, at | *l* | newspaper | *nzp* |
| keep | *kp* | nice | *ns* |
| kind | *ki* | north | *N* |
| known | *no* | not | *n* |
| labor | *Lab* | note | *nt* |
| large | *lj* | object | *ob* |
| latter | *Ll* | of | *v* |
| learn | *ln* | on | *o* |
| liberty | *Lb* | once | *s* |
| life | *lf* | only | *nl* |
| like | *lk* | open | *op* |
| line | *li* | opinion | *opn* |
| little | *ll* | opportunity | *opt* |
| look | *lo* | organize, -ation | *og* |
| magazine | *mag* | our | *r* |
| man | *m-* | out | *ou* |
| many | *m* | over | *V* |

| | | | |
|---|---|---|---|
| particular, -ly | *Pl* | school | *skl* |
| peace | *ps* | several | *sv* |
| piece | *ps* | shall | *?* |
| place | *pl* | she | *?* |
| please | *p* | ship | *?* |
| popular | *pop* | situation | *sul* |
| price | *ps* | small | *sra* |
| probable, -bly | *pbl* | south | *S* |
| prove | *pv* | strength | *S* |
| public | *pb* | subject | *sj* |
| publish | *pb* | succeed | *suc* |
| pull | *pu* | success, -ful, -ly | *suc* |
| put | *p* | table | *tab* |
| question | *q* | that | *ta* |
| real, -ly | *rl* | the | *.* |
| regular, -ly | *rg* | their | *z* |
| remember | *Rb* | there | *z* |
| represent | *rep* | they | *ly* |
| representative | *rep* | this | *th* |
| result | *rsl* | those | *los* |
| room | *r* | thought | *tt* |
| satisfy | *sal* | thousand | *J* |
| satisfaction | *sal* | throughout | *Tu* |
| satisfactory | *sal* | time | *li* |

| | | | |
|---|---|---|---|
| to, too | *lo* | what | *a* |
| turn | *ln* | where | *r* |
| until | *ul* | while | *l* |
| up | *p* | whole, hole | *hl* |
| upon | *pn* | whom | *h* |
| usual,-ly | *x* | will | *l* |
| very | *v* | with | |
| voice | *vy* | without | |
| war | *r* | woman | |
| was | *3* | work | *ke* |
| we | *e* | world | *o* |
| well | *l* | would | *d* |
| were | | year | *y* |
| west | | your | *u* |

# MEDICAL PREFIXES AND SUFFIXES

## JOINED PREFIXES
### Small Letters

A or *Ab*—from
*Acr*—pertaining to extremity
*Aden*—pertaining to a gland
*Ante*—before
*Anti*—against
*Auto*—self
*Bi*—two
*Bio*—pertaining to life
*Bleph*—pertaining to eyelid
*Brady*—slow
*Cardi*—pertaining to heart
*Cephal*—pertaining to head
*Cheil*—pertaining to lip
*Cheir*—pertaining to hand
*Chondr*—pertaining to cartilage
*Cleid*—pertaining to clavicle
*Crani*—pertaining to skull
*Crypt*—pertaining to anything hidden
*Cyst*—pertaining to the bladder or any fluid-containing sac
*Di*—two
*Dys*—pertaining to pain or difficulty
*En*—in
*Encephal*—pertaining to brain
*End*—within
*Epi*—above or upon
*Eu*—well
*Ex*—out
*Extra*—without
*Gastr*—pertaining to stomach
*Gyne*—pertaining to woman
*Hem* or *hemat*—pertaining to the blood
*Hemi*—half
*Hyper*—above
*Hyster*—pertaining to uterus
*In*—in
*Kopr*—pertaining to feces

*Leuk*—pertaining to anything white
*Mes*—middle
*Met*—beyond, over
*My*—pertaining to muscle
*Myc*—pertaining to fungi
*Neo*—new
*Nephr*—pertaining to kidney
*Odont*—pertaining to tooth
*Olig*—little
*Omo*—pertaining to shoulder
*Oss*—pertaining to bone
*Oste*—pertaining to bone
*Ot*—pertaining to ear
*Path*—pertaining to disease
*Pneum* or *pneumon*—pertaining to lung
*Polio*—gray
*Poly*—many
*Pre*—before
*Pro*—before
*Pseud*—false
*Psych*—pertaining to soul or mind
*Py*—pertaining to pus
*Pyel*—pertaining to pelvis
*Rach*—pertaining to spine
*Rhin*—pertaining to nose
*Semi*—half
*Septic*—pertaining to poison
*Sub*—under
*Super*—above
*Supra*—above
*Tox* or *toxi*—pertaining to poison
*Trache*—trachea
*Tri*—three
*Trich*—pertaining to the hair
*Uni*—one
*Zoo*—pertaining to animal

# JOINED SUFFIXES
## Small Letters

-*algia*—pertaining to pain
-*blast*—germ
-*cyst*—bladder or sac containing fluid
-*cyte*—cell
-*dynia*—pain
-*ec* or *ect*—out
-*ectasis*—dilation, stretching
-*ectomy*—excision
-*esthesia* (noun)—relating to sensation
-*esthetic* (adj.)—a drug producing lack of feeling
-*iatrics*—pertaining to a physician
-*itis*—signifying inflammation of
-*lysis*—losing, flowing, dissolution
-*ology*—science of biology
-*oma*—tumor
-*osis*—condition of being affected with
-(*o*)*stomy*—creation of an opening
-(*o*)*tomy*—cutting into
-*pathy*—disease
-*phagia*—eating
-*phasia*—speech
-*phobia*—fear
-*ptosis*—falling
-*rrhythmia*—rhythm
-*rrhagia*—flowing
-*rrhaphy*—suture of
-*scope*—to see
-*sthen*—pertaining to strength
-*taxia* or *taxic*—order, arrangement of
-*trophia*—nourishment

## JOINED PREFIXES
### Capitals

*K*    *Contra*—against
*K*    *Counter*—against
*n*    *Enter*—pertaining to intestine
*H*    *Hetero*—other
*n*    *Inter*—between
*N*    *Intra*—within
*V*    *Ovar*—pertaining to ovary
*P*    *Para*—beyond or round about
*P*    *Peri*—around

## DISJOINED PREFIXES

*kl*    *Chole*—pertaining to bile
*k*    *Colp*—pertaining to vagina
*d*    *Dermat*—pertaining to skin
*gl*    *Galact*—pertaining to milk
*hp*    *Hypo*—under
*k*    *Kerat*—pertaining to horn, cornea
*a*    *Macr*—large
   *Micr*—small
*o*    *Oophor*—pertaining to ovary
*ol*    *Ophthalm*—pertaining to eye
*sl*    *Salping*—pertaining to a tube
*s*    *Sapr*—root for putrid
   *Example: dermatography*
         *dermatitis*

## DISJOINED SUFFIXES
### Small Letters

*s*    *-cele*—tumor, hernia
*kk*    *-coccus*—round bacterium
*su*    *-cytosis*—having to do with the cell
*l*    *-emia*—blood
*sl*    *-malacia*—softness
*r*    *-rrhea*—discharge or flowing
*u*    *-uria*—to do with urine
   *Example: hysterocele*
         *cystocele*